BEST AMERICAN
POLITICAL WRITING 2009

PRESIDENTS OF THE UNITED STATES

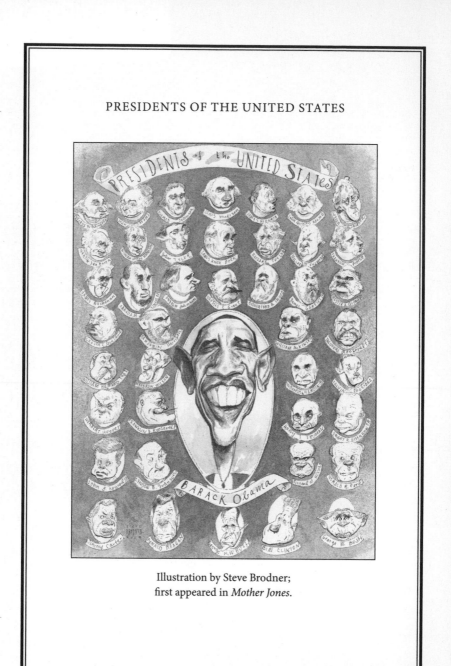

Illustration by Steve Brodner;
first appeared in *Mother Jones*.

BEST AMERICAN POLITICAL WRITING 2009

Edited by Royce Flippin

with an Introduction by
Matt Taibbi

PublicAffairs
New York

Copyright © 2009 Compilation by Royce Flippin
Copyright © 2009 Introduction by Matt Taibbi
Copyright © 2009 Cartoon Illustrations by Steve Brodner

Published by Public Affairs,
A Member of the Perseus Books Group

Public Affairs books are available at special discounts for bulk purchases
in the United States by corporations, institutions, and other
organizations. For more information, please contact the Special Markets
Department at the Perseus Books Group, 2300 Chestnut Street, Suite
200, Philadelphia, PA 19103, or call (800) 810-4145, ext. 5000, or e-mail
special.markets@perseusbooks.com.

Designed by Timm Bryson

CIP catalog information for this book is available from The Library
of Congress.
ISBN: 978-1-58648-783-3
10 9 8 7 6 5 4 3 2 1

This book is dedicated to the American voter

CONTENTS

Voting for Change

Over There

LIST OF ILLUSTRATIONS BY STEVE BRODNER

ACKNOWLEDGMENTS

I'd like to thank all the contributors to this year's edition, as well as their literary agents and the permissions representatives of their respective publications, for allowing such a terrific collection of writing to grace these pages. I particularly want to thank Steve Brodner for generously agreeing once again to enliven this anthology with his wonderful artwork, and Matt Taibbi for contributing his perceptive introduction. I also want to thank everyone at PublicAffairs Books who has contributed to this book—including, first and foremost, my editor, Morgen Van Vorst, whose invaluable support and judgment make her an essential partner in this enterprise. Thanks, too, to Laura Stine and her production team. Finally, a heartfelt thank-you to my wife, Alexis, for her unwavering love and encouragement.

INTRODUCTION
Matt Taibbi

George W. Bush has been blamed for a lot of things in the last eight years or so, and rightly so for the most part, but no one has bothered yet to talk about the awful effect he had on our national political journalism—an intellectual discipline that during the eight years of his reign sank somewhere beneath check kiting and truck-stop prostitution on the list of things America has to be proud of.

It shouldn't have been this way. A generation ago the similarly polarizing and outrageous Richard Nixon inspired some of the greatest political journalism ever—the Nixon presidency was bookended by two classics, kicking off with Joe McGinniss's *The Selling of the President 1968* and ending with *All the President's Men*, and in between were mountains of great stuff from the likes of Michael Herr, Seymour Hersh, and Hunter Thompson.

Bush was the same kind of president as Nixon in so many ways: self-obsessed and defiant and unnervingly willing to sacrifice young lives for personal political gain, a serial line-crosser who found laws boring and defined morality according to what he happened to be doing at the time. Like Nixon, Bush built a decidedly confrontational presidency, a presidency that didn't even pay lip service to the notion of being "for" everyone—under Bush the ship of state was set on a very definite course, and those who did not completely agree with the navigational plan were invited in no uncertain terms to get the hell off the deck.

It was a presidency that fostered fierce political disagreements, very often dividing families and erstwhile friends, and even leaving a kind of geographic scar on the national landscape as the states turned deeper and deeper blue and red—completing the national cultural divorce that began back with the "Southern Strategy" in 1968 that made Nixon, as McGinniss wrote, "president of everyplace that doesn't have a bookstore."

But while the Nixon era inspired all sorts of profound and passionate work from writers and journalists of all stripes, conservative and progressive alike, in the Bush era the divisions were so stark and entrenched that political writing became 100 percent about the cultural war. Journalism under George W. Bush devolved into a relentlessly boring exercise in side-taking and finger-pointing.

The conservatives who supported Bush were remarkably disciplined in presenting a unified front with the journalists who counted themselves in their camp—the flag-wavers for the right whom James Wolcott called "Attack Poodles." Together they spoke as if with one voice, pounding home the same White House–generated talking points on the radio and in news-papers day after day in what was an extremely effective, if not particularly interesting, propaganda method. The Bush-era conservative media icons, the Limbaughs and Hannitys and O'Reillys, were towering, powerful mammoths whose reach and influence were perhaps unprecedented, at least as far as private-sector media figures go.

Meanwhile, progressive media in the Bush years experienced a great awakening as well, with the president in effect laying ground for new forms of popular political entertainment based largely on anti-Bush riffing, the most notable being *The Daily Show* and *The Colbert Report*. Unlike Nixon, who had a face like an old shoe sole and whose exploits even at their most outrageous were grim and extremely unfunny (try making a joke about the bombing of Cambodia), Bush to his ideological opponents was an enormously entertaining figure, bumbling and absurd and embarrassing. Books and websites dedicated entirely to Bush's unique diction achieved tremendous popularity, and the public consumed anti-conservative invective at a feverish clip, ultimately sending at least one anti-Bush pundit, Al Franken, to the U.S. Senate.

The problem with the political literature of both of these camps was that the content was essentially decided upon in advance. When you tuned in to a conservative radio station, you knew what opinions you were going to hear; and when you listened to Air America or picked up *The Nation*, you knew what was coming there too. With such a polarizing president in office, few pundits found a way to get past the divisions and speak to a broad audience about the underlying issues (particularly economic issues) that affected both groups equally. Virtually every major political book written during the Bush years offered unbroken culture-war cheerleading from start to finish for one side or the other; when you went into bookstores, there was usually one rack full of titles like *Why Liberals Should Be Beaten with Iron Rods*, and another with titles like *Bush Sucks Ass* or *Religious Midwesterners Are Fucking Stupid*. I even wrote one of those books.

The problem most political writers faced in those years was that the audience hunger for culture-war invective was seemingly endless, and any writer who was even half-clever could score one book deal after another just by stringing together enough red-meat one-liners to keep the crowds happy. Writers who tried to escape the cheerleading paradigm had a much tougher time getting work, so most just took sides and went from there. By being such an awesomely polarizing figure, and using the bully pulpit of the White House to stoke the culture war to red-hot intensity, Bush made political journalism too easy. Attacking Bush in print was like picking low-hanging fruit all year round, and defending him was much the same thing.

But that came to an end in 2009, for two reasons. One was that Bush was replaced by a new political icon, a smooth-talking young superstar named Barack Obama. The other was that at the tail end of the Bush years, the entire system of international capitalism imploded.

Both developments left journalists scrambling for a new literary paradigm. The story of the financial crisis in particular blasted the old culture-war paradigm to smithereens, if for no other reason than the fact that its causes were so markedly bipartisan in nature; the Obama era therefore highlighted the work of reporters who were able to look past ideology in their economic reporting. Whereas the tendency in the Bush years with economic issues was to either back or oppose a presidential policy and end the discussion there, the writers in this year's volume, like James K. Galbraith ("No Return to Normal") were now paying careful attention to the fine print of the new president's policies and judging the new chief's moves on their merits.

Likewise, Paul Krugman ("Obama's Bailout"), famous as a withering critic of Bush during his presidency, showed that the financial crisis had rendered the culture war irrelevant when he took on Obama's stimulus package. The red-blue thing just didn't mean a whole hell of a lot when everyone was broke: The days when people had enough money to really care about issues like Terri Schiavo's brain-lump seemed very far away.

Obama's personality, meanwhile, was diametrically opposed to that of Bush's: He was smooth and articulate, his surface so pleasingly clean and nonstick that a great many pundits were tempted to gloss him over and sell him as pure pop icon. In the summer of 2008 I witnessed journalists on the Obama campaign plane literally swooning when the candidate strode back to the press section of the aircraft. The angle of the first black president was inspirational to many and to some reporters proved irresistible, and it was not long before the Obama of most political coverage began to seem like a human T-shirt, an unconvincingly two-dimensional piece of marketing. The *New Republic*'s Michelle Cottle ("The Cool Presidency") keenly examines both the good and the creepy aspects of Obama's coolness.

Then there were the journalists who sidestepped the image issue to pursue hard questions about Obama's policies, people like Michael Hastings ("Obama's War"), who wondered aloud about what happens when a campaign meme—Obama's emphasis on fighting in Afghanistan instead of Iraq—clashes with the reality on the ground. Some, like Dexter Filkins ("Right at the Edge") were in line with this trend of moving away from simple storylines even before the election. In his case, Filkins trenchantly waded through the maddening gray areas and hall-of-mirror deceptions of the U.S.-Pakistani relationship in an attempt to determine what the hell it is we are actually doing over there.

Granted, there are journalists out there who miss the Bush years already, who miss the pitched ideological battles and the easy water-cooler controversies and dread the low-temperature atmosphere of the over-mellow Obama presidency. But the exit of George W. Bush is good for journalism, as this volume reveals. The Obama era will bring political writers back to their real job of examining issues, digging up facts, and using the written word not as a means of pushing established opinions but rather as a means of discovering the truth about things. It's more of a challenge, but challenging times are good for pundits—or they should be, anyway.

PREFACE

Royce Flippin

Welcome to the eighth edition of *Best American Political Writing*, the first installment in this series to see print with someone other than George W. Bush occupying the White House. It covers the period from June 2008 through May 2009—a twelve-month stretch that began with Barack Obama and John McCain squaring off at the start of their battle to replace outgoing President Bush and ended with Obama installed as the nation's first African American president, the Democrats in firm control of both Houses of Congress, and defeated Democratic primary opponent Hillary Clinton steering America's foreign policy as secretary of state.

The prospect of an administration headed by the progressive but pragmatic Obama has left Democrats somewhat giddy, while conservative politicians and pundits have taken to issuing dark warnings about America's drift toward socialism and the country's increased vulnerability to terrorist attacks. But in fact, the early moves of President Obama—which included a bank bailout not all that different from the one outlined by President Bush's team, a stimulus bill that passed over almost unanimous opposition from congressional Republicans, and an endorsement of President Bush's proposed military tribunals for the prisoners on Camp Guantánamo—underscored the truism that change in Washington comes grudgingly, at best.

Meanwhile, the U.S. economy continues to founder in the grip of a historic recession, with unemployment rising and the stock market struggling to recoup some portion of the huge losses it incurred in 2008. Overseas, Iraq seems to have achieved a tenuous stability, but Afghanistan and Pakistan are more problematic than ever, with the resurgent Taliban exerting control over significant parts of both countries—a development that can only embolden its al Qaeda houseguests. At the same time, Iran and Korea both appear to be moving inexorably toward their goals of becoming nuclear powers.

To put it mildly, our new chief executive has a lot on his plate. And whatever the GOP opposition lacks in terms of substantive policy alternatives, they're making up for in their blatant determination to fight his agenda tooth and nail—backed by a Republican base that, while electorally diminished, is more disgruntled than ever.

The twenty-two pieces in *Best American Political Writing 2009* provide an apt record and a thorough analysis of how this transformative year has affected our politics and our nation. The opening section, "Voting for Change," covers the general election contest between Obama and McCain. It begins with "Battle Plans," Ryan Lizza's report on how the Obama team formulated and executed their winning strategy; "The Making (and Remaking and Remaking) of McCain," Robert Draper's chronicle of the losing candidate's struggle to craft a clearly defined image; and "The Front-Runner's Fall," Joshua Green's behind-the-scenes look at the slow disintegration of Hillary Clinton's primary campaign. "The Insiders," by Jane Mayer, explores the maneuverings that led to the surprising selection of Sarah Palin as John McCain's running mate, while Lisa Taddeo's "The Man Who Made Obama" offers a close-up look at David Plouffe, Obama's youthful (and relatively unknown) campaign manager. In "The Spreadsheet Psychic," Adam Sternbergh zeroes in on Nate Silver, the young, statistics-minded creator of one of the most influential blogs to emerge during the 2008 race, FiveThirtyEight.com.

The second section, "Economy in Crisis: Postcards from the Edge," covers the issue that dominated the presidential campaign and continues to loom large during the early days of Obama's presidency: The U.S. economy. In "Capitalist Fools," Nobel Prize–winning economist Joseph E. Stiglitz explains how our political leaders' trust in the marketplace and distaste for government regulation—dating back to the early days of Ronald Reagan's presidency—got America into its current mess. Meanwhile, his fellow Nobel laureate, economist Paul Krugman continues to serve as gadfly to the new administration with "Obama's Bailout," in which he warns that the Obama team isn't moving aggressively enough to address the economic crisis. "No

Return to Normal," by University of Texas economist James K. Galbraith, looks at the current crisis in historical terms and suggests that a true recovery will be more elusive than today's policy-makers want to believe. In his concluding piece, "The New Liberalism," George Packer reflects on how the economic crisis has created new opportunities for the progressive wing of American politics.

Section Three, "The New New Presidency," offers insight into the post-election landscape. Michelle Cottle's "The Cool Presidency" is a meditation on Barack Obama's trademark air of equilibrium, whereas Jennifer Senior's "Regarding Michelle Obama" examines the underrated political savvy of America's new first lady. In "President of Everything," Brian Doherty interrupts the administration's honeymoon to point out that Obama, despite his criticism of George W. Bush's overreaching, has been no more shy about wielding power than his predecessor. "Joe Biden, Advisor in Chief," by John H. Richardson, is an affectionate portrait of our new vice president, and Larissa MacFarquhar's "Ms. Kennedy Regrets" chronicles Caroline Kennedy's brief bid for Hillary Clinton's senate seat. "The Man Who Ate the GOP," from Michael Wolff, parses the ongoing Rush Limbaugh phenomenon, and "Specter's Epilogue" by Terence Samuel analyzes long-time Republican Senator Arlen Specter's recent defection to the Democratic side of the aisle.

The last section, "Over There," is devoted to international affairs. "Obama's Foreign Policy at 100," by Ilan Goldenberg, is a brief overview of the new administration's initial steps on the world stage. Michael Hastings' "Obama's War" and Dexter Filkins' "Right at the Edge," offer firsthand reports from either side of the Afghanistan-Pakistan border, the region that's certain to be America's most pressing overseas concern over the next several years. *Best American Political Writing 2009* concludes with two very different articles on the gnawing issue of the "enhanced interrogation" techniques employed by the Bush administration on suspected terrorists in the years following the September 11 attacks. In "Believe Me, It's Torture," Christopher Hitchens pushes the boundaries of investigative journalism by voluntarily undergoing the simulated-drowning procedure known as waterboarding. Mark Danner's extended review of the recently released Red Cross report on U.S. interrogation techniques, meanwhile, stands as a definitive and sobering summary of the human consequences of the

Bush anti-terror policy—detailing a catalog of cruelties meted out in the name of American security, for which we are all partly responsible.

As of this writing, America's battered economy is starting to show signs of a recovery, Pakistan—with its nuclear arsenal hanging in the balance—has launched a counteroffensive in its western provinces to reclaim territories captured by the Taliban, and North Korea is reportedly about to launch an intercontinental ballistic missile capable of reaching U.S. territory. Meanwhile, the Obama administration has promised to reform health care and tackle climate change, and the Republicans have vowed to resist these endeavors every step of the way. In other words, it's business as usual in Washington.

VOTING FOR CHANGE

ELECTION DAY DOGS, 2008

Illustration by Steve Brodner; first appeared in *The New Yorker*.

1

BATTLE PLANS: HOW OBAMA WON

RYAN LIZZA
The New Yorker   November 17, 2008

By the time Election Day 2008 arrived, all but the most diehard GOP partisans were acknowledging that an Obama victory was in the bag. Still, the election itself—the first in fifty-six years not to feature a sitting president or vice-president as one of the candidates—was one of the most exciting in recent memory: A record 131 million votes were cast, representing well over 60 percent of eligible voters, the highest proportional turnout in the past forty years. When the dust settled, Barack Obama had been elected forty-fourth President of the United States by a solid margin, capturing twenty-eight states plus the District of Columbia and racking up 365 electoral votes to John McCain's 173. His 69.5-million vote total was a record, and his 53.2 percent share of the popular vote was the best showing for a Democrat since Lyndon Johnson in 1964.

It was a historic victory, and a resounding one, with Obama's biracial parentage making him the first person of color ever elected to America's highest office. But a landslide it wasn't. Consider, for instance, that Obama's 6.4 percent margin over McCain was just one percentage point more than Bill Clinton's spread over George H. W. Bush in 1992, and less than Bush Sr.'s margin over Michael Dukakis in 1988 (7.7 percent), and Clinton's over Bob Dole in 1996 (8.5 percent). Obama's electoral vote tally was also less than the winning total in those other three races.

That said, Obama's triumph was impressive in many ways. It's easy to forget, for example, that most polls had McCain slightly ahead coming out of the Republican convention in early September. Remember, also, that many experts had flatly predicted the nation would never elect an African American president. Obama not only proved them wrong but also managed to turn a number of once-solidly-red states blue, picking up nine states that had sided with George W. Bush in 2004. He is also only the third sitting senator ever to get elected president (the others were Warren Harding and John Kennedy).

Most of all, however, Obama's win was the culmination of a finely crafted and superbly executed campaign—something we can only hope is a harbinger of his administration. The New Yorker's ace political reporter Ryan Lizza followed the 2008 contest every step of the way, beginning with the earliest primaries. In this piece, written just after the election, Lizza displays his trademark mastery of the mechanics and personal dynamics of the political game as he provides the definitive recap of how Obama and his team made history.

Last June, Joel Benenson, who was Barack Obama's top pollster during his presidential run, reported on the state of the campaign. His conclusions, summed up in a sixty-slide PowerPoint presentation, were revealed to a small group, including David Axelrod, Obama's chief strategist, and several media consultants, and, as it turned out, some of this research helped guide the campaign through the general election. The primaries were over, Hillary Clinton had conceded, and Obama had begun planning for a race against Senator John McCain.

There was good news and bad in Benenson's presentation. Obama led John McCain, forty-nine per cent to forty-four per cent, among the voters most likely to go to the polls in November, but there was also a large group of what Benenson called "up-for-grabs" voters, or U.F.G.s, who favored McCain, forty-eight per cent to thirty-six per cent. The U.F.G.s were the key to the outcome; if the election had been held then, Obama would have probably lost.

Benenson, who is fifty-six, is bearded and volatile. He speaks with a New York accent, and in the movie version of the Obama campaign he might be played by Richard Lewis. He is considered the star pollster in the Democratic Party. Like several of Obama's other top advisers—David Axelrod; Rahm Emanuel, the Illinois congressman who is his new chief of staff; Bill Burton, the campaign's national press secretary—Benenson was deeply involved in helping Democrats win in the 2006 midterm elections, an experience that put the Obama team more in touch with the mood of the electorate going into 2008. (The top strategists for Clinton and McCain had not been involved in difficult races in 2006.)

The data from Benenson's June presentation contained some reasons to be optimistic. The conventional wisdom was that Obama, as the newest of the candidates, had an image that was malleable and thus highly vulnerable to negative attacks. But that was not what the polling showed. As the presentation explained, "Obama's image is considerably better defined than McCain's, even on attributes at the core of McCain's reputation," such as "stands up to lobbyists and special interests," "puts partisan politics aside to get things done," and "tells people what they need to hear, not what they want to hear."

For Obama aides, who viewed McCain as the one Republican with the potential to steal the anti-Washington bona fides of their candidate, Benenson's polling was revelatory. "Voters actually did not know as much as I think the press corps thought they did about John McCain," Anita Dunn, a senior adviser to Obama, told me. "What they'd heard about McCain most recently, and certainly during the primary process, was that he was like every other Republican—fighting to sound more like George Bush." Benenson said, "What we knew at the start of the campaign was that the notion of John McCain as a change agent and independent voice didn't exist anywhere outside the Beltway."

Another finding from this initial poll had clear strategic implications: the economy concerned the U.F.G.s more than any other issue, and on that question neither candidate showed particular strength. In addition, the U.F.G.s were fed up with Washington and, especially, with George W. Bush. Based on those insights, Benenson came up with some recommendations, among them "Own the economy" and "Maintain an emphasis on changing Washington."

As a practical matter, this meant that, after the Democratic National Convention, in Denver, the campaign would do all that it could to focus attention on economic matters. It had no idea, of course, how fully both the economy and John McCain would cooperate with that goal.

⊷ ● ⊶

There was an almost obsessive singularity in the way that Obama and his chief strategists—Axelrod and David Plouffe, the campaign's manager—saw the contest. In their tactical view, all that was wrong with the United States could be summarized in one word: Bush. The clear alternative, then, was not so much a Democrat or a liberal as it was *anyone* who could credibly define himself as "not Bush." Axelrod had a phrase that he often used to describe this approach: America was looking for "the remedy, not the replica." The appeal of the strategy was that, with only minor alterations, it could work in the primaries as well as in the general election, and that, in turn, allowed Obama to finesse the perpetual problem of presidential politics: having one message to win over a party's most ardent supporters and another when trying to capture independents and U.F.G.s—the voters who decide a general election. Experience? That was George W. Bush. Hillary Clinton? She could be portrayed as polarizing and as a Washington insider—just like Bush. When Obama gave economic speeches during the primaries and caucuses—which continued over five months, in fifty-five states and territories—he lumped together the Clinton and Bush years as one long period of decline. And John McCain? Four more years of Bush, of "the same."

"We were fortunate," Anita Dunn said. Both Clinton and McCain were "Washington insiders, people who for different reasons you could argue weren't going to bring change."

The incessant repetition of Obama's change message had its drawbacks, though, and Benenson described to me the ongoing debate inside and outside the campaign about whether the candidate should move away from that theme—for instance, during the summer and fall of 2007, when Obama's poll numbers in Iowa were stagnant. "We had people in Iowa in the summer of '07 saying, 'All we're getting asked about is experience! We've got to have an answer on experience!'" Benenson recalled.

Polling in the summer and fall of 2007 led the campaign to a choice between trying to win the debate that the Clinton campaign was eager to have—about Obama's perceived lack of experience—and sharpening the debate about change in a way that could undermine Clinton. Once again, change trumped experience. "The much shorter path for us," Benenson said, going into the jargon of political consulting, "was to eliminate Senator Clinton from the decision set as a change agent. We defined change in a way that Barack Obama had to be the answer." Larry Grisolano, whose job was to oversee all spending on TV ads and mail, the largest part of the campaign's budget, posed the question this way: "How do we talk about change in a way that makes Hillary Clinton pay a price for her experience?"

On October 10, 2007, less than three months before the Iowa caucuses, Axelrod, Grisolano, Benenson, and other members of Obama's "message team" distilled several weeks' worth of polling and internal debate into a twelve-page memo that laid out Obama's strategy for the weeks leading up to the Iowa caucuses. "The fundamental idea behind this race from the start has been that this is a 'change' election, and that has proven out," the memo said. "Everything in our most recent research has confirmed this premise, as has the fact that other campaigns have adapted to try and catch—or survive— the wave." The plan adopted by Obama was to raise character issues about Clinton that would disqualify her from employing Obama's message. "We cannot let Clinton especially blur the lines on who is the genuine agent of change in this election," the memo said. It argued that, in voters' minds, Clinton "embodies trench warfare vs. Republicans, and is consumed with beating them rather than unifying the country," and that "she prides herself on working the system, not changing it." Obama raised all these issues with some delicacy; he framed the choice as "calculation" versus "conviction," and was careful not to use Clinton's name. But the campaign wanted to be sure that reporters got the message. "We also can't drive the contrasts so subtly or obtusely that the press doesn't write about them and the voters don't understand that we're talking about HRC," the memo advised Obama.

The new strategy was unveiled on November 10th, at the annual Jefferson Jackson Dinner, the biggest event of the Iowa-caucus season. Candidates could not use notes or a teleprompter at the dinner, and, in the weeks leading up to it, Obama stayed up late each night memorizing a new speech based on the strategy memo. "The Iowa Jefferson Jackson Dinner ended up being a tipping point in the election," Dan Pfeiffer, Obama's communications director, said. "That's when we took the lead in our internal polling in Iowa for the first time."

Axelrod believed that the argument about change versus experience would also apply in a race against McCain, and he laid out his argument to Obama in a strategy memo in late 2006, when Obama was still planning his presidential race. "I was assessing potential opponents," Axelrod told me. "I got to McCain and said that the McCain of 2000 would be a formidable opponent in a year that was all about change, but that he would almost certainly have to make a series of Faustian bargains in order to be the nominee, and that would make him ultimately a very vulnerable candidate in a year when people were looking for change. And so we started the general election, and by then he had made the Faustian bargains, and he had turned himself into a Bush supporter." Axelrod continued, "So we had a very simple premise about the general election, which is that these Bush policies had failed, that McCain was essentially carrying the tattered banner of a failed administration, and that we represented a change from all that. There have been zigs and zags in the road, but that's essentially the strategy that we have executed from the start."

The campaign's faith in the strength of such a simple message was constant. Not only was it the answer for an electorate exhausted with Bush; it turned Obama's vulnerabilities into assets. "He was at that point a couple of years out of the Illinois Senate, and he was a black guy named Barack Hussein Obama," Axelrod said. "You don't have to load up the wagon with too many more bricks than that. But, in a year that was poised for big change, those things were less of an obstacle than you might find in a traditional year. As is often the case, your strength is your weakness, and your weakness is your strength." Obama almost never delivered a speech from a lectern unless it was festooned with the word "change." On Election Day, thirty-four per cent of the voters said that they were looking for change, and nearly ninety per cent of those voters chose Obama.

⤛ • ⤜

Like many campaign teams, Obama's was young. The communications department—made up mostly of guys in their twenties and thirties—had a fraternity-house quality. On weekends, they would often drink beer together and play the video game Rock Band at a group house in Chicago's Lincoln Park neighborhood. They had been brought up in Democratic politics in the previous two decades with an understanding that the people who worked for Bill and Hillary Clinton were the best operatives in Washington, especially when it came to dealing with the media. They had watched *The War Room*, the documentary about the 1992 Clinton campaign, which featured strategists like James Carville and George Stephanopoulos manically responding to every negative story and trying to win every news cycle.

Several Obama aides believe that a crucial moment came after a debate sponsored by YouTube and CNN in July of 2007. During the debate, Obama was asked, "Would you be willing to meet separately, without preconditions, during the first year of your administration, in Washington or anywhere else, with the leaders of Iran, Syria, Venezuela, Cuba, and North Korea, in order to bridge the gap that divides our countries?" Obama answered simply, "I would." Hillary Clinton pounced on the remark as hopelessly naïve, and her aides prepared to emphasize what appeared to be a winning argument. Obama's aides had much the same reaction. "We know this is going to be the issue of the day," Dan Pfeiffer, recalling a conference call the following morning, said. "We have the sense they're going to come after us on it. And we're all on the bus trying to figure out how to get out of it, how not to talk about it." Obama, who was listening to part of the conversation, took the telephone from an aide and instructed his staff not to back down. According to an aide, Obama said something to the effect of "This is ridiculous. We met with Stalin. We met with Mao. The idea that we can't meet with Ahmadinejad is ridiculous. This is a bunch of Washington-insider conventional wisdom that makes no sense. We should not run from this debate. We should have it."

The episode gave Obama's communications aides a boost of confidence. "Instead of writing a memo explaining away our position to reporters, we changed our memo and wrote an aggressive defense of our position and went on the offense," Pfeiffer said. The aftermath taught them that they could take on the dreaded Clinton machine—"the most impressive, toughest, most ruthless war room in the world," as Pfeiffer put it. "It was like we had taken our first punch and kept on going," he said.

The anti-Washington message of their candidate started to influence the way that some staffers saw themselves. "We are, I think, as a group, different from folks in Washington in that we signed up for this campaign and moved to Chicago not knowing a clear path to victory," Bill Burton, Obama's press secretary, said. "But, at the same time, we are all still creatures of Washington in the sense that when something happens like that"— the back-and-forth at the YouTube debate—"it lends itself to us thinking, Well, maybe that's something that we clarify, because the grownups in Washington were all saying you can't do that. And those are the people that we came up listening to. The Clinton administration people were saying, 'O.K., kids, you can't do that.'"

-<+- • ->->-

Campaigns are divided in two. On one side are the ad-makers, speechwriters, press secretaries, and assorted spinners, who manage a candidate's image. On the other side are the field operatives, who find voters and deliver them to the polls. While the communications people operate almost exclusively in the world of perceptions, the field people operate in the world of hard data. David Plouffe, the Obama campaign's publicity-shy manager, whom Obama praised as "the unsung hero" of his campaign in his victory speech last Tuesday [election] night, comes out of the field side of campaigns. "Politics is about numbers," Plouffe said to me a few days before the election.

Plouffe, who is forty-one, is thin and discreet, and his low profile in the press sent a message throughout the Obama organization that staffers were to be similarly reticent about attracting publicity. The catchphrase inside the campaign was "No drama with Obama," and Plouffe channeled the low-key temperament of the candidate himself. "Barack went out and sought people who had a certain personality type," Pfeiffer said. "They were people who had intentionally low profiles in Washington." Of Plouffe, Pfeiffer said, "If he had wanted to spend the past five years of his life on *Crossfire* and CNN, he could do that. He's chosen not to do that." When, in January 2007, Pfeiffer interviewed for his job, Obama told him, "What I want around me are people who are calm, who don't get too high and don't get too low, because that's how I am."

Jon Favreau, a twenty-seven-year-old speechwriter who had worked for John Kerry in 2004, told me, "People were drawn to him and inspired by him in a way that you knew this was about electing Barack Obama. People had come from places where they were probably disappointed in politics. I was, after 2004. It was painful, and I didn't know if I was going to do it again." He added, "Even during tough times, everyone sticks together. There are not a lot of Washington assholes on this campaign."

Alyssa Mastromonaco, the director of scheduling and advance, who had also worked for Kerry in 2004, said that she had some trouble getting used to the quieter vibe of the Obama operation. "When I first started on the campaign, at the very beginning of this one, I was one of the only people who had actually done a presidential before," Mastromonaco, who is thirty-two, told me. "And so we were on some conference call, and I was just completely irritated by something someone was saying. After the call, they came in and were, like, 'Alyssa, this is a campaign where you need to respect other people's opinions and you can't be a bitch.' I was, like, 'Oh, my God, these guys are serious!'"

Obama, who is not without an ego, regarded himself as just as gifted as his top strategists in the art and practice of politics. Patrick Gaspard, the campaign's political director, said that when, in early 2007, he interviewed for a job with Obama and Plouffe, Obama said that he liked being surrounded by people who expressed strong opinions, but he also said, "I think that I'm a better speechwriter than my speechwriters. I know more about policies on any particular issue than my policy directors. And I'll tell you right now that I'm gonna think I'm a better political director than my political director." After Obama's first debate with McCain, on September 26th, Gaspard sent him an e-mail. "You are more clutch than Michael Jordan," he wrote. Obama replied, "Just give me the ball." Obama's confidence filtered down through the campaign and gave comfort to his staff during the bleaker moments of 2008, such as when Obama learned that he had lost the New Hampshire primary. After that, he told his longtime friend and adviser Valerie Jarrett, "This will turn out to have been a good thing." Jarrett told me, "You would think you would have a lot of other things to say before you might get to that." Favreau said. "His demeanor when he won the Iowa caucuses and his demeanor when he lost New Hampshire were not much different."

⊰– • –⊱

David Plouffe's field director was Jon Carson. When we spoke, five days before the election, it was at a cafeteria-style Italian restaurant in the food court of the office building that housed Obama's headquarters. He wore a gray button-down shirt and khakis, and told me that we had exactly forty-five minutes. Carson has a civil-engineering degree and spent time in Honduras working as a water and sanitation engineer. He, like Plouffe, made me think of the focused men in white shirts and narrow black ties who, in the nineteen-sixties, ran the space program. When Carson hired field organizers for the campaign, he said that he looked for people with unusual backgrounds—"I try to throw out all the political-science majors when I do hiring." During a lull in the primary season, he set up a three-week "data camp" in Oregon for Obama staffers. "We had the best data operation of any campaign," he said. "You can have the most inspirational candidate, you can have the best organizing philosophy in the world, but if you can't organize your data to take advantage of it and get lists in front of the canvassers and take these volunteers and use it in a smart way and figure out who it is we're going to talk to—I mean, the rest of it is all pointless."

Carson was part of the team that made the important decision, during the race against Clinton, to target small caucus states where Clinton had virtually no presence. Carson and Plouffe realized that the cost-per-delegate in caucus states was very low. "I remember the day when we said, 'Look at this, we could win more delegates in Idaho than in New Jersey,'" he told me. Obama's original plan was to win the Iowa caucuses and use momentum from that victory to catapult him through the three other early states—New Hampshire, Nevada, and South Carolina—and then on to February 5th, Super Tuesday, when twenty-four states voted. It was clear that the campaign would need a backup plan if Clinton and Obama split the first four states, which is what happened. Obama won Iowa and South Carolina, and Clinton won New Hampshire and Nevada.

As the campaign got ready for Super Tuesday, Carson called upon the volunteers—in particular, those he called the "super-volunteers," people who had left their jobs or dropped out of school to help. He estimated that there were about fifteen thousand super-volunteers working full time for Obama. Carson recalled the moment when the campaign figured out what it would cost to put a hundred organizers out in the February 5th states. "It was the first time that we took an enormous leap of faith in our grass-roots network that was already out there," he said.

On October 1st, a field organizer named Joey Bristol, a recent graduate of Princeton's Woodrow Wilson School, who had delayed a career at the State Department and was working as an intern at the Chicago campaign headquarters, was sent to Idaho to organize the state for Obama. When he arrived, he learned that much of his work had already been done by a local group, Idaho for Obama. "When Joey gets there, a hundred people are waiting for him," Carson said. "They've got meetings planned for him for the next month, they've got little subgroups by county all across the state, they've already gone to the state party, gotten the rules of the caucus, figured out a plan." On February 5th, Clinton won a net total of eleven delegates from New Jersey, which had a primary, and Obama won a net total of twelve delegates from the caucus state of Idaho.

⤙ • ⤚

In hindsight, it seems that the most important decision that Obama made during the campaign was to remove himself from the restrictions of the public-financing system. The decision held risks. He had, after all, promised to stay in the system, and his reversal had the potential to damage the reform image that Benenson's polling showed was a vital advantage over McCain. But there were collateral benefits; namely, making the campaign more of a person-to-person enterprise, by keeping it tied to the Internet grass roots. Much of the intimacy that the campaign created with its supporters was driven by its need—its ravenous appetite—for money. Plouffe, who rarely spoke to reporters on the record, communicated with donors via amateurish videos in which he explained campaign strategy. "You can't just ask for money," Jim Messina, Obama's chief of staff, said. "You've got to involve them. That's why the famous videos with Plouffe were so important. People felt like insiders. They felt like they knew what we were doing."

Some Obama advisers couldn't quite believe that McCain decided not to follow them in opting out of the system. McCain, during the campaign, criticized Obama for going back on his pledge, but the issue did not seem to hurt Obama. The financial gap between the two campaigns was striking. Budgets that were drawn up in June at Obama headquarters were discarded in September, after the Conventions, when online fund-raising soared. "I spend the money, so everything's gotta go through me to get spent, which is the best job ever," Messina, the keeper of the budget, told me. "It's like getting the keys to a fucking Ferrari." Messina's Ferrari got more turbocharged every week. "On my whiteboard in front of me, I have the money we added to the media and field budgets by day," he said. "We ended up adding tens of millions to the media budget and twenty-five million to the mail budget over the course of September and the first week of October." By the end of September, Messina said, the money for Obama "was just raining down." Though McCain was aided by outside groups and by the Republican National Committee, his entire budget for the general election was the amount provided by the government—eighty-four million dollars.

One day in September, Plouffe asked Messina if he could find seven million dollars more in the budget—for a thirty-minute advertorial that was to air on the Wednesday before Election Day. He found it. (The Obama commercial attracted an estimated thirty-three million viewers, nearly twice the number for the top-rated *Dancing with the Stars*.) There was still money left over, so the campaign bought ads in video games, like Guitar Hero and Madden NFL 09, and scheduled some get-out-the-vote concerts aimed at the youth vote and featuring the rapper Jay-Z and the NBA star LeBron James. "I mean, dude," Messina said, "when you're buying commercials in video games, you truly are being well funded."

But television remained the key advertising medium. And the volume of TV ads that Obama was broadcasting in late October was unprecedented in a presidential campaign. "In a battleground state like Virginia, we're at thirty-five hundred points," Messina said, by which he meant that an average viewer sees a spot thirty-five times a week. "I've worked on two of the closest U.S. Senate races in the country," he continued. "I helped do Jon Tester last time in Montana," he said, adding that, at the end of the Tester campaign, an average viewer was seeing pro-Tester spots twenty times a week. For Obama, he said, "we've been at two thousand points in Montana since the end of September." Obama narrowly lost the state, but Republicans were forced to use resources to defend it.

McCain couldn't keep up. "From the second week in September to the middle of October, we were doing two or three to one against McCain, and at least three to one in some of these battleground states," Messina said. "Republicans couldn't play in North Carolina. They couldn't play in Indiana. They weren't in Florida for forever, and so we're up by ourselves just kicking the shit out of them." Obama won all three states.

The Obama campaign became so flush with cash that one of its trickiest political problems was dealing with other Democrats who wanted Obama to campaign for them and spend money on their races. Pete Rouse, who was Obama's Senate chief of staff and an architect of his presidential campaign, spent hours handling such calls. "When we announced that we raised a hundred and fifty-one million in one month"—in October—"every Democratic senator in America called Rouse and had an idea how to spend it on winning the Senate, or whatever race," one senior Obama aide said. Senator Charles Schumer, who ran the committee in charge of Democratic senatorial campaigns, was particularly aggressive. "The only Senate ad Obama did was in Oregon," the aide continued. "Schumer rolled Barack. He just got him at an event and made him promise. Barack is really good about not making those promises, but Schumer was begging for money."

◄◄ • ►►

Like being too rich, seeming to be too popular—as exemplified by the enormous crowds that Obama attracted—also vexed the campaign. "We had a rally problem during the primaries," Anita Dunn said. "It was like he was on a pedestal." As far back as the earliest primaries, the campaign went back and forth between embracing the crowds to show off Obama's mass appeal and shunning them to emphasize his regular-guy credentials. Hillary Clinton's campaign discovered that it could make Obama's popularity work against him. "Once the Clinton campaign figured out how it wanted to run against Obama, she started doing these town halls," Dunn said. "Her visuals were she was with people, she was working her heart out, and he's floating into these rallies with all these adoring people."

McCain's aides adopted the same strategy in the general election. In July, after Obama toured the Middle East and Europe, and spoke in Berlin at a rally where two hundred thousand people came to cheer him, a McCain ad compared Obama to Paris Hilton. What seemed to outsiders like a trivial, even ridiculous attack had an enormous impact inside Obama's headquarters.

"We've had a 'presumptuous watch' on since then," Dunn said. Alyssa Mastromonaco, who was in charge of putting on all of Obama's events, said, "After that, people started thinking that he's like this celebutante. You have to make it pretty clear through your pictures every day that you aren't, that this is not easy for you."

The campaign kept Obama away from celebrities as much as possible. A Hollywood fund-raiser with Barbra Streisand became a source of deep anxiety and torturous discussions. The campaign was on the phone for days trying to make sure it was going to work, and almost cancelled it. In Denver, celebrities who in past presidential campaigns would have had major speaking roles were shielded from public view. "We spent hours trying to celebrity-down the Democratic National Convention," the aide said.

Two days before Obama's acceptance speech, in Denver, Jim Margolis, a top media consultant to the campaign, went to inspect the stage at Invesco Field. McCain's aides had successfully turned the Greek columns ringing the stage at the stadium into a story about how a godlike Obama would be speaking from a "temple." But when Margolis arrived he realized that it was even worse than that. "I walked in and turned to look at the stage, and they had put in purple runway lights all the way around the whole stage, up across all the columns and it looked like a set from *Deal or No Deal*," he said. "And in back of them, where he would walk out, there was a colored horseshoe that was lit that would have gone around him. And in back of that was a sixty-five-inch plasma monitor that would change colors. And for a guy who is being torpedoed every day about celebrity and Hollywood this was straight out of a Hollywood set. My mouth just dropped open." Margolis ordered the producer and the set designer, who had worked for months on the design, to remove the screen and the purple lights and generally make the stage look less like a Hollywood production.

Obama's rallies had a strategic purpose beyond their visual impact, and, by putting pressure on Obama to scale down these events, Clinton and then McCain were able to take away one of the campaign's most useful organizational tools—a chance to capture personal information about potential voters and campaign volunteers, and, toward the end, a means of encouraging supporters to vote early. The battle between the communications staff, which was spooked by the Paris Hilton ad, and the field organizers, who needed the rallies to help identify Obama voters, was decided in favor of the organizers. "Finally, at the end of September we got back to saying, 'Look, we're gonna do this again because we need to push early voting,' and if you're gonna push early voting and voter registration you've gotta do big events," Messina said.

In the closing weeks of the campaign, crowds of fifty, sixty, and seventy thousand people greeted Obama at every stop—almost as if there were a pent-up demand to see him. At Obama's final rally, in Manassas, Virginia, the night before Election Day, ninety thousand people came to a dusty fairground. Traffic was snarled for miles on the main highway leading to the site, and people simply abandoned their cars on the side of the road so as not to miss Obama's speech. Obama's grandmother, Madelyn Dunham, had died that morning. He seemed subdued, and when he finished his speech he did something unusual. He stood on the stage for what seemed like a long time, a solitary figure in a simple black jacket with his arms at his sides, as if simply absorbing the intensity of a crowd illuminated by high-powered spotlights. A man standing next to me pointed up at Obama. "Look," he said. "He doesn't want it to end."

⤙ • ⤚

Much of the Obama campaign was consumed with making the candidate look presidential. The theory was that the U.F.G.s wanted to be for Obama, but needed some help visualizing him as Commander-in-Chief. His aides had a term for the process of getting voters comfortable with a President Obama: "building a permission structure." Bill Burton explained it this way: "There were a lot of questions about Senator Obama from the start. Who is he? What's with the name? Is America ready to vote for a black guy for president?" There were four major moments in the general election—Obama's trip to the Middle East and Europe, his selection of a running mate, his Convention speech, and the debates—and each was designed to add another plank to the permission structure. For instance, the foreign trip was designed to show Obama in meetings with world leaders, the strategy that the McCain campaign employed when it sent Sarah Palin to the United Nations to meet people like Henry Kissinger and President Asif Ali Zardari of Pakistan. "If he looks like a president, and you put him in presidential settings, then people will get more comfortable with the idea that he could be president," Anita Dunn said.

To Obama's aides, the most important moment of the campaign occurred when Obama had to actually *be* president. It was not totally obvious how he would perform. Many who cheered for Obama from the moment he gave the keynote address at the 2004 Democratic National Convention have had reservations. Michelle Obama once talked to me about the doubts that would need to be addressed before people could vote for her husband.

"It is a leap of faith," she said finally. "We talk about it all the time. It is a leap of faith."

No matter how much confidence one has in Obama, support for him is often based on such intangibles as his temperament and his intelligence, not on a real record of successful decision-making. The campaign helped affirm supporters' faith in him, but running a successful campaign can't predict whether someone will be a good president; after all, most presidents, whether good or bad, have won a presidential race.

The September financial crisis, which confronted Congress with the task of trying to rescue the economy from collapse, gave Obama's aides the clearest indication that he might indeed be as good at governing as he has been at campaigning. It forced Obama to do something unusual and difficult for a candidate: he needed to separate politics and governance in the midst of a political campaign in which there was often no distinction. Obama's aides say that that was the moment they won the election—the moment that any lingering doubts were erased.

The Obama campaign was organized around a series of conference calls, the most important of which was a nightly call involving Obama and some dozen senior advisers. There was always a mixture of the serious and the absurd. For instance, on October 10th the agenda included an update on the message for rallies in Philadelphia, an update on the collapsing economy, and, just as important then, an "Ayers update"—how to respond to attacks on Obama's limited contacts with the former Weatherman William Ayers. On these calls, Obama's advisers had a chance to watch their candidate grapple with complex economic problems. During one, Obama laid out the steps in negotiating the bailout package: he would call the Treasury Secretary, Henry Paulson, and the Federal Reserve chairman, Ben Bernanke, and consult with Senate Majority Leader Harry Reid. Pfeiffer said, "We all got off the phone and I was, like, 'You know what? That was the first call that felt like that's what it's going to be like if he's president.' That was the moment where he began looking like a president and not a presidential candidate."

Ever since the Benenson PowerPoint presentation in June, Obama's aides had been looking for ways to show that McCain was just another Washington politician; this was the strategy that had helped defeat Hillary Clinton. At the start of the financial crisis, when McCain announced that he would "suspend" his campaign, Obama's team knew that McCain had stumbled—

and that it could highlight his mistake. "We tested right away as to whether people thought it was a genuine attempt to solve the crisis or more of a political maneuver," Benenson said. "The numbers started out as even, maybe a two-point edge on 'genuine intent,' but, five days later, it swung against him, with a ten-point deficit toward 'political maneuver.'" Obama was surprised by McCain's move. Earlier that day, September 24th, he had spoken with McCain and asked him to release a joint statement about principles that both men wanted to see in a financial rescue package. McCain seemed interested but also told Obama about possibly suspending his campaign; he asked Obama to join him. Obama was noncommittal, but he ended the conversation with the belief that they had agreed about the joint statement and called Jason Furman, a top economic adviser.

"I picked up the phone, and he basically said, 'Jason, I just got off the phone with Senator McCain and we're going to come out with a joint statement to help move the financial rescue package forward, because it looks like it's in a lot of trouble,'" Furman told me. "'I know you know his economic adviser, and I'd like you to call him up and make it a really substantive statement.'" Furman, glancing at a television, saw McCain walking up to a lectern; a caption at the bottom of the screen said that he was suspending his campaign and might not attend the first debate. When Furman told Obama what McCain was doing, Obama used a salty expression to describe the move and hung up the phone.

As the financial crisis dragged on, Obama and his aides began to realize what it meant for their prospects. Staffers eagerly soaked up the latest polling, which showed a growing lead for Obama, and the conference calls at night only increased their confidence in the candidate. There was some pressure on Obama to come out against the rescue bill, a position that would have been more consistent with the campaign's themes. "On a purely political calculation, it would have been easy to be against that bill," Anita Dunn said. "If you look at all the polls, right? People were thinking, They made a mess and they're trying to stick you, and they're going to bail out Wall Street. I mean, what would have been easier?"

David Axelrod, who has known Obama longer than most of Obama's other campaign aides, said that he had always wondered how Obama would fare at such a moment. "Barbaric and sometimes ridiculous as is this process of running for president, the thing that I love about it is at the end of the day you can't hide who you are," Axelrod said. "I'd known him for six-teen years, I have huge confidence in him, but you never know how some-one's gonna handle the vagaries and vicissitudes of a presidential race, so you hope that they do well."

-‹‹ • ›-

A lingering question about Barack Obama's run for the presidency was whether this inspirational figure—more so even than the candidate John F. Kennedy—would be transformed by consultants and a sophisticated cam-paign apparatus into someone no longer recognizable. "Most of us do this and then we go away," Dan Pfeiffer said at the end of a conversation at Obama's Chicago headquarters. "The first Wednesday in November, we're off doing something else. We got the horse to the water, and someone else can make him drink. We're about winning elections, not actually governing the country, and because he has not done campaigns—he has not run for re-election five times; he's actually really only ever had one hard race, this one—he doesn't have all the bad habits of career politicians."

It is already being said by the great army of bloggers and commentators that the Obama campaign was the best-run in modern history. Much the same thing was said about James Carville's work for Bill Clinton in 1992 and Karl Rove's for Bush in 2000. But campaigns can change a candidate, too. Axelrod said to me that, early in the process, Obama told aides, "I'm in this to win, I want to win, and I think we will win. But I'm also going to emerge intact. I'm going to be Barack Obama and not some parody." At another point, in early 2007, Obama returned from a forum about health care know-ing that he had not done well against Hillary Clinton. "She was very good, and I need to meet that standard, meet that test," he told Axelrod. "I am not a great candidate now, but I am going to figure out how to be a great can-didate." One of Obama's achievements as a politician is that he somehow managed to emerge intact, after navigating two years of a modern and oc-casionally absurd presidential race, while also becoming a great candidate. On Election Night, as he once again invoked the words of Lincoln, he seemed to be saying that he was going to figure out how to be a great president.

2

THE MAKING (AND REMAKING AND REMAKING) OF MCCAIN

ROBERT DRAPER

The New York Times Magazine   October 26, 2008

You wouldn't think that a bona fide war hero who's also been a high-profile U.S. senator for more than two decades would have trouble defining himself in the eyes of the American public. Yet that was exactly what John McCain found himself struggling to do in the 2008 presidential campaign. In this age of focus groups, micro-polling and the "framing" of issues and candidates for maximum psychological effect, a candidate's personal narrative is often less about his or her actual life history than it is an attempt to create and sell a political brand that will appeal to the largest possible slice of the electorate.

McCain had already had to battle his own "maverick" image in the primary in order to win over the more conservative elements of the Republican Party. In the general election, he was confronted with an opponent who not only had a well-defined brand but one that was selling like hotcakes: At a time when the nation was clearly weary of GOP leadership, Barack Obama was change personified. The age gap between the two presidential candidates—almost twenty-five years, the biggest differential in the history of presidential politics—didn't help either. But as you'll see from this blow-by-blow account of McCain's campaign by Robert Draper (whose profile of John Edwards appeared in Best American Political Writing 2003*), the biggest reason Candidate McCain had so much difficulty establishing a consistent persona was that his campaign could never settle on exactly what brand they were selling.*

On the morning of Wednesday, September 24, John McCain convened a meeting in his suite at the Hilton hotel in Midtown Manhattan. Among the handful of campaign officials in attendance were McCain's chief campaign strategist, Steve Schmidt, and his other two top advisers: Rick Davis, the campaign manager; and Mark Salter, McCain's longtime speechwriter. The senator's ears were already throbbing with bad news from economic advisers and from House Republican leaders who had told him that only a small handful in their ranks were willing to support the $700 billion bailout of the banking industry proposed by Treasury Secretary Henry Paulson. The meeting was to focus on how McCain should respond to the crisis—but also, as one participant later told me, "to try to see this as a big-picture, leadership thing."

As this participant recalled: "We presented McCain with three options. Continue offering principles from afar. A middle ground of engaging while still campaigning. Then the third option, of going all in. The consensus was that we could stay out or go in—but that if we're going in, we should go in all the way. So the thinking was, do you man up and try to affect the outcome, or do you hold it at arm's length? And no, it was not an easy call."

Discussion carried on into the afternoon at the Morgan Library and Museum as McCain prepared for the first presidential debate. Schmidt pushed for going all in: suspending the campaign, recommending that the first debate be postponed, parachuting into Washington and forging a legislative solution to the financial crisis for which McCain could then claim credit. Exactly how McCain could convincingly play a sober bipartisan problem-solver after spending the previous few weeks garbed as a populist truth teller was anything but clear. But Schmidt and others convinced McCain that it was worth the gamble.

Schmidt in particular was a believer in these kinds of defining moments. The smartest bit of political wisdom he ever heard was dispensed by George W. Bush one spring day at the White House residence in 2004, at a time when his reelection effort was not going especially well. The strategists at the meeting—including Schmidt, who was directing the Bush campaign's rapid-response unit—fretted over their candidate's sagging approval ratings and the grim headlines about the war in Iraq. Only Bush appeared thoroughly unworried. He explained to them why, polls notwithstanding, voters would ultimately prefer him over his opponent, John Kerry.

There's an accidental genius to the way Americans pick a president, Schmidt remembers Bush saying that day. By the end of it all, a candidate's true character is revealed to the American people.

Had Schmidt been working for his present client back in 2000, he might have disputed Bush's premise. After all, in McCain's first run for the presidency, "true character" was the one thing the Vietnam hero and campaign-finance-reform crusader seemed to have going for him eight years ago in the Republican primaries. Bush had everything else, and he buried McCain. What campaigns peddle is not simply character but character as defined by story—a tale of opposing forces that in its telling will memorably establish what a given election is about. In 2000, the McCain effort played like that of a smart and plucky independent film that ultimately could not compete for audiences against the Bush campaign's summer blockbuster. Four years later, in the race against John Kerry, Schmidt and the other Bush strategists had perfected their tradecraft. With a major studio's brutal efficiency, they distilled the campaign into a mega-budget melodrama pitting an unwavering commander in chief against a flip-flopper, set in a post–9/11 world where there could be no room for error or equivocation.

Schmidt has been in charge of strategy for the McCain campaign since early this summer, and his effort to prevail in the battle of competing story lines has been considerably more problematic. The selling of a presidential "narrative," the reigning buzzword of this election cycle, has taken on outsize significance in an age in which a rush of visuals and catchwords can cripple public images overnight. Mitt Romney, it is said, lost because he could not get his story straight. Hillary Clinton found her I'm-a-fighter leitmotif too late to save her candidacy. By contrast, the narrative of Barack Obama has seemed to converge harmonically with the shifting demographics and surging discontent of the electorate. It may well be, as his detractors suggest, that Obama is among the least-experienced presidential nominees in our nation's history. But to voters starved for change, the 47-year-old biracial first-term Democratic senator clearly qualifies. That, in any event, is his story, and he has stuck to it.

John McCain's biography has been the stuff of legend for nearly a decade. And yet Schmidt and his fellow strategists have had difficulty explaining how America will be better off for electing (as opposed to simply admiring) a stubborn patriot. In seeking to do so, the McCain campaign has changed its narrative over and over. Sometimes with McCain's initial resistance but always with his eventual approval, Schmidt has proffered a candidate who is variously a fighter, a conciliator, an experienced leader and a shake-'em-up rebel. "The trick is that all of these are McCain," Matt McDonald, a senior adviser, told me. But in constantly alternating among story lines in order to respond to changing events and to gain traction with voters, the "true character" of a once-crisply-defined political figure has become increasingly murky.

Schmidt evidently saw the financial crisis as a "true character" moment that would advance his candidate's narrative. But the story line did not go as scripted. "This has to be solved by Monday," Schmidt told reporters that Wednesday afternoon in late September, just after McCain concluded his lengthy meeting with his advisers and subsequently announced his decision to suspend his campaign and go to Washington. Belying a crisis situation, however, McCain didn't leave New York immediately. He spent Thursday morning at an event for the Clinton Global Initiative, the non-profit foundation run by former President Bill Clinton. As McCain headed for Washington later that morning, he was sufficiently concerned about the situation that Schmidt felt compelled to reassure him. "Remember what President Clinton told you," Schmidt said, referring to advice Clinton had dispensed that morning: "If you do the right thing, it might be painful for a few days. But in the long run it will work out in your favor."

After arriving on Capitol Hill nearly 24 hours after his announcement, McCain huddled with three of his closest political allies: fellow senators Lindsey Graham, Joe Lieberman and Jon Kyl. Later that day at a White House meeting convened by Bush and also attended by Congressional leaders of both parties as well as both candidates, McCain said almost nothing, even when House Republicans declared that they were not yet willing to sign onto the administration's $700 billion proposal. Despite the fact that the deal maker had produced no deal, McCain announced the next day that his campaign would resume—"optimistic that there has been significant progress towards a bipartisan agreement," as a campaign statement put it—and traveled to Mississippi that Friday afternoon to debate Obama. On Sunday morning, Schmidt went on *Meet the Press* to insist that his boss's foray had been crucial in bringing "all of the parties to the table," with the result that "there appears to be a framework completed." The next day—Monday, September 29, the day by which Schmidt had earlier warned the crisis "has to be solved"—the House Republicans played the key role in defeating the bailout legislation.

Scene by scene, McCain failed to deliver the performance that had been promised. Of course, this was no mere movie. America was in crisis. Perhaps with the Bush theory in mind, Steve Schmidt had advised McCain to "go in all the way" on the financial crisis so as to reveal his candidate's true character. But given a chance to show what kind of president he might be, McCain came off more like a stymied bystander than a leader who could make a difference. Judging by the polls, the McCain campaign has yet to recover.

In reporting on the campaign's vicissitudes, I spoke with a half-dozen of McCain's senior-most advisers—most of them more than once and some of them repeatedly—over a period that began in early August. I spoke as well to several other midlevel advisers and to a number of former senior aides. Virtually all of these individuals had spoken with me for previous articles concerning McCain. Their insights and recollections enabled me to piece together conversations and events. My repeated requests to interview McCain and his running mate, Sarah Palin, were denied, and with only a couple of exceptions those who spoke to me did so with the stipulation that most or all of their comments not be attributed to them.

Despite their leeriness of being quoted, McCain's senior advisers remained palpably confident of victory—at least until very recently. By October, the succession of backfiring narratives would compel some to reappraise not only McCain's chances but also the decisions made by Schmidt, who only a short time ago was hailed as the savior who brought discipline and unrepentant toughness to a listing campaign. "For better or for worse, our campaign has been fought from tactic to tactic," one senior adviser glumly acknowledged to me in early October, just after Schmidt received authorization from McCain to unleash a new wave of ads attacking Obama's character. "So this is the new tactic."

NARRATIVE 1: THE HEROIC FIGHTER VS. THE QUITTERS

Steve Schmidt is 38, bald and brawny, with a nasal, deadpan voice and a relentless stare. He is also a devoted husband and father of two young children, introspective and boyishly vulnerable for someone of such imposing stature. On mornings, he can be seen standing outside the McCain campaign headquarters in Arlington, Va., smoking a cigarette while he scowls at his BlackBerry. After campaign events in the evening, he often hangs out at a hotel bar drinking beer with fellow campaign workers and members of the media. Whenever possible, he flies back to California to spend the weekend with his family. He is not a hothead and tends to hesitate for several beats before offering a well-tailored, often wry answer to a question. Though commonly described in the press as a Karl Rove protégé, Schmidt was a Republican operative for a dozen years before he ever worked for Rove. When Bush returned to the White House, Schmidt was not among those from the 2004 reelection effort who were rewarded with plum jobs, despite his well-regarded work overseeing the campaign's rapid-response unit. After spending the first half of 2005 heading up the press office for Vice President Dick Cheney, Schmidt was sent to Baghdad to improve the administration's anemic communications strategy in Iraq. He also orchestrated the Senate confirmation hearings of the Supreme Court nominees John Roberts and Samuel Alito and their presentation to the outside world. Along the way, Schmidt never really developed the personal relationship with Bush that would have enabled him to advance in accordance with his talents. In early 2006, when an opportunity came to jump ship, Schmidt took it, departing the Bush administration to spearhead the successful reelection campaign of Gov. Arnold Schwarzenegger in California. He still lives outside Sacramento, far from Washington. Though Schmidt often brandishes his geographical remove from the Beltway and his lack of interest in another White House job as proof of his equanimity, you get the sense that a McCain victory would bring him no small measure of personal vindication.

For a man who seems to relish Rove-like alley fighting, Schmidt is not an ideologue and claims he harbors no ambition of delivering the Republican Party to a state of lasting supremacy. He also displays great nuance in office politics. Until Schmidt consolidated his power this summer, McCain, it's fair to say, was not a big believer in organization. The important decisions were all made by him, with various confidants of ambiguous portfolio orbiting around him and often colliding with one another (and often staying in the picture well after their departure—as was the case of Mike

Murphy, a strategist from the 2000 campaign, who remained close enough to McCain that rumors of his return persisted until fairly recently).

A year earlier, in the summer of 2007, the McCain campaign all but collapsed under the weight of financial woes, vicious infighting and the conservative base's fury over his moderate stance on immigration. Among the senior staff members who walked out were McCain's longtime political guru John Weaver and several alumni of the well-oiled 2004 Bush campaign. Schmidt—who until that point was not particularly influential—decided to stick around, even without pay. He began to earn McCain's trust while also befriending the senator's two closest advisers, who happened not to care for each other.

One was Rick Davis, a charming Southern lobbyist and Republican jack-of-all-trades who had assumed control of the campaign's day-to-day operations. McCain and Davis have for years called each other a half-dozen times a day, but Davis has also cultivated a close bond with Cindy McCain, who once when talking to Katie Couric referred to Davis as "our best friend." The other adviser was 53-year-old Mark Salter, a brilliant, pugnacious writer who has composed all of McCain's books and major speeches and in a more encompassing sense is McCain's definer, looking after what Salter himself calls the "metanarrative" of McCain's transformation from a reckless flyboy and P.O.W. to a courageous patriot. The complicated interdependence between McCain and Salter could be glimpsed during the candidate's acceptance speech at the Republican convention. Salter sat in the front row, dead center, no more than 15 feet from McCain. I watched as Salter gazed intently at McCain throughout, making subtle motions with his hands and face, and when McCain came to the pivotal line in his P.O.W. tale—"I was no longer my own man; I was my country's"—its author leapt to his feet and applauded.

But in the summer of 2007, Salter and McCain's relationship frayed when Salter and others tried to marginalize Davis, and McCain resisted. While Salter brooded and Davis spent his hours at headquarters begging donors and volunteers not to jump ship, Schmidt stepped into the void. There was still more than a year until the election, he figured. The problem was that McCain was spending his time talking about Iraq, in distinctly funereal tones. "It's long and it's hard and it's tough," the senator told one audience in Gilford, N.H., that summer. "I could recommend books on it that'll make you cry. . . . I know how frustrated you are. I know the sorrow you experience." Virtually all of his senior staff members, Schmidt and Davis among them, had been begging McCain to focus on the economy, health care and tax policy. Anything, really, except Bush's war. But according to several senior advisers, the candidate felt a deep sense of responsibility to cheerlead for the troop surge, which he believed would turn the tide in Iraq. It began to dawn on Schmidt that McCain's stubborn patronage of an unpopular war wasn't impeding the campaign's quest for narrative—it *was* the narrative.

"Sir, is the surge working?" he said he asked McCain one day. "Are we winning?"

"Yes," McCain said.

"That's not what you're saying on the trail."

"It is!"

"No, sir. It's not. You're saying things are getting better. Do you believe we're actually winning now?"

McCain indicated that he did.

"Well, going forward, that's what you should say," Schmidt replied. He encouraged McCain to denounce the Democrats for advocating a withdrawal of troops—a kind of surrender in the face of victory. Thus did Schmidt initiate the No Surrender Tour late in the summer of 2007, a push through the early primary states that saw John McCain surrounded by war veterans while he lashed out at weak-kneed war critics. Employing considerable artistic license, Schmidt linked McCain's stance on Iraq with his bravery during his years in captivity in Vietnam, something the candidate had shied away from. Indeed, as McCain told me two years ago, he decided to write his Vietnam memoir, *Faith of My Fathers*, with Salter largely to put the subject to rest once and for all: "I just got bored telling the same old story over and over again. . . . After the 3,000th time, you think, Hey, I'd rather talk about something else."

As one adviser told me two months ago: "It's against his better nature to be self-aggrandizing. But everybody was telling him, 'This is about the election, the election's about your character and this stuff goes along with your narrative.'" Schmidt warned McCain that declining to discuss personal matters like his P.O.W. days and his religious faith would very likely have ramifications at the polls. The candidate acquiesced. In speeches, debates and advertising, the McCain campaign made liberal use of his war-hero meta-narrative. On March 28, 2008, with the Republican nomination secured, McCain's first national ad was shown. It concluded with grainy black-and-white footage of the wounded P.O.W. reciting his serial number to his captors, followed by a spoken line that Schmidt loved and adamantly defended, even when others inside the campaign argued that it made no sense: "John McCain. The American President Americans have been waiting for." Thereafter, McCain seldom wasted an opportunity to extol his own patriotism.

NARRATIVE 2: COUNTRY-FIRST DEAL MAKER VS. NONPARTISAN PRETENDER

Schmidt spent this spring futilely trying to broaden the story line. Americans, he knew, did not share McCain's devotion to the surge in Iraq. Their concerns lay at home. Accordingly, Schmidt toured McCain through Annapolis, Alexandria and Jacksonville, the towns of his beginnings (an idea conceived by Karl Rove, according to a senior adviser), and then made an empathy swing through poor regions of the country. Both came off as contrivances. McCain's speech in New Orleans on June 3 of this year—the night Obama effectively clinched the nomination—was delivered against a sickly green backdrop, a poorly executed version of an idea Schmidt borrowed from the eco-friendly 2006 Schwarzenegger campaign. Contrasted with Obama's ringing articulation of change in St. Paul that very night, McCain's speech (with its "That's not change we can believe in" refrain) struck even some Republicans as churlish. McCain was so frustrated by his own, at times, stumbling performance that he vowed never to deliver another teleprompter speech again.

The campaign was in the throes of an identity crisis by June 24, when a number of senior strategists gathered at 9:30 A.M. in a conference room of McCain's campaign headquarters in Arlington. As one participant said later, the meeting was convened "because we still couldn't answer the question, 'Why elect John McCain?'" Considering that the election was less than five months away, this was not a good sign.

"We had a narrative problem," Matt McDonald recalls. "Obama had a story line: 'Bush is the problem. I'm not going to be Bush, and McCain will be.' Our story line, I argued, had to be that it's not about Bush—it's Congress, it's Washington. And Obama would be more about partisanship, while John McCain would buck the party line and bring people together."

The others could see McDonald's line of reasoning—and above all, the need to separate McCain from Bush. But the message seemed antiseptic, impersonal. That was when the keeper of McCain's biography, Mark Salter, took the floor. There's a reason McCain bucks his party, McDonald remembers Salter arguing. It's because he puts his country ahead of party. Then the speechwriter, who is not known for his dispassion, began to yell: "We're talking about someone who was willing to *die* before losing his honor! He *would die!*"

Salter stalked out of the meeting to have a cigarette and didn't return. But he had said enough. The metanarrative of Heroic Fighter was now joined with one that evoked postpartisan statesmanship. The new narrative needed a label. The first version was "A Love for America." Then "America First." And finally, the one that stuck: "Country First."

The McCain campaign maintained that in contrast to Obama, their candidate had taken on his own party while working with Democrats on such issues as immigration and campaign-finance reform. "Obama pays no price from his party—never has," Salter told me. "My guy has made a career out of it. So, how can you get people to believe that if you can't get the press to make an honest assessment of it? You tell a story. 'When it came down to a choice between my very life and my country, I chose my country.' That's why the story's important. Just as Obama's story is important to him. I don't gainsay it. You know, tell your story!"

Salter and Schmidt had hoped that the mainstream press would warm to this new narrative. But the matter of which candidate had shown more acts of bipartisan daring failed to become Topic A. The two advisers—each of whom had friendly relations with the media but had grown increasingly convinced that Obama was getting a free ride—took this as further proof that today's reporters were primarily young, snarky, blog-obsessed and liberal. To Schmidt's and Salter's minds, John McCain had always been honest and straightforward with the press, and the press in turn was not acting in good faith toward their candidate. As such it was now undeserving of McCain's unfettered "straight talk."

But this rationale for shutting out the press has its limitations. For one, when McCain's Straight Talk Express first rolled out in 1999, the notion was not conceived simply out of the sense that being transparent with the media—and by extension the voters—was just the right thing to do. Instead, it was implemented because the 2000 campaign lacked the money to compete with Bush's ad campaign. As John Weaver, McCain's former strategist told me, "We needed the coverage." For another, McCain happened to like passing the time with reporters, whom he would sometimes refer to as his "base." In addition, talking openly with the press had some important advantages early on for McCain. According to some of his aides, McCain's victory in the make-or-break New Hampshire primary in January of this year might not have transpired had he not spent time talking to and overtly courting every editorial board in the state for their endorsements.

Regardless, this summer Schmidt sought to convince his voluble candidate that the press was no longer his friend. By July, a curtain was literally drawn to separate McCain from the reporters traveling on his plane. He no longer mingled with them, and press conferences were drastically curtailed. The Bushian concept of message discipline—the droning repetition of a single talking point—that had been so gleefully mocked by McCain's lieutenants in 2000 now governed the Straight Talk Express.

NARRATIVE 3: LEADER VS. CELEBRITY

"Gentlemen, let me put a few things on the table for observation and discussion," Steve Schmidt said to his fellow strategists while sitting in a conference room in the Phoenix Ritz-Carlton. "Would anyone here disagree with the premise that we are not winning this campaign?"

No one disagreed. It was Sunday, July 27, and Obama had just concluded an eight-day swing through the Middle East and Europe that received practically round-the-clock media coverage. "Would anyone disagree with the premise," Schmidt went on, "that Mr. Obama has scored the most successful week in this entire campaign? I mean, they treated him like he was a head of state! So tell me, gentlemen: how do we turn this negative into a positive?"

"It's third and nine," Bill McInturff, a pollster, observed. "Time to start throwing the ball down field."

Eventually, it was Schmidt who blurted out the epiphany concerning Obama. "Face it, gentlemen," he said. "He's being treated like a celebrity."

The others grasped the concept—a celebrity like J-Lo! or Britney!—and exultation overtook the room.

John and Cindy McCain showed up at the end of the daylong meeting, and Schmidt took the opportunity to run the celebrity concept by them. The McCains liked it—though the candidate was otherwise cranky: he was tired of being overscheduled and always late and demanded that this change immediately. (It did, according to a senior adviser: "After that meeting, you will rarely see McCain do an event before 9 in the morning.")

Three days later, the new ad went up. "He's the biggest celebrity in the world," a female voice intoned, as images of Britney Spears and Paris Hilton flashed on the screen. "But: is he ready to lead?" In a conference call with reporters that morning, Schmidt framed the issue with a binary choice straight out of the 2004 playbook: "Do the American people want to elect the biggest celebrity or an American hero?"

The idea, McDonald told me, was "to exalt Obama's eloquence. Push it up to a place where there's no oxygen. Make it an Icarus thing." The notion of Obama's apparent presumptuousness seemed to grow on viewers. And when Russia invaded the fledgling republic of Georgia on August 8, McCain's strategists saw an opportunity for another stark binary choice—albeit one that abruptly shifted the story line back to the international arena: combat-ready leader versus unready celebrity.

The execution of the new narrative left something to be desired, however. Three days after the invasion, McCain made a statement to reporters in Erie, Pa., intended to showcase his mastery of the Russia-Georgia situation. Instead, the candidate mispronounced the name of the Georgian president, Mikheil Saakashvili, three times. The next day, I watched as McCain appeared in York, Pa., to engage in one of his free-form town-hall meetings. But he began the event by standing next to a lectern and reciting Russia-Georgia talking points from prepared notes. Though no doubt this was intended to avoid his previous flubs, McCain's scripted performance seemed more like that of a foreign-policy novice than a sure-handed sage.

When I mentioned this episode later to one of McCain's advisers, he winced and said: "This is part of the Schmidt gotta-have-absolute-message-discipline thing. That's one of the disagreements. And John can be really resistant. He's always worried about being put in a box. He's got a very sensitive nerve about it. A lot of times I would hear him say: 'Don't control me.

This is my campaign.' But I think Steve has convinced him that we've got to do this if we're going to win."

NARRATIVE 4: TEAM OF MAVERICKS VS. OLD-STYLE WASHINGTON

On Sunday, August 24, Schmidt and a few other senior advisers again convened for a general strategy meeting at the Phoenix Ritz-Carlton. McInturff, the pollster, brought somewhat-reassuring new numbers. The Celebrity motif had taken its toll on Obama. It was no longer third and nine, the pollster said—meaning, among other things, that McCain might well be advised to go with a safe pick as his running mate.

Then for a half-hour or so, the group reviewed names that had been bandied about in the past: Governor Tim Pawlenty (of Minnesota) and Governor Charlie Crist (of Florida); the former governors Tom Ridge (Pennsylvania) and Mitt Romney (Massachusetts); Senator Joe Lieberman (Connecticut); and Mayor Michael Bloomberg (New York). From a branding standpoint, they wondered, what message would each of these candidates send about John McCain? McInturff's polling data suggested that none of these candidates brought significantly more to the ticket than any other.

"What about Sarah Palin?" Schmidt asked.

After a moment of silence, Fred Davis, McCain's creative director (and not related to Rick), said, "I did the ads for her gubernatorial campaign." But Davis had never once spoken with Palin, the governor of Alaska. Since the Republican Governors Association had paid for his work, Davis was prohibited by campaign laws from having any contact with the candidate. All Davis knew was that the R.G.A. folks had viewed Palin as a talent to keep an eye on. "She'd certainly be a maverick pick," he concluded.

The meeting carried on without Schmidt or Rick Davis uttering an opinion about Palin. Few in the room were aware that the two had been speaking to each other about Palin for some time now. Davis was with McCain when the two met Palin for the first time, at a reception at the National Governors Association winter meeting in February, in the J. W. Marriott Hotel in Washington. It had not escaped McCain's attention that Palin had blasted through the oleaginous Alaska network dominated by Frank

Murkowski and Ted Stevens, much in the same manner that McCain saw himself doing when he was a young congressman. Newt Gingrich and others had spoken of Palin as a rising star. Davis saw something else in Palin— namely, a way to reestablish the maverick persona McCain had lost while wedding himself to Bush's war. A female running mate might also pick off some disaffected Hillary Clinton voters.

After that first brief meeting, Davis remained in discreet but frequent contact with Palin and her staff—gathering tapes of speeches and interviews, as he was doing with all potential vice-presidential candidates. One tape in particular struck Davis as arresting: an interview with Palin and Governor Janet Napolitano, the Arizona Democrat, on *The Charlie Rose Show* that was shown in October 2007. Reviewing the tape, it didn't concern Davis that Palin seemed out of her depth on health-care issues or that, when asked to name her favorite candidate among the Republican field, she said, "I'm undecided." What he liked was how she stuck to her pet issues—energy independence and ethics reform—and thereby refused to let Rose manage the interview. This was the case throughout all of the Palin footage. Consistency. Confidence. And . . . well, *look at her*. A friend had said to Davis: "The way you pick a vice president is, you get a frame of *Time* magazine, and you put the pictures of the people in that frame. You look at who fits that frame best—that's your V.P."

Schmidt, to whom Davis quietly supplied the Palin footage, agreed. Neither man apparently saw her lack of familiarity with major national or international issues as a serious liability. Instead, well before McCain made his selection, his chief strategist and his campaign manager both concluded that Sarah Palin would be the most dynamic pick. Despite McInturff's encouraging new numbers, it remained their conviction that in this ominous election cycle, a Republican presidential candidate could not afford to play it safe. Picking Palin would upend the chessboard; it was a maverick type of move. McCain, the former Navy pilot, loved that sort of thing. Then again, he also loved familiarity—the swashbuckling camaraderie with his longtime staff members, the P.O.W. band of brothers who frequently rode the bus and popped up at his campaign events, the Sedona ranch where he unwound and grilled wagonloads of meat. By contrast, McCain had barely met Palin.

That evening of August 24, Schmidt and Davis, after leaving the Ritz-Carlton meeting, showed up at McCain's condominium in Phoenix. They informed McCain that in their view, Palin would be the best pick. "You never know where his head is," Davis told me three weeks later. "He doesn't betray a lot. He's a great poker player. But he picked up the phone." Reached at the Alaska State Fair, Palin listened as McCain for the first time discussed the possibility of selecting her as his running mate.

These machinations remained thoroughly sub rosa. McCain's close friend, Lindsey Graham, the South Carolina senator, continued to argue passionately for Lieberman—"a McCain-Plus ticket," he would say. McCain, referring to Romney, at one point said that "Mitt's been awfully helpful with fund-raising," according to a senior aide who was present during the discussion. "And he'd bring us Michigan." Pawlenty's name frequently came up in internal discussions, says that aide. But as for Palin, says another: "She just wasn't one of the names. I mean, we heard more about Bloomberg."

On Tuesday, August 26, Schmidt picked up the phone around noon and called Jon Berrier, an old friend and partner at Schmidt's consulting business in Northern California. Berrier was asked to get on a plane to Anchorage, check into a hotel, await further details and tell no one. The next morning, Davis White, who oversaw all of McCain's travel logistics, met Berrier for breakfast in Anchorage. White informed Berrier that they would meet Palin at a private airstrip that afternoon, and that White would fly with Palin to Arizona to meet with Schmidt and Salter that evening—and then, the following morning, with McCain. If McCain offered the vice-president slot to Palin, White told Berrier, then Berrier would surreptitiously fly Palin's husband, Todd, and their children to Ohio on Thursday evening, and a public announcement would be made there the next morning. The final decision wasn't to be made until Thursday morning, but they should proceed as if it was going to happen.

Palin and her assistant, Kris Perry, met Schmidt and Salter on Wednesday evening in Flagstaff, at the house of Bob Delgado, the chief executive of Hensley & Company, Cindy McCain's beer distributorship. McCain's speechwriter had never spoken with Palin before. A senior adviser said: "Salter was always a big Pawlenty fan—son of a truck driver, salt of the earth, genuine guy. Just thought he was a good, honest addition to the McCain brand as opposed to, say, Romney." That so much momentum had been building in Palin's favor was likely a surprise to Salter, says one of the few individuals privy to the vice-presidential selection process: "Mark was new to it, and so it was important to us to make sure that he was in on the situation that was brewing."

For two hours, Salter and Schmidt asked Palin questions based on the vetting material. Salter says they discussed her daughter's pregnancy and the pending state investigation regarding her role in the controversy surrounding the state trooper who had been married to her sister. The two advisers warned her that nothing was likely to stay secret during the campaign. Salter says that he was impressed. "The sense you immediately get is how tough-minded and self-assured she is," he recalled three weeks after meeting her. "She makes that impression in like 30 seconds."

Now all three of McCain's closest advisers were on board. The next morning was Thursday, August 28. Salter and Schmidt drove Palin to McCain's ranch. According to Salter, the senator took the governor down to a place where he usually had his coffee, beside a creek and a sycamore tree, where a rare breed of hawk seasonally nested. They spoke for more than an hour. Then the two of them walked about 40 yards to the deck of the cabin where the McCains slept. Cindy joined them there for about 15 minutes, after which the McCains excused themselves and went for a brief stroll to discuss the matter. When they returned, McCain asked for some time with Schmidt and Salter. "And we did our pros and cons on all of them," Salter told me. "He just listened. Asked a couple of questions. Then said, 'I'm going to offer it to her.'"

Late that same evening, a McCain spokeswoman, Nicolle Wallace, and the deputy speechwriter, Matthew Scully, were ferried to the Manchester Inn in Middletown, Ohio. Schmidt instructed them to turn off their cell phones and BlackBerrys. Then he opened the door of Room 508 and introduced them to McCain's running mate. The two aides were surprised. Palin and Scully spoke for about 45 minutes, and the governor handed him a copy of the speech she had intended to give as one of the Republican convention's many guest speakers. With this scant information in hand, Scully began his all-night drafting of Palin's first speech to a national audience.

During the evening, Scully also traded e-mail messages with Matt McDonald, who had just gotten the news from Schmidt that the vice-presidential pick was someone who did not quite fit the campaign's current emphasis on "readiness." The story line, Schmidt informed McDonald, was now Change. The two of them, along with Rick Davis, talked through this rather jolting narrative shift. What they decided upon was workable, if inelegant. First, define the problem as Washington, not Bush. Second, posit both McCain and Palin as experienced reformers. And third, define Obama and his 65-year-old running mate, Senator Joe Biden, as a ticket with no real record of change. McDonald in turn transmitted this formulation to Scully and Salter, who was busily drafting McCain's announcement speech.

The spunky hockey mom that America beheld the next morning instantly hijacked Obama's narrative of newness. ("Change is coming!" McCain hollered, almost seeming startled himself.) And five days later, in the hours after Palin's stunningly self-assured acceptance speech at the GOP convention, I watched as the Republicans in the bar of the Minneapolis Hilton rejoiced as Republicans had not rejoiced since Inauguration Night three and a half long years ago. Jubilant choruses of "She knocked it out of the park" and "One of the greatest speeches ever" were heard throughout the room, and some people gave, yes, Obama-style fist bumps. When the tall, unassuming figure of Palin's speechwriter, Matthew Scully, shuffled into the bar, he was treated to the first standing ovation of his life. Nicolle Wallace confessed to another staff member that she had cried throughout Palin's speech. Allowing his feelings to burst out of his composed eggshell of a face, Schmidt bellowed to someone, "Game on!"

Just as quickly, he resumed his natural state of arch contemplativeness. "Arguably, at this stage?" he observed. "She's a bigger celebrity than Obama."

A commotion erupted, followed by outright hysteria. It was 11:45, and the Palins had entered the bar. Dozens of staff members and delegates flocked to the governor, cell phone cameras outstretched. Todd and Sarah Palin posed, shook hands and extended their gracious appreciation for 15 minutes. Then, no doubt realizing that they would never be able to enjoy a drink in peace, they withdrew for the evening, again to raucous applause.

While all of this was going on, an elegant middle-aged woman sat alone at the far end of the bar. She wore beige slacks and a red sweater, and she picked at a salad while talking incessantly on her cell phone. But for the McCain/Palin button affixed to her collar and the brief moment that Tucker Eskew, Palin's new counselor, spoke into her ear, she seemed acutely disconnected from the jubilation swelling around her.

In fact, the woman was here for a reason. Her name was Priscilla Shanks, a New York–based stage and screen actress of middling success who had found a lucrative second career as a voice coach. Shanks's work with Sarah

Palin was as evident as it was unseen. Gone, by the evening of her convention speech, was the squeaky register of Palin's exclamations. Gone (at least for the moment) was the Bushian pronunciation of "nuclear" as "nook-you-ler." Present for the first time was a leisurely, even playful, cadence that signaled Sarah Palin's inevitability on this grand stage.

In the ensuing two and a half weeks (which surely felt longer to the Obama campaign), the Palin Effect was manifest and profound. McCain seemed, if not suddenly younger—after all, the woman standing to his side was nearly the same age as his daughter, Sidney—then freshly boisterous as he crowed, "Change is coming, my friends!" Meanwhile, Palin's gushing references to McCain as "the one great man in this race" and "exactly the kind of man I want as commander in chief" seemed to confer not only valor but virility on a 72-year-old politician who only weeks ago barely registered with the party faithful.

But just as you could make too much of Shanks's quiet coaching of Palin, you could also make too little of it. The new narrative—the Team of Mavericks coming to lay waste the Beltway power alleys—now depended on a fairly inexperienced Alaska politician. The following night, after McCain's speech brought the convention to a close, one of the campaign's senior advisers stayed up late at the Hilton bar savoring the triumphant narrative arc. I asked him a rather basic question: "Leaving aside her actual experience, do you know how informed Governor Palin is about the issues of the day?"

The senior adviser thought for a moment. Then he looked up from his beer. "No," he said quietly. "I don't know."

NARRATIVE 5: JOHN MCCAIN VS. JOHN MCCAIN

In the period before the campaign's decision earlier this month to wage an all-out assault on Obama's character as the next narrative tactic, McCain was signaling to aides that it was important to run an honorable campaign. People are hurting now, McCain said to his convention planners as Hurricane Gustav whirled toward the Gulf Coast. It's a shame we have to have a convention at all. But because we have to do this, tone it down. No balloons, nothing over the top. When his media team suggested running ads that highlighted Obama's connection with the Rev. Jeremiah Wright, McCain reminded them that he pledged months earlier not to exploit the matter, and John McCain was not about to go back on his word. In such moments, the man who renounced negative ads during the 2000 campaign because he wanted (as he told his aghast advisers back then) "to run a campaign my daughter can be proud of" has been thoroughly recognizable.

But that John McCain had lost. Of the noble but perhaps naïve decision in 2000 to unilaterally take down his attack ads, Rick Davis would vow: "That's not gonna happen a second time. I mean, the old dog can learn a few new tricks." And yet on this landscape of new tricks—calling your opponent a liar; allowing your running mate to imply that the opponent might prefer terrorists over Americans—McCain sometimes seemed to be running against not only Barack Obama but an earlier version of himself.

The flipside to John McCain's metanarrative of personal valor has always been palpable self-righteousness. In this campaign, his sense of integrity has been doubly offended. First, an adviser said, "He just really thinks the media is completely in the tank for Obama and doesn't feel like he's getting a fair shake at all." And second, another said, "I don't think John likes people who try to do jobs they're not qualified for"—referring, in this case, to Barack Obama.

In June, McCain formally proposed that he and his Democratic opponent campaign together across America in a series of town-hall-style meetings. He had in fact suggested the same thing to Joe Biden three years earlier, Biden told me back then: "He said: 'Let's make a deal if we end up being the nominees. Let's commit to do what Goldwater and Kennedy committed to do before Kennedy was shot.' We agreed that we would campaign together, same plane, get off in the same city and go to 30 states or whatever together." According to Biden, he and McCain sealed their agreement with a handshake. When McCain extended the same offer to Obama in 2008, the Democrat said that he found the notion "appealing" but then did little to make it happen. Since that time, McCain has repeatedly told aides what he has also said in public—that had Obama truly showed a determination to have a series of joint appearances, the campaign would not have degenerated to its current sorry state.

But to McCain, that Obama failed to do so carries a deeper significance. Authenticity means everything to a man like McCain who, says Salter, "has an affinity for heroes, for men of honor." Conversely, he reserves special contempt for those he regards as arrogant phonies. A year after Barack Obama was sworn into the Senate, Salter recalls McCain saying, "He's got a future,

I'll reach out to him"—as McCain had to Russ Feingold and John Edwards, and as the liberal Arizona congressman Mo Udall had reached out to Mc-Cain as a freshman. McCain invited Obama to attend a bipartisan meeting on ethics reform. Obama gratefully accepted—but then wrote McCain a letter urging him to instead follow a legislative path recommended by Harry Reid, the Democratic leader in the Senate. Feeling double-crossed, McCain ordered Salter to "send him a letter, brush him back a little." Since that experience, says a Republican who has known McCain for a long time, "there was certainly disdain and dislike of Obama."

A senior adviser to McCain said: "The town halls, the ethics bill, immigration reform—all are examples. I think McCain finds it galling that Obama gets credit for his impressive talk about bipartisanship without ever having to bear the risk that is a part of that. It is so much harder to walk the walk in the Senate than to talk the talk." By extension, then, if the McCain campaign's conduct would appear to be at odds with the man's "true character," it is only because the combination of a dishonorable opponent and a biased media has forced his hand. Or so goes the rationale for what by this month was an increasingly ugly campaign.

The worry among his aides had long been that McCain would let his indignation show. Going into the debates, an adviser expressed that very concern to me: "If he keeps the debates on substance, he's very good. If it moves to the personal, then I think it's a disaster." Accordingly, Salter advised McCain before the first debate to maintain, one person privy to the sessions put it, "a very generous patience with Obama—in terms of, 'I'm sure if he understood. . . .'"

"The object wasn't to appear condescending at all—really, the opposite," an adviser said of Salter's tactic, which judging by the post-debate polls seemed to backfire. "You put a bullet in a gun, figuring it'll get shot once. We had no idea it would be shot 10 times."

NARRATIVE 6: THE FIGHTER (AGAIN) VS. THE TAX-AND-SPEND LIBERAL

Having fallen back on the most clichéd of political story lines—the devil you know versus the devil you don't—only to see the negative tactic boomerang, Schmidt and his colleagues cobbled together one last narrative with less than a month to go. Kicking it off at an event in Virginia Beach on October 13, McCain delivered a speech that did not mention "maverick," or "country first," or "no surrender." The new motif was a hybrid of the previous five story lines, especially the first. Mentioning some version of the word "fight" 19 times, McCain was once again a warrior—only more upbeat, more respectful of his opponent, more empathetic to suffering Americans and far more disapproving of the president. Rick Davis told me in September, "The worst scenario for Obama is if he winds up running against the McCain of 2000," an authentic independent. But if this was the McCain that was now emerging, it was awfully late in the game, and he was encumbered by other versions of McCain gone awry.

In the final debate on October 15 at Hofstra University on Long Island, McCain barely mentioned any version of the word "fight" but performed forcefully, perhaps even indignantly. By the time Steve Schmidt entered the post-debate spin room, his Obama counterpart, David Axelrod, had already been holding the floor for 20 minutes. Schmidt wore a pinstripe suit and his blue eyes carried a victor's gleam. Like every other McCain aide I encountered that night, he was convinced not only that the senator had turned in his best performance but that viewers would see him as the clear winner.

Schmidt vowed that McCain would spend the final days of the campaign focused on the economy—and on Joe the plumber, the kind of entrepreneur (so McCain thought at the time) who would become an endangered species in an Obama administration. But that did not stop Schmidt from a lengthy monologue questioning Obama's character and assailing the opposition's "vicious" and "racially divisive" ads. At a certain point, when a member of the foreign media asked him if all of this spinning was likely to help McCain, Schmidt allowed himself a small grin and said: "Well, look. One of the things I always wonder is why we come in here at the end. . . . It doesn't really matter, to be totally truthful with you. It's just part of the ritual. Like eating turkey on Thanksgiving."

A few minutes later, his close friend and colleague Nicolle Wallace tugged Schmidt away from the scrum. They exited the spin room while Axelrod was still holding forth and flew back to Washington late that night.

McCain and a number of his advisers remained at their hotel on Long Island. At the hotel bar where many of them lingered into the late hours, I asked one of them whether the debate could make a difference at this late stage. The adviser maintained that regardless of the instant-poll numbers, Joe the plumber and other talking points would likely resonate in the weeks to come.

Then the adviser said with a helpless smile, "Hopefully that'll change the narrative."

3

THE FRONT-RUNNER'S FALL

JOSHUA GREEN

The Atlantic Monthly   September 2008

Now that Barack Obama is in the White House, it's become accepted wisdom that his biggest accomplishment wasn't defeating John McCain in November but rather his primary upset of the well-financed Hillary Clinton juggernaut. Clinton was so heavily favored, in fact, that her campaign staff—which hadn't anticipated the primary lasting past Super Tuesday on February 5, when twenty-four states and American Samoa held primaries or caucuses—had difficulty waking up to the fact that they were being outmaneuvered by Obama's operation. A dysfunctional management structure and a failure to grasp the importance of the caucus states didn't help matters. In this Atlantic Monthly *article, published in the middle of the general election contest, Joshua Green uses his access to Clinton campaign communiqués to deconstruct how her primary effort ran off the rails.*

For all that has been written and said about Hillary Clinton's epic collapse in the Democratic primaries, one issue still nags. Everybody knows *what* happened. But we still don't have a clear picture of *how* it happened, or why.

The after-battle assessments in the major newspapers and newsweeklies generally agreed on the big picture: the campaign was not prepared for a lengthy fight; it had an insufficient delegate operation; it squandered vast sums of money; and the candidate herself evinced a paralyzing schizophrenia—one day a shots-'n'-beers brawler, the next a Hallmark Channel mom. Through it all, her staff feuded and bickered, while her husband distracted.

But as a journalistic exercise, the "campaign obit" is inherently flawed, reflecting the viewpoints of those closest to the press rather than empirical truth.

How did things look on the inside, as they unraveled?

To find out, I approached a number of current and former Clinton staffers and outside consultants and asked them to share memos, e-mails, meeting minutes, diaries—anything that would offer a contemporaneous account. The result demonstrates that paranoid dysfunction breeds the impulse to hoard. Everything from major strategic plans to bitchy staff e-mail feuds was handed over. (See for yourself: much of it is posted online at www.theatlantic.com/clinton.)

Two things struck me right away. The first was that, outward appearances notwithstanding, the campaign prepared a clear strategy and did considerable planning. It sweated the large themes (Clinton's late-in-the-game emergence as a blue-collar champion had been the idea all along) and the small details (campaign staffers in Portland, Oregon, kept tabs on Monica Lewinsky, who lived there, to avoid any surprise encounters). The second was the thought: *Wow, it was even worse than I'd imagined!* The anger and toxic obsessions overwhelmed even the most reserved Beltway wise men. Surprisingly, Clinton herself, when pressed, was her own shrewdest strategist, a role that had never been her strong suit in the White House. But her advisers couldn't execute strategy; they routinely attacked and undermined each other, and Clinton never forced a resolution. Major decisions would be put off for weeks until suddenly she would erupt, driving her staff to panic and misfire.

Above all, this irony emerges: Clinton ran on the basis of managerial competence—on her capacity, as she liked to put it, to "do the job from Day One." In fact, she never behaved like a chief executive, and her own staff proved to be her Achilles' heel. What is clear from the internal documents is that Clinton's loss derived not from any specific decision she made but rather from the preponderance of the many she did not make. Her hesitancy and habit of avoiding hard choices exacted a price that eventually sank her chances at the presidency. What follows is the inside account of how the campaign for the seemingly unstoppable Democratic nominee came into being, and then came apart.

2003–2006: LAYING THE GROUNDWORK

As long ago as 2003, the Clintons' pollster, Mark Penn, was quietly measuring Hillary's presidential appeal, with an eye toward the 2004 election. Polling suggested that her prospects were "reasonably favorable," but Clinton herself never seriously considered running. Instead, over the next three years, a handful of her advisers met periodically to prepare for 2008. They believed the biggest threat was John Edwards.

Decisions made before her 2006 reelection to the Senate were to have important consequences downstream. Perhaps the biggest was Clinton's choosing to forgo the tradition of visiting early states like Iowa and New Hampshire. Even if she was presumed to be the heavy favorite, Clinton needed to win Iowa to maintain the impression of invincibility that she believed was her greatest advantage. And yet Iowa was a vulnerability. Both husband and wife lacked ties there: Bill Clinton had skipped the 1992 caucuses because Iowa's Senator Tom Harkin was running; in 1996, Clinton had run unopposed.

With her Senate race looming, she feared a backlash if she signaled her presidential intentions. If New Yorkers thought her presumptuous, they could punish her at the polls and weaken her national standing. A collective decision was made not to discuss a presidential run until she had won reelection, leaving the early pursuit of Iowa to John Edwards and Barack Obama.

The effect of these choices in Iowa became jarringly clear when Penn conducted a poll just after Clinton's Senate reelection that showed her running a very distant third, barely ahead of the state's governor, Tom Vilsack. The poll produced a curious revelation: Iowans rated Clinton at the top of the field on questions of leadership, strength, and experience—but most did not plan to vote for her, because they didn't like her. This presented a basic conundrum: Should Clinton run a positive campaign, to persuade Iowans to reconsider her? Or should she run a negative campaign that would accuse her opponents of being untrustworthy and under-qualified? Clinton's top advisers never agreed on the answer. Over the course of the campaign, they split into competing factions that drifted in and out of Clinton's favor but always seemed to work at cross purposes. And Clinton herself could never quite decide who was right.

MARCH 2007: THE STRATEGY

Penn had won the trust of both Clintons by guiding Bill Clinton to reelection in 1996 and through the impeachment saga that followed. But his poll-tested centrism and brusque manner aroused suspicion and contempt among many of their advisers. In the White House and during Hillary's Senate races, Penn often prevailed in internal disputes by brandishing his own poll numbers (which his opponents distrusted) and pointing out that he had delivered a Clinton to the White House once before.

In light of this history, he got off to an inauspicious start when Clinton entered the race in January 2007, by demanding the title "chief strategist" (previously he had been one of several "senior advisers") and presenting each of his senior colleagues with a silver bowl inscribed with the words of Horace Mann: "Be ashamed to die until you have won some victory for humanity."

Penn had clear ideas about how to engineer a win for Clinton, in Iowa and beyond. Obama had eclipsed Edwards right out of the gate and was experiencing the full measure of "next JFK" hype. In a memo dated March 19, 2007, Penn laid out an "Overall Strategy for Winning" built upon a coalition of voters he called "Invisible Americans," a sort of reprise of Bill Clinton's "forgotten middle class":

> As this race unfolds, the winning coalition for us is clearer and clearer. There are three demographic variables that explain almost all of the voters in the primary—gender, party, and income. Race is a factor as well, but we are fighting hard to neutralize it.
>
> We are the candidate of people with needs.
>
> We win women, lower classes, and Democrats (about 3 to 1 in our favor).
>
> Obama wins men, upper class, and independents (about 2 to 1 in his favor).
>
> Edwards draws from these groups as well.
>
> Our winning strategy builds from a base of women, builds on top of that a lower and middle class constituency, and seeks to minimize his advantages with the high class democrats.

If we double perform with WOMEN, LOWER AND MIDDLE CLASS VOTERS, then we have about 55% of the voters.

The reason the Invisible Americans is so powerful is that it speaks to exactly how you can be a champion for those in needs [*sic*]. He may be the JFK in the race, but you are the Bobby.

Clinton was already under attack for an attitude of "inevitability"—the charge being that she imperiously viewed the primary process as a ratifying formality and would not deign to compete for what she felt she was owed. Penn's memo makes clear that what she intended to project was "leadership" and "strength," and that he had carefully created an image for her with that in mind. He believed that he had identified a winning coalition and knew which buttons to press to mobilize it:

1) Start with a base of women.
   a. For these women you represent a breaking of barriers
   b. The winnowing out of the most competent and qualified in an unfair, male dominated world
   c. The infusion of a woman and a mother's sensibilities into a world of war and neglect
2) Add on a base of lower and middle class voters.
   a. You see them; you care about them
   b. You were one of them, it is your history
   c. You are all about their concerns (healthcare, education, energy, child care, college, etc.)
   d. Sense of patriotism, Americana
3) Play defensively with the men and upper class voters.
   a. Strength to end the war the right way
   b. Connect on the problems of the global economy, economics
   c. Foreign policy expert
   d. Unions

Contest the black vote at every opportunity. Keep him pinned down there.

Organize on college campuses. We may not be number 1 there, but we have a lot of fans—more than enough to sustain an organization in every college.

Penn's prescription is notable because it is the rare instance of a Clinton campaign goal that panned out—the coalition she ended up winning a year later is the one described here. Penn's memo is also notable for its tone: it reinforces rather than confronts the Clintons' biases. "The biggest problem we have is the troika that has been set up to tear Hillary down," he wrote.

It is a vast right and left wing conspiracy. Listening to Brit Hume say that Obama is surging while Hillary failed to do X is almost comical and certainly transparent. The right knows Obama is unelectable except perhaps against Attila the Hun, and a third party would come in then anyway.

By contrast, top consultants like Karl Rove usually aim to temper their clients' biases with a cold dose of realism. I suspect the damaging persecution complex that both Clintons displayed drew much of its sustenance from memos like this one.

Penn also left no doubt about where he stood on the question of a positive versus negative strategy. He made the rather astonishing suggestion to target Obama's "lack of American roots":

All of these articles about his boyhood in Indonesia and his life in Hawaii are geared towards showing his background is diverse, multicultural and putting that in a new light.

Save it for 2050.

It also exposes a very strong weakness for him—his roots to basic American values and culture are at best limited. I cannot imagine America electing a president during a time of war who is not at his center fundamentally American in his thinking and in his values. He told the people of NH yesterday he has a Kansas accent because his mother was from there. His mother lived in many states as far as we can tell—but this is an example of the nonsense he uses to cover this up.

How we could give some life to this contrast without turning
negative:

Every speech should contain the line you were born in the middle of America to the middle class in the middle of the last century.
And talk about the basic bargain as about the deeply American values you grew up with, learned as a child and that drive you today.
Values of fairness, compassion, responsibility, giving back.

Let's explicitly own 'American' in our programs, the speeches and
the values. He doesn't. Make this a new American Century, the American Strategic Energy Fund. Let's use our logo to make some flags we
can give out. Let's add flag symbols to the backgrounds.

Clinton wisely chose not to go this route. But the defining clash within
her campaign quickly became the disagreement over how hard to attack
Obama, if at all. Invariably, Penn and Bill Clinton pressed for aggressive
confrontation to tear Obama down, while senior advisers like Harold Ickes,
Patti Solis Doyle, Mandy Grunwald, and Howard Wolfson counseled re-
straint and an emphasis on her softer side that would lift her up. The two
strategies were directly at odds.

On March 29, Ickes, who oversaw the targeting and budget operation
with the campaign's manager, Solis Doyle, circulated a list of the campaign's
"Key Assumptions." (Though Penn was "chief strategist," he was a paid con-
tractor, and thus barred from most targeting and budget planning.) Ickes
believed that Iowa and New Hampshire could determine Clinton's fate, and
that the February 5 Super Tuesday primaries would determine the nominee.
No mention was made of the delegates or the later-caucus states that actually figured so decisively.

Ickes seemed attuned to the asymmetric risk that accompanies overwhelming front-runner status: the collapse of momentum that would accompany an unexpected loss. He posited that Edwards and Obama could
sustain losing Iowa and New Hampshire but worried that Clinton could
not; he urged that she spend "substantial" time in Iowa; and he recommended a contingency plan that would haunt the campaign when his own
budget team didn't fulfill it. Noting the difficulty of raising more than $75
million before Iowa, Ickes stressed the need to maintain a $25 million re-
serve, presumably as insurance against a setback. The campaign wound up

raising more than $100 million—but, according to *The New York Times*, by the time Iowa was lost, $106 million had been spent. The $25 million reserve had vanished, and the campaign was effectively insolvent.

APRIL-MAY 2007: PUZZLING OVER IOWA

By April 8, Penn seemed to have absorbed the criticism of Clinton as behaving imperiously, as well as the emerging importance of the "change" theme Obama was touting. "Show more of the happy warrior," he counseled in a memo. "Let's talk more about a movement for change coming from the people. It's not a Republican movement or a Democratic movement, but a broad-based movement centered on the idea that America is ready for change."

He also seemed cognizant of the growing power of the Web, and, straining for hipness, took at a stab at brainstorming a "viral" strategy:

> I CAN BE PRESIDENT. This idea has potential for a viral campaign among moms—it is about your sons and your daughters believing that they too can be president. Your success paves the way for them. . . . We are making a video with celebrities to launch this program in a FUN way, with great clips from kids and from celebrities saying what they would do if president.

Once again, he returned to the "Invisible Americans":

> Invisibles—need to use this as a creative vehicle to involve people— This can be a cool button where people appear/disappear. Mandy is working on an early spot that would give this some drama to the idea that it's the people's turn to be seen again.

With Obama's popularity and fund-raising strength becoming clearer by the day, Penn started advising Clinton in areas technically outside his purview. He began what would become a contentious, and ultimately unsuccessful, push to persuade Clinton to hire "a friendly TV face"—a clear jab at Howard Wolfson, the chief spokesman. He also urged Clinton to gather more data about the voters in Iowa and New Hampshire and suggested major "issue speeches" in both states.

Penn wasn't the only one worried about Iowa. On May 21, the deputy campaign director, Mike Henry, wrote a prescient memo noting the cost and difficulty of running there and proposing that Clinton skip the caucus. The memo was leaked to *The New York Times*. Henry had estimated (conservatively, as it turned out) that Iowa would require more than $15 million and 75 days of the candidate's presence, and would not provide any financial or organizational edge. "This effort may bankrupt the campaign and provide little if any political advantage," he warned. When the story appeared, Clinton felt compelled to publicly recommit, thereby upping Iowa's significance even further.

SUMMER-FALL 2007: BATTLING OVER IRAQ

Clinton's staff spent the summer battling itself over how to take on Obama, and battling the media over her record on Iraq and just about everything else. Penn had confronted Obama's chief strategist, David Axelrod, at a Harvard symposium in March with the charge that since arriving in the Senate, Obama had voted no differently on Iraq than Clinton had. "Are we going to . . . tell everyone out there the truth about . . . who voted for what, when, or are we going to selectively tell people?" he demanded.

The gambit failed, because Penn was practically the only Clinton adviser eager to push the Iraq issue; the rest believed it was a debate Clinton would lose. The fact that Edwards had apologized for having voted for the war resolution further isolated her. Penn insisted that an apology would be "a sign of weakness," and Clinton never seriously entertained the notion. But the lingering contrast with Obama did not favor her, particularly among Iowa's liberal caucus-goers, and the attacks she did launch only highlighted this fundamental disparity.

The internal discord over whether to attack Obama led some of her own staff to spin reporters to try to downplay the significance of her criticisms. The result for Clinton was the worst of both worlds: the conflicting message exacerbated her reputation for negativity without affording her whatever benefits a sustained attack might have yielded.

Clinton's epic and costly battles with the press—and her husband's, as well—had their genesis in this incoherence. About the only thing the campaign's warring factions *did* agree on was that the press ought to be criticizing

Obama more severely. The more the Clinton team became paralyzed by conflict, the more it was forced to rely on the press to write negative stories that would weaken Obama—to, in effect, perform the very function it was unable to do for itself. This led the campaign to aggressively pressure reporters throughout 2007 and launch the outright attacks against the press that backfired once the primaries began.

DECEMBER 2007: DISASTER LOOMS

Inside the campaign, Penn was losing the debate. His insistence that Obama's mounting attacks called for an expanded press operation was seen as an attempt to weaken his rivals, and he was punished with leaks suggesting that Clinton might dump him as chief strategist. Meanwhile, Clinton had nervously accepted the advice from her Iowa campaign staff that negative attacks would backfire.

On December 1, Clinton and her husband attended a private dinner with the influential *Des Moines Register* editorial board. Seated at opposite ends of a long table, they were stunned to hear journalists praise the skill and efficiency of the Obama and Edwards campaigns and question why Clinton's own operation was so passive.

On the next morning's staff conference call, Clinton exploded, demanding to know why the campaign wasn't on the attack. Solis Doyle was put on a plane to Iowa the next day to oversee the closing weeks. Within hours of the call, the panicked staff produced a blistering attack on Obama for what it characterized as evidence of his overweening lust for power: he had written a kindergarten essay titled "I Want to Become President." The campaign was mocked for weeks.

One story line that has featured prominently in the postmortems is Harold Ickes's attempts to alert the campaign to the importance of the party's complicated system of allotting delegates—a system that Obama's campaign cleverly exploited, by focusing on delegate-rich caucus states. Ickes wrote a series of memos, fatefully ignored, that drew attention to this matter. Nothing I was privy to suggests that anyone else gave it more than passing attention until just before Iowa (though as a cost-saving measure, the budget team halted polling in many of the caucus states they expected Obama to win). Then, on December 22—just 12 days before Iowa—Ickes tried again, in a memo that seems to be introducing the subject of delegates for the first time:

> Assuming that after Iowa and New Hampshire the presidential nominating contest narrows to two competitive candidates who remain locked in a highly contested election through 5 February, the focus of the campaign and press will shift to the delegate count. The dedication of resources (including candidate time) should be influenced, in part, by factors that will afford HRC an advantage in acquiring more delegates compared to her opponent(s).

The advice finally registered—but it was too late.

JANUARY 2008: COLLAPSE AND COMEBACK

In the hours after she finished third in Iowa, on January 3, Clinton seized control of her campaign, even as her advisers continued fighting about whether to go negative. The next morning's conference call began with awkward silence, and then Penn recapped the damage and mumbled something about how badly they'd been hurt by young voters.

Mustering enthusiasm, Clinton declared that the campaign was mistaken not to have competed harder for the youth vote and that—overruling her New Hampshire staff—she would take questions at town-hall meetings designed to draw "comparative," but not negative, contrasts with Obama. Hearing little response, Clinton began to grow angry, according to a participant's notes. She complained of being outmaneuvered in Iowa and being painted as the establishment candidate. The race, she insisted, now had "three front-runners." More silence ensued. "This has been a very instructive call, talking to myself," she snapped, and hung up.

In the days leading up to her stunning New Hampshire comeback, on January 8, Clinton's retail politicking, at last on full display, seemed to make the most difference. But any hope of renewal was short-lived. Not long after New Hampshire, in a senior-staff meeting that both Clintons attended at the campaign's Arlington headquarters, Ickes announced to his stunned colleagues, "The cupboard is empty." The campaign had burned through its money just getting past Iowa. And the news got worse: despite spending

$100 million, it had somehow failed to establish ground operations in all but a handful of upcoming states. Now, urgently needing them, it lacked the money.

Clinton ended up agreeing to lend the campaign $5 million. But even this would enable it to compete in only some of the February 5 states. Though under heavy pressure to fire her campaign manager and chief strategist, Clinton wouldn't drop the ax. She layered on still more advisers, including her former White House chief of staff, Maggie Williams, who settled uncomfortably alongside Solis Doyle.

On January 21, Guy Cecil, a veteran operative who had been brought aboard in September, circulated a memo laying out the game plan for February 5. Now fully alive to the challenge ahead, Cecil split the map into three categories: Obama base states, battleground states, and Clinton base states (of which there were four—Arkansas, California, New Jersey, and New York).

To maximize delegates cheaply, Cecil fell back on trying to drive up voter turnout in Clinton states. He also seems to have been the first person to spot the alarming possibility that blowout wins in weak Clinton districts could yield huge delegate gains for Obama. But here he was essentially flying blind. The Clinton campaign had long since ceased polling in unfriendly states, and now had to make do with guesswork. Cecil estimated that Clinton could net 58 delegates on February 5, significantly expanding her narrow lead.

FEBRUARY 2008: CHAOS

On February 4, Ickes circulated a "framework" of the post–Super Tuesday strategy, stoically noting that "given the lack of polling information for post–5 Feb states, these projections are based on best estimates." The campaign was collectively holding its breath. Ickes wrote:

> Assuming HRC's lead in super delegates holds and continue [*sic*] to increase even slowly, she will continue to lead BO in total delegates at every step. We are in for a real fight, but assuming she at least achieves the projections for Tuesday and given some breaks, it is a fight that she can win.

On Super Tuesday, however, Clinton fell well short of projections, and according to NBC News, Obama finished the day having netted about 10 delegates and narrowed the gap. The slow-motion collapse of Clinton's candidacy began to accelerate.

On February 10, Clinton finally fired Solis Doyle and moved Williams in—but did not heed calls to fire Penn, enraging Solis Doyle's many loyalists. At this crucial point, long-simmering feuds burst into the open. On February 11, Williams's first day on the job, Phil Singer, Wolfson's deputy and a man notorious for his tirades at reporters, blew up in Wolfson's office and screamed obscenities at his boss before throwing open the door to direct his ire at the campaign's policy director, Neera Tanden, an ally of Solis Doyle. "Fuck you and the whole fucking cabal!" he shouted, according to several Clinton staffers. In the end, he climbed onto a chair and screamed at the entire staff before storming out.

The same day, Philip Bennett, the managing editor of the *Washington Post*, sent Williams a letter formally complaining that Singer had maligned one of his reporters by spreading unfounded rumors about her (apparently in retaliation for an accurate—and prescient—story that had noted, long before anyone else, Clinton's tendency to burn through money). Fearing for his deputy's job, Wolfson intercepted the letter, though Bennett eventually got a copy to Williams. Singer disappeared and was presumed fired. But a week later, he made amends and rejoined the campaign. "When the house is on fire, it's better to have a psychotic fireman than no fireman at all," Wolfson explained to a colleague.

As the days wore on, morale deteriorated. In state after state, the staff watched helplessly as huge leads dwindled to nothing in the face of Obama's massive outlays. Toward the end of a February 21 debate, amid what would prove to be a string of 12 straight losses, Clinton spoke of the race wistfully, as though resigned to losing. The press took this as a signal that the end was near—not at all what she meant.

On the call two days later, the candidate was furious, this time at a press corps she accused of purposely misreading her designs in an effort to force her from the race. "They're taking out their revenge on Bill," she fumed, according to a participant's notes. Later that day at a press conference, Clinton left no doubts about her purpose, lighting into Obama. Penn's star was ascendant.

MARCH-APRIL 2008: PENN TAKES COMMAND

Penn believed that white men ("beer drinkers") had been up for grabs since Edwards had bowed out, on January 30; one basis for his disagreement with colleagues who wanted to showcase Clinton's softer side was that doing so would not attract white men. "The idea," he wrote, "that this can be won all on smiles, emotions, and empathy is simply wrong."

Penn created his infamous "3 A.M." ad, questioning Obama's readiness for a crisis, with these voters in mind. Before presenting the ad to the senior staff, he secured Hillary Clinton's approval to broadcast it. But even Clinton's newfound willingness to attack did not prevent Penn from being challenged. His detractors had two rationales: that attacks would look desperate and drive up Clinton's already lofty "unfavorable" ratings; and that if she continued down this path she would irreparably damage her reputation and possibly that of her party's nominee.

In the days leading up to Ohio and Texas, the campaign kept arguing over whether to air the ad. With the deadline looming, Bill Clinton, speaking from a cell phone as his plane sat on a runway, led a conference call on Thursday, February 28, in which he had both sides present their case. As his plane was about to lift off, it was Bill Clinton—not Hillary—who issued the decisive order: "Let's go with it."

On March 4, Clinton carried the primaries in Ohio and Texas, and vowed to remain on the offensive. She chided her reluctant advisers: "A general alone cannot assault a hill." In a triumphant memo afterward, Penn brandished his sword: "We have begun, but must now in earnest, show that their image of Obama Camelot is simply nothing but campaign pitter-patter."

The celebration was dampened, however, by a front-page headline in the *Washington Post*: "Even in Victory, Clinton Team Is Battling Itself." Rather than spotlighting the resurgent candidate, the March 6 piece examined "the battle on the inside"—particularly the towering contempt for Penn.

At nine o'clock that morning, Robert Barnett, the eminent Washington attorney prized by the Clintons for his years of wisdom and discretion, finally blew his top and fired off an e-mail to Hillary Clinton and her senior staff:

> STOP IT!!!! I have help [*sic*] my tongue for weeks. After this morning's WP story, no longer. This makes me sick. This circular firing

squad that is occurring is unattractive, unprofessional, unconscionable, and unacceptable. . . . It must stop.

Yet the clashes and paralysis continued. In the aftermath of Obama's historic race speech on March 18, Sheila Jackson Lee, a Texas congresswoman, urged Clinton to deliver a speech of her own on gender. Clinton appeared very much to want to do this, and solicited the advice of her staff, which characteristically split. The campaign went back and forth for weeks. Opponents argued that her oratory couldn't possibly match Obama's, and proponents countered that she would get credit simply for trying, inspire legions of women to her cause, and highlight an issue that everyone in the campaign fiercely believed was hurting them—sexism. But Clinton never made a decision, and seemed troubled by the concern of Ann Lewis, perhaps her most venerable feminist adviser, who opposed such a speech for fear that it would equate sexism with racism—another contrast with Obama that Clinton feared she would lose.

Even in the midst of chaos, Penn was at last where he wanted to be: steering the campaign. After the death-defying wins in Texas and Ohio, he delivered a strategy update on March 30 charting Clinton's "Path to Victory":

1. Win PA, WV, KY, PR
2. Perform well in OR, NC, SD, MONT, GUAM
3. Pick up 25 Delegates
4. Resolve or Revote MI, FL to close at least 30 Delegates including Supers
5. Be ahead in Popular Vote inc. MI and FL
6. Be ahead in delegates from primaries (his lead will be entirely from caucuses)
7. Be ahead of him against McCain (why we will contrast with McCain on ec[onomy], Iraq)
8. Increase concern about what he would do to Congressional Races (trying test now in white rural districts)
9. Will have won every big state and have coalition of Catholics, working class, Latinos, and women—the key electorates.
10. Super-delegates must see Obama as a doomsday scenario to vote en masse for HRC

Then he shifted gears and went after his colleagues within the campaign:

> Does anyone believe it is possible to win the nomination without,
> over these two months, raising all these issues on him? A "nice" cam-
> paign that wins the states along [*sic*] that can be won—will that be
> enough or do serious issues have to be raised about him?
>
> If you believe that serious issues need to be raised then we have
> to raise them without continual hesitation and we should be push-
> ing the envelope. Won't a single tape of [the Reverend Jeremiah]
> Wright going off on America with Obama sitting there be a game
> ender?
>
> Many people (Peter Hart excluded) believe under the surface
> that 20 years sitting there with Goddamn America would make him
> unelectable by itself.

Four days later, Penn's momentum collided with *The Wall Street Journal*, when the paper exposed his lobbying activity on behalf of a free-trade
agreement with Colombia that Clinton opposed. He was stripped of the
"chief strategist" title, though he maintained an advisory role, and Geoff
Garin, a veteran Democratic operative, replaced him at the helm of the
campaign.

⤛ . ⤜

The absence of clear lines of authority meant that another lurking problem
was ignored for too long. The Democratic National Committee had disal-
lowed the results from Florida and Michigan, to punish the states for holding primaries earlier than its rules permitted. Though Ickes had monitored
the developments throughout 2007, the status of the delegates from the two
states did not become vitally important until Clinton fell behind. Because
she had won both states (even though it was clear that they were technically meaningless "beauty contests"), her campaign made the assumption,
routinely reflected in e-mails and memos from top strategists, that it would
be able to formalize her claim to the delegates.

On February 25, a pair of Clinton advisers began sending a series of increasingly urgent memos, which were given to me by a recipient sympa-

thetic to Solis Doyle as a way of illustrating that strategic mistakes contin-ued even after her dismissal. The first memo, from Philippe Reines and An-drew Shapiro, worried that Clinton's anticipated wins in Texas and Ohio on March 4 would not meaningfully narrow Obama's delegate lead—a fact sure to sap momentum once the initial excitement of victory passed. They pro-posed that Clinton, from a position of strength immediately after her wins, challenge Obama to accept Michigan and Florida revotes. Such a move "pre-empts Obama's reiteration on March 5th that they are still up 100 plus del-egates and that we can't win," they noted. "The press will love the rematch, like *Rocky II*."

On March 4, as Ohio and Texas were voting, the advisers, who now in-cluded senior strategist Doug Hattaway, circulated another memo formal-izing what they now called the "Florigan Plan." Absent a revote, the memo warned, "we cannot secure enough delegates to win; we cannot overtake him; the math simply doesn't work . . . it is imperative that we provide . . . a clear and tenable answer to the single most important question we face." But March 5 passed without any action. On March 10, sensing that the op-portunity to reclaim the Florigan delegates had already vanished, the group again urged pressure for a revote. On the next day's call, Clinton asked for an update on Florida and Michigan. Exasperated by the meager response, she erupted once again and insisted that something be done. A week later, Clinton made an impromptu visit to Detroit to publicly highlight the lack of a resolution.

The campaign did not launch an organized offensive until nine weeks later, on May 21. But by then Clinton was operating from a position of weakness. Rather than greeting it as *Rocky II*, the press covered her bid for a revote as a "last-gasp strategy," which soon failed.

MAY 2008: LAST CHANCE

Geoff Garin, the new leader, soon encountered the old problems. Obama re-mained the front-runner, and Clinton's communications staff disagreed on how to turn back the tide of tough stories. Garin was appalled at the open feuding and leaking. "I don't mean to be an asshole," he wrote in an e-mail to the senior staff. "But . . . Senator Clinton has given Howard Wolfson both the responsibility and the authority to make final decisions about how this campaign delivers its message." On the strategic front, Garin sided with the coalition opposed to Penn's call to confront Obama, and he had numbers to support his reasoning. Polls showed that a majority of voters now distrusted Clinton.

Though Clinton carried Pennsylvania on April 22, aided by Obama's "bitter" comment, Garin believed that a positive strategy could rebuild trust in her in North Carolina and Indiana, the next big hurdles. The campaign was deeply in debt, but Garin convinced Clinton that if she committed several million dollars to his strategy, they would win Indiana, pull to within single digits in North Carolina, and live to fight on. In an April 25 e-mail outlining his approach, which would be very different from Penn's, he wrote:

> We are definitely moving in the right direction, and I believe we are on track to narrow this to single digits—especially if we fund a competitive effort in [North Carolina].
>
> Our white targets are slightly more male than female, and definitely skew under age 50. . . . About 20% of all whites are still moveable to Clinton.

But on May 6, the narrowness of Clinton's victory in Indiana and her blowout loss in North Carolina effectively ended the race. She finished out the primary calendar, with Garin gently steering the campaign into port on June 3.

That evening, as she delivered the non-concession speech that awkwardly preceded the real one several days later, Clinton seemed to finally embrace the ideas of her erstwhile chief strategist (who was, even in his reduced role, preparing one final attempt to win the argument, this time in a formal presentation for the super-delegates). Her campaign at an end, Clinton seemed to reach all the way back to the beginning, to Penn's "Invisible Americans":

> I want to turn this economy around. I want health care for every American. I want every child to live up to his or her God-given potential, and I want the nearly 18 million Americans who voted for me to be respected, to be heard, and no longer to be invisible.

4

THE INSIDERS: HOW JOHN MCCAIN CAME TO PICK SARAH PALIN

JANE MAYER
The New Yorker   October 27, 2008

If you had to pick the media highlight of the 2008 presidential campaign, it was John McCain's selection of Sarah Palin as his running mate, hands down. Most Americans had never heard of the Alaska governor, but the nation's fascination with the conservative Christian ex–small-town mayor and former Miss Alaska contestant was immediate. Everything about her was intriguing, from her high school basketball team's state championship and her "pit bull with lipstick" stump style to her snowmobile-racing husband, Todd, and the rest of her very Alaskan family. The fascination quickly took on a partisan tinge, with conservatives embracing her frontier values and her unapologetic defense of her teenage daughter's unplanned pregnancy and the left quick to pan her inarticulate performance in a series of television interviews.

As the campaign moved forward, it became apparent that Palin's lack of preparation was a net negative for McCain, especially because of his campaign's emphasis on "experience" and because of his own advanced age (if elected, he would have been the oldest president to enter the White House at age seventy-two), which gave extra weight to the qualifications of any potential successor. With the media sifting through every detail of Palin's life, however, one question remained largely unanswered: exactly how did "Sarah Barracuda" make it onto the short list of McCain's possible veep picks in the first place? In this illuminating and entertaining New Yorker *article, Jane Mayer (author of the book The Dark Side, and a frequent contributor to this anthology) takes a break from reporting on the Bush administration's enhanced-interrogation program to reveal how Palin has been cultivating ties with Washington since she was first elected governor—and how two cruise ships filled with vacationing Republicans may have played a crucial role in ushering her onto the national stage.*

[Editor's note: In the article, Mayer refers to both the corruption trial and reelection campaign of U.S. Senator Ted Stevens. In late October 2008, Stevens was found guilty of seven counts of ethics violations. Several days later, he lost his bid for a seventh Senate term. His conviction was overturned five months later by a federal judge, on the grounds that federal prosecutors had mishandled evidence.]

"Here's a little news flash," Sarah Palin, the governor of Alaska and the Republican candidate for vice-president, announced in September, during her debut at the party's convention, in St. Paul. "I'm not a member of the permanent political establishment. And I've learned quickly these past few days that if you're not a member in good standing of the Washington elite then some in the media consider a candidate unqualified for that reason alone." But, she added, "I'm not going to Washington to seek their good opinion."

In subsequent speeches, Palin has cast herself as an antidote to the elitist culture inside the Beltway. "I'm certainly a Washington outsider, and I'm proud of that, because I think that that is what we need," she recently told Fox News. During her first interview as John McCain's running mate, with ABC's Charlie Gibson, Palin was asked about her lack of experience in foreign policy. She replied, "We've got to remember what the desire is in this nation at this time. It is for no more politics as usual, and somebody's big fat résumé, maybe, that shows decades and decades in the Washington establishment. . . . Americans are getting sick and tired of that self-dealing, and kind of that closed-door, good-ol'-boy network that has been the Washington elite."

Palin's sudden rise to prominence, however, owes more to members of the Washington elite than her rhetoric has suggested. Paulette Simpson, the head of the Alaska Federation of Republican Women, who has known Palin since 2002, said, "From the beginning, she's been underestimated. She's very smart. She's ambitious." John Bitney, a top policy adviser on Palin's 2006 gubernatorial campaign, said, "Sarah's very conscientious about crafting the story of Sarah. She's all about the hockey mom and Mrs. Palin Goes to

Washington—the anti-politician politician." Bitney is from Wasilla, Palin's hometown, and has known her since junior high school, where they both played in the band. He considers Palin a friend, even though after becoming governor, in December, 2006, she dismissed him. He is now the chief of staff to the speaker of the Alaska House.

Upon being elected governor, Palin began developing relationships with Washington insiders, who later championed the idea of putting her on the 2008 ticket. "There's some political opportunism on her part," Bitney said. For years, "she's had D.C. in mind." He added, "She's not interested in being on the junior-varsity team."

During her gubernatorial campaign, Bitney said, he began predicting to Palin that she would make the short list of Republican vice-presidential prospects. "She had the biography, I told her, to be a contender," he recalled. At first, Palin only laughed. But within a few months of being sworn in she and others in her circle noticed that a blogger named Adam Brickley had started a movement to draft her as vice-president. Palin also learned that a number of prominent conservative pundits would soon be passing through Juneau, on cruises sponsored by right-leaning political magazines. She invited these insiders to the governor's mansion, and even led some of them on a helicopter tour.

Throughout the campaign, Palin has mocked what she calls "the mainstream media." Yet her administration made a concerted effort to attract the attention of East Coast publications. In late 2007, the state hired a public-relations firm with strong East Coast connections, which began promoting Palin and a natural-gas pipeline that she was backing in Alaska. The contract was for thirty-seven thousand dollars. The publicist on the project, Marcia Brier, the head of MCB Communications, in Needham, Massachusetts, was asked to approach media outlets in Washington and New York, according to the *Washington Post*. "I believe Alaska has a very small press organization," Brier told me. "They hired an outside consultant in order to get that East Coast press." Brier crafted a campaign depicting Palin as bravely taking on powerful oil interests by choosing a Canadian firm, Trans-Canada, rather than an American conglomerate such as ExxonMobil, to build the pipeline. ("Big Oil Under Siege" was the title of a typical press release.) Brier pitched Palin to publications such as the *Times*, the *Washington Post*, and *Fortune*.

From the start of her political career, Palin has positioned herself as an insurgent intent on dislodging entrenched interests. In 1996, a campaign pamphlet for her first mayoral run—recently obtained by *The New Republic*—strikes the same note of populist resentment that Palin did at the Convention: "I'm tired of 'business as usual' in this town, and of the 'Good Ol' Boys' network that runs the show here." Yet Palin has routinely turned to members of Washington's Old Guard for help. After she became the mayor of Wasilla, Palin oversaw the hiring of a law firm to represent the town's interests in Washington, D.C. The Wasilla account was handled by Steven Silver, a Washington-area lobbyist who had been the chief of staff to Alaska's long-serving Republican senator Ted Stevens, who was indicted in July on charges of accepting illegal gifts and is now standing trial. (Silver declined to discuss his ties to Palin.) As the *Washington Post* reported, Silver's efforts in the capital helped Wasilla, a town of sixty-seven hundred residents, secure twenty-seven million dollars in federal earmarks. During this election season, however, Palin has presented herself as more abstemious, saying, "I've championed reform to end the abuses of earmark spending by Congress."

⋖ • ⋗

In February, 2007, Adam Brickley gave himself a mission: he began searching for a running mate for McCain who could halt the momentum of the Democrats. Brickley, a self-described "obsessive" political junkie who recently graduated from the University of Colorado at Colorado Springs, told me that he began by "randomly searching Wikipedia and election sites for Republican women." Though he generally opposes affirmative action, gender drove his choice. "People were talking about Hillary at the time," he recalled. Brickley said that he "puzzled over every Republican female politician I knew." Senator Kay Bailey Hutchison, of Texas, "waffled on social issues"; Senator Olympia Snowe, of Maine, was too moderate. He was running out of options, he recalled, when he said to himself, "What about that lady who just got elected in Alaska?" Online research revealed that she had a strong grassroots following; as Brickley put it, "I hate to use the words 'cult of personality,' but she reminded me of Obama."

Brickley registered a Web site—palinforvp.blogspot.com—which began getting attention in the conservative blogosphere. In the month before Palin was picked by McCain, Brickley said, his Web site was receiving about three thousand hits a day. Support for Palin had spread from one right-of-center Internet site to the next. First, the popular conservative blogger InstaPundit mentioned Brickley's campaign. Then a site called the American Scene said that Palin was "very appealing"; another, Stop the A.C.L.U., described her as "a great choice." The traditional conservative media soon got in on the act: *The American Spectator* embraced Palin, and Rush Limbaugh, the radio host, praised her as "a babe."

Brickley's family, once evangelical Christians, now practice what he calls "Messianic Judaism." They believe that Jesus is the Messiah, but they also observe the Jewish holidays and attend synagogue; as Brickley puts it, "Jesus was Jewish, so to be like Him you need to be Jewish, too." Brickley said that "the hand of God" played a role in choosing Palin: "The longer I worked on it the less I felt I was driving it. Something else was at work."

Brickley is an authentic heartland voice, but he is also the product of an effort by wealthy conservative organizations in Washington to train activists. He has attended several workshops sponsored by the Leadership Institute, a group based in the Washington area and founded in 1979 by the Christian conservative activist Morton Blackwell. "I'm building a movement," Blackwell told me. Brickley also participated in a leadership summit held by Young America's Foundation (motto: "The Conservative Movement Starts Here") and was an intern at the Heritage Foundation. He currently lives in a dormitory, on Capitol Hill, run by the Heritage Foundation, and is an intern with townhall.com, a top conservative Web site.

While Brickley and others were spreading the word about Palin on the Internet, Palin was wooing a number of well-connected Washington conservative thinkers. In a stroke of luck, Palin did not have to go to the capital to meet these members of "the permanent political establishment"; they came to Alaska. Shortly after taking office, Palin received two memos from Paulette Simpson, the Alaska Federation of Republican Women's leader, noting that two prominent conservative magazines—*The Weekly Standard*, owned by Rupert Murdoch's News Corporation, and *National Review*, founded by William F. Buckley, Jr.—were planning luxury cruises to Alaska in the summer of 2007, which would make stops in Juneau. Writers and editors from these publications had been enlisted to deliver lectures to politically minded vacationers. "The Governor was more than happy to meet these guys," Joe Balash, a special staff assistant to Palin, recalled.

On June 18, 2007, the first group disembarked in Juneau from the Holland America Line's M.S. *Oosterdam*, and went to the governor's mansion, a white wooden Colonial house with six two-story columns, for lunch. The contingent featured three of *The Weekly Standard*'s top writers: William Kristol, the magazine's Washington-based editor, who is also an op-ed columnist for the *Times* and a regular commentator on *Fox News Sunday*; Fred Barnes, the magazine's executive editor and the co-host of *The Beltway Boys*, a political talk show on Fox News; and Michael Gerson, the former chief speechwriter for President Bush and a *Washington Post* columnist.

By all accounts, the luncheon was a high-spirited, informal occasion. Kristol brought his wife and daughter; Gerson brought his wife and two children. Barnes, who brought his sister and his wife, sat on one side of Governor Palin, who presided at the head of the long table in the mansion's formal dining room; the Kristols sat on the other. Gerson was at the opposite end, as was Palin's chief of staff at the time, Mike Tibbles, who is now working for Senator Stevens's reelection campaign. The menu featured halibut cheeks—the choicest part of the fish. Before the meal, Palin delivered a lengthy grace. Simpson, who was at the luncheon, said, "I told a girlfriend afterwards, 'That was *some* grace!' It really set the tone." Joe Balash, Palin's assistant, who was also present, said, "There are not many politicians who will say grace with the conviction of faith she has. It's a daily part of her life."

Palin was joined by her lieutenant governor and by Alaska's attorney general. Also present was a local woman involved in upholding the Juneau school system's right to suspend a student who had displayed a satirical banner—"Bong Hits 4 Jesus"—across the street from his school. The student had sued the school district, on First Amendment grounds, and, at the time of the lunch, the case was before the Supreme Court. (The school district won.)

During the lunch, everyone was charmed when the Governor's small daughter Piper popped in to inquire about dessert. Fred Barnes recalled being "struck by how smart Palin was, and how unusually confident. Maybe because she had been a beauty queen, and a star athlete, and succeeded at almost everything she had done." It didn't escape his notice, too, that she was "exceptionally pretty."

According to a former Alaska official who attended the lunch, the visitors wanted to do something "touristy," so a "flight-seeing" trip was arranged. Their destination was a gold mine in Berners Bay, some forty-five miles north of Juneau. For Palin and several staff members, the state leased two helicopters from a private company, Coastal, for two and a half hours, at a cost of four thousand dollars. (The pundits paid for their own aircraft.) Palin explained that environmentalists had invoked the Clean Water Act to oppose a plan by a mining company, Coeur Alaska, to dump waste from the extraction of gold into a pristine lake in the Tongass National Forest. Palin rejected the environmentalists' claims. (The Ninth Circuit Court of Appeals ruled against Coeur Alaska, and the dispute is now before the Supreme Court.) Barnes was dazzled by Palin's handling of the hundred or so mineworkers who gathered to meet the group. "She clearly was not intimidated by crowds—or men!" he said. "She's got real star quality."

By the time the *Weekly Standard* pundits returned to the cruise ship, Paulette Simpson said, "they were very enamored of her." In July, 2007, Barnes wrote the first major national article spotlighting Palin, titled "The Most Popular Governor," for *The Weekly Standard*. Simpson said, "That first article was the result of having lunch." Bitney agreed: "I don't think she realized the significance until after it was all over. It got the ball rolling."

The other journalists who met Palin offered similarly effusive praise: Michael Gerson called her "a mix between Annie Oakley and Joan of Arc." The most ardent promoter, however, was Kristol, and his enthusiasm became the talk of Alaska's political circles. According to Simpson, Senator Stevens told her that "Kristol was really pushing Palin" in Washington before McCain picked her. Indeed, as early as June 29th, two months before McCain chose her, Kristol predicted on *Fox News Sunday* that "McCain's going to put Sarah Palin, the governor of Alaska, on the ticket." He described her as "fantastic," saying that she could go one-on-one against Obama in basketball, and possibly siphon off Hillary Clinton's supporters. He pointed out that she was a "mother of five" and a reformer. "Go for the gold here with Sarah Palin," he said. The moderator, Chris Wallace, finally had to ask Kristol, "Can we please get off Sarah Palin?"

The next day, however, Kristol was still talking about Palin on Fox. "She could be both an effective vice-presidential candidate and an effective president," he said. "She's young, energetic." On a subsequent *Fox News Sunday*, Kristol again pushed Palin when asked whom McCain should pick: "Sarah Palin, whom I've only met once but I was awfully impressed by—a genuine reformer, defeated the establishment up there. It would be pretty wild to pick a young female Alaska governor, and I think, you know, McCain might as well go for it." On July 22nd, again on Fox, Kristol referred to Palin as "my heartthrob." He declared, "I don't know if I can make it through the next three months without her on the ticket." Reached last week, Kristol pointed out that just before McCain picked Palin he had ratcheted back his campaign a little; though he continued to tout her, he also wrote a *Times* column promoting Senator Joe Lieberman, of Connecticut.

On October 6th, in another *Times* column, Kristol cryptically acknowledged having been entertained by the Governor. He mentioned meeting Palin "in far more relaxed circumstances, in Alaska over a year ago." The column featured one of the few interviews that Palin has granted to the national media since becoming McCain's running mate. Kristol quoted Palin saying that the debate had been a "liberating" experience, then wrote, "Shouldn't the public get the benefit of another Biden-Palin debate, or even two? If there's difficulty finding a moderator, I'll be glad to volunteer."

On August 1, 2007, a few weeks after the *Weekly Standard* cruise departed from Juneau, Palin hosted a second boatload of pundits, this time from a cruise featuring associates of *National Review*. Her guests, arriving on the M.S. *Noordam*, included Rich Lowry, the magazine's editor and a syndicated columnist; Robert Bork, the conservative legal scholar and former federal judge; John Bolton, who served as the Bush administration's Ambassador to the United Nations from 2004 to 2006; Victor Davis Hanson, a conservative historian who is reportedly a favorite of Vice-President Dick Cheney; and Dick Morris, the ideologically ambidextrous political consultant, who writes a column for *The Hill* and appears regularly on Fox News.

As Jack Fowler, *National Review*'s publisher, recalled it, when the guest speakers were invited to come to a special reception at the governor's mansion, "We said, 'Sure!' There's only so much you can do in Juneau." The mansion itself, he said, was modest—"not exactly Newport." But the food was great, and included an impressive spread of salmon. Palin, who circulated nimbly through the room, and spoke admiringly of *National Review*, made a good impression. Fowler said, "This lady is something special. She connects. She's genuine. She doesn't look like what you'd expect. My thought was, Too bad she's way up there in Alaska, because she has potential, but to make things happen you have to know people."

Hanson, the historian, recalled Palin in high heels, "walking around this big Victorian house with rough Alaska floors, saying, 'Hi, I'm Sarah.'" She was "striking," he said. "She has that aura that Clinton, Reagan, and Jack Kennedy had—magnetism that comes through much more strongly when you're in the same room." He was delighted that Palin described herself as a fan of history, and as a reader of *National Review*'s Web site, for which he writes regularly. She spoke about the need to drill for oil in Alaska's protected wilderness areas, arguing that her husband had worked in nearby oil fields and knew firsthand that it wasn't environmentally hazardous. Hanson, a farm owner, found it appealing that she was married to an oil worker, rather than to an executive. Bolton, for his part, was pleased that Palin, a hunting enthusiast, was familiar with his efforts to stave off international controls on the global flow of small weapons. She spoke knowledgeably about missile defense, too, he said, and discussed his role, in 2001, in guiding the Bush administration's withdrawal from the Anti-Ballistic Missile Treaty. Jay Nordlinger, a senior editor at *National Review*, had a more elemental response. In an online column, he described Palin as "a former beauty pageant contestant, and a real honey, too. Am I allowed to say that? Probably not, but too bad."

According to several accounts, however, no connection made that day was more meaningful than the one struck between Palin and Dick Morris. "He had this *very* long conversation with her," Fowler recalled. Lowry laughed in remembering it: "The joke going around was that he was going to take credit for making her." (Nordlinger's column went on to say, "Her political career will probably take her beyond Alaska. Dick Morris is only one who thinks so.")

In fact, in an admiring column published in the *Washington Post* two days after Palin was chosen, Morris wrote, "I will always remember taking her aside and telling her that she might one day be tapped to be vice-president, given her record and the shortage of female political talent in the Republican Party. She will make one hell of a candidate, and hats off to McCain for picking her."

Morris offered Palin some advice during their encounter in Juneau, several of those present recollected, which he shared with the rest of the gathering in a short speech. As Lowry recalled it, Morris had warned her that a reformer, in order to be successful, needed to maintain her "outsider cred." In a similar vein, Simpson recalled that Morris "gave a little speech" in which he warned that "what happens to most people is that they campaign as outsiders, but when they get into power they turn into insiders. If you want to be successful, you have to stay an outsider."

Clearly, Palin has taken this advice to heart. Still, when the moment came for Morris and other guests to depart, Palin was sad to see the Washington insiders go. Hanson recalled, "She said, 'Hey—does anyone want to stay for dinner? We're going to eat right now.' She also invited everyone to come back the next day. 'If any of you are in the area, all you have to do is knock. Yell upstairs, I'll be right down.'"

⤛ • ⤜

By the end of February, 2008, the chorus of conservative pundits for Palin was loud enough for the mainstream media to take note. Chris Cillizza, reporting for the Web site of the *Washington Post*, interviewed Palin and asked her if she'd accept an offer to be McCain's running mate. Though she dismissed the notion as a virtual "impossibility this go-round," Palin, who had been in office for only fourteen months, said, "Is it generally something that I would want to consider? Yes."

By the spring, the McCain campaign had reportedly sent scouts to Alaska to start vetting Palin as a possible running mate. A week or so before McCain named her, however, sources close to the campaign say, McCain was intent on naming his fellow-senator Joe Lieberman, an independent, who left the Democratic Party in 2006. David Keene, the chairman of the American Conservative Union, who is close to a number of McCain's top aides, told me that "McCain and Lindsey Graham"—the South Carolina senator, who has been McCain's closest campaign companion—"really wanted Joe." But Keene believed that "McCain was scared off" in the final days, after warnings from his advisers that choosing Lieberman would ignite a contentious floor fight at the Convention, as social conservatives revolted against Lieberman for being, among other things, pro-choice.

"They took it away from him," a longtime friend of McCain—who asked not to be identified, since the campaign has declined to discuss its selection process—said of the advisers. "He was furious. He was pissed. It wasn't what he wanted." Another friend disputed this, characterizing McCain's mood as one of "understanding resignation."

With just days to go before the Convention, the choices were slim. Karl Rove favored McCain's former rival Mitt Romney, but enough animus lingered from the primaries that McCain rejected the pairing. "I told Romney not to wait by the phone, because 'he doesn't like you,'" Keene, who favored the choice, said. "With John McCain, all politics is personal." Other possible choices—such as former Representative Rob Portman, of Ohio, or Governor Tim Pawlenty, of Minnesota—seemed too conventional. They did not transmit McCain's core message that he was a "maverick." Finally, McCain's top aides, including Steve Schmidt and Rick Davis, converged on Palin. Ed Rogers, the chairman of B.G.R., a well-connected, largely Republican lobbying firm, said, "Her criteria kept popping out. She was a governor—that's good. The shorter the Washington résumé the better. A female is better still. And then there was her story." He admitted, "There was concern that she was a novice." In addition to Schmidt and Davis, Charles R. Black, Jr., the lobbyist and political operative who is McCain's chief campaign adviser, reportedly favored Palin. Keene said, "I'm told that Charlie Black told McCain, 'If you pick anyone else, you're going to lose. But if you pick Palin you *may* win.'" (Black did not return calls for comment.) Meanwhile, McCain's longtime friend said, "Kristol was out there shaking the pom-poms."

McCain had met Palin once, but their conversation—at a reception during a meeting of the National Governors Association, six months earlier—had lasted only fifteen minutes. "It wasn't a real conversation," said the longtime friend, who called the choice of Palin "the fucking most ridiculous thing I've ever heard." Aides arranged a phone call between McCain and Palin, and scrutinized her answers to some seventy items on a questionnaire that she had filled out. But McCain didn't talk with Palin in person again until the morning of Thursday, August 28th. Palin was flown down to his retreat in Sedona, Arizona, and they spoke for an hour or two. By the time he announced her as his choice, the next day, he had spent less than three hours in her company.

"It certainly was a risk—a risk a lot of people wouldn't take," Dan Coats, a former Indiana senator and now a volunteer with the McCain campaign, said. "But that's what I like about John. There's a boldness there."

The thoroughness of the campaign's vetting process, overseen by the Washington lawyer and former White House counsel Arthur B. Culvahouse, Jr., remains in dispute. The campaign insists that Palin's record and personal history were carefully examined. (Culvahouse declined to comment for this story.) The *Los Angeles Times*, however, reported that the campaign never contacted several obvious sources of information on Palin, including Lyda Green—a Republican state senator in Alaska, and a former ally turned opponent. Also in dispute is whether Palin disclosed to the campaign, as she and officials have said, that her unwed teenage daughter was pregnant. "I am a hundred per cent sure they didn't know," McCain's longtime friend said. Another campaign source, however, insisted that McCain's team knew about the pregnancy.

The selection of Palin thrilled the Republican base, and the pundits who met with her in Juneau have remained unflagging in their support. But a surprising number of conservative thinkers have declared her unfit for the vice-presidency. Peggy Noonan, the *Wall Street Journal* columnist, recently wrote, "The Palin candidacy is a symptom and expression of a new vulgarization in American politics. It's no good, not for conservatism and not for the country. And yes, it is a mark against John McCain." David Brooks, the *Times* columnist, has called Palin "a fatal cancer to the Republican Party." Christopher Buckley, the son of *National Review*'s late founder, defected to the Obama camp two weeks ago, in part because of his dismay over Palin. Matthew Dowd, the former Bush campaign strategist turned critic of the president, said recently that McCain "knows in his gut" that Palin isn't qualified for the job, "and when this race is over, that is something he will have to live with. . . . He put the country at risk."

Palin initially provided the McCain campaign with a boost, but polls now suggest that she has become a liability. A top Republican close to the campaign said that McCain's aides have largely kept faith with Palin. They have been impressed by her work ethic, and by what a quick study she is. According to the Republican close to the campaign, she has sometimes discomfited advisers by travelling with a big family entourage. "It kind of changes the dynamic of a meeting to have them all in the room," he told me. John McCain's comfort level with Palin is harder to gauge. In the view of the longtime McCain friend, "John's personal comfort level is low with everyone right now. He's angry. But it was his choice."

5

THE MAN WHO MADE OBAMA

LISA TADDEO

Esquire   March 2009

While Barack Obama's chief strategist, David Axelrod, was the public face of the Obama campaign, campaign manager David Plouffe remained largely out of sight throughout the primary and general election contests. Plouffe's effectiveness, on the other hand, could be seen everywhere: in the smooth-running central campaign staff; in the tight coordination with regional campaign efforts; and, above all, in the deft, omnipresent, and persistent use of the Internet to organize and capitalize on a ground-up, grassroots effort to elect Plouffe's candidate. One benefit of this web-based operation was that it left Obama well positioned to score heavily in the states that had primary caucuses—victories that ended up providing the decisive advantage in his defeat of Hillary Clinton. Another benefit was financial: Obama raised a staggering $750 million dollars during the course of the campaign, much of it through online donations.

In this engaging profile, Esquire's *Lisa Taddeo catches up with the elusive Plouffe postelection to learn a little more about what makes him tick—and what he plans to do with his massive database of Obama supporters, now that their candidate is safely ensconced in the Oval Office.*

When you have been to the moon, you can't come back to Earth and stand in line at Starbucks. You can't order a coffee, and pay for it, and drink it beside someone wearing Sarah Palin glasses and a cruise visor. The regression to mediocrity is stunning and sapping. You would die inside.

After de-mooning, Buzz Aldrin got depressed and divorced. He drank and he returned to the Air Force. But the Air Force doesn't fly to the moon; it's glad to clear the clouds.

Campaign consultant Paul Begala landed Bill Clinton the most powerful job on the ground. That's a moon trip, too. Once, Begala sent Buzz Aldrin a fan letter. What Begala wondered—because it's the same question that bedevils the people who get other people elected president—is what you do after you come back down. What in the world do you do now?

"Buzz was the second man on the moon, and the guy comes back and he can't get out of bed in the morning," says Begala. "What the fuck do you do after you get on the moon? What the *fuck* do you do?"

⤙ • ⤚

There is a picture of large-eared David Plouffe in his college newspaper. It's 1988 at the University of Delaware, and there's a story on the student who, two decades later, would design a black man's winning campaign for president that at its most linear was described by its opposition as "perfect." At its most cultish, it was "breathtaking," "golden," "justice."

The seven-hundred-word article is about beer pong. Plouffe and his college roommate were prolific. "For two years," says Barack Obama's campaign manager, "that's all we did." Classes, he wasn't that into them. He never graduated.

Today Plouffe, forty-one, is wearing a bargain-colored henley shirt and smiling into his grouper sandwich. It's a cold day in early December in Washington, D.C., and Plouffe's face has a windburned clean to it. Life has become the whirlwind that happens when you have publicly done something very good, or bad. His mouth becomes a cartoon shape when he smiles, a sunny crescent.

"You have to use a paddle, or you can use a saucepan, but where do you think the word *pong* comes from? It's not just about the ball," he says. In fact, if you think it's just about the ball, you're missing most of the game.

An old college buddy says that Plouffe was far more skilled at the hanging out and drinking than at the game. He also loved Roger Clemens and the Democratic Party. Originally from Wilmington, he cleaned chimneys and sold knives during college summers.

This is not the sort of man who looks as if he's good at asking for money. He's calm and has a pent-up grin. He says "Listen" a lot. It's moderately jarring. It makes you think that what he's about to say is essential, so come closer. "Listen." But really it's only a blinking cursor, a half beat of an inflection.

You might describe this shy middleman by not describing him. He has a widow's peak, which today has been gelled into rigid formation, and the teeth of a man who has never smoked a cigarette. He's small and lean and always seems to be folded into a gesture of lanky politeness, arms crossed, and legs. He wears T-shirts under his button-down shirts, like the small boys in high school did to feign bulk with cotton. On his first appearance on *Fox News Sunday*, he swallowed hard in between answers. He looked thirsty.

He is a modest champion, puppy-loyal, and wholly inoffensive. His friends and colleagues, both in and outside the party, unfailingly call him brilliant and kind and inspiring and inspired. "If he wanted to go invent cold fusion, he'd figure out a way to do it," says Jim Messina, who ran the campaign's budget and is now deputy chief of staff to Obama. Others suggest that General Motors, bleeding America in Detroit, could clot the hemorrhage by popping Plouffe in as C.E.O.

Here at this lunch table, David Plouffe is soft-spoken, and he is quick. He is nice to the waitress, but she is barely there, invisible on his radar, and the clang of the dishes and the laughter of lunchtime are inaudible. He keenly concentrates on describing his strategy. He is focused, meditative. He is yours for this hour, because this is what he has allotted. He is exact, and he is frank.

But also, David Plouffe is very quiet. No, not quiet, because quiet isn't strong enough. Try reticent. David Plouffe is preternaturally reticent. Some might even say secretive.

"He is such a guarded person, *intensely* private," says David Axelrod, Plouffe's partner and Obama's campaign strategist and now senior advisor. "The one thing I would say, if he ever invites you to a friendly game of poker, you shouldn't go. You never know what's going on in his head. . . . He's got eyes that are like headlights, and you know that he's taking in everything that he's seeing."

These are the qualities—the poker face and the hush, in the service of his also-quiet master—that helped him make winning Barack Obama the presidency look not just easy but preordained. Yes, there was some luck to it. A once-in-a-lifetime candidate, a fast-unspooling economy, a low point for national self-esteem, an opponent who, aside from a brief moment over the summer, was all but inept. But still, it takes impossible talent to make it look so easy. It takes genius and discipline. A campaign-season's worth of silence.

But David Plouffe has something else now. Something that Aldrin lacked, something that eluded Begala and Carville and Atwater and even Karl Rove, who rode his success into the White House. A magic beanstalk that will keep you on the moon, even while you're back down at Starbucks. David Plouffe has a list.

⤙ • ⤚

It was Plouffe (rhymes with *bluff*) who gathered the president's unprecedented thirteen-million-name contact list, which has grown into a fulsome pulsing beast, and it is Plouffe who now owns it and keeps it under lock and key. Plouffe sent those thirteen million people an e-mail in mid-November and they replied, *Yes, I still want to be involved, and yes, David Plouffe, I'll have house parties when you tell me to. Here is who I am socioeconomically and socially. I am* boxers; *my next-door neighbor is* briefs. Now the president has instructed him to make that list a new lever of government.

No president has ever entered office with this much information. The closest thing to it, Begala says, were direct-mail lists like Ronald Reagan's back in 1980. But, he says, "it's a different thing than Reagan writing, 'Send me thirty-five bucks if you want to fight the Commies.'" This list is granular. And it is flexible and transferable to myriad media outlets—even those not yet invented. Begala believes it could potentially "revolutionize progressive politics."

The idea is a national operation, likely named Organizing for America, that will resemble Obama's grassroots operation in reach and love. It will be as finely tuned as the campaign behemoth and funded the same way—no money from third parties. If Obama has a policy initiative he wants to push, or a message he needs to disseminate, or a gaffe he wants to bat down, he will call David Plouffe and Plouffe will unleash the many-million-mouthed dog, just as he did all across America for these past two years.

If you believe in Obama and in the need for change and for a new, streamlined, hyperlinked Democratic Party, then this is a watershed idea. It is a mechanism that could truly morph the power structure in Washington—waking up the unused, overslept public, as Plouffe successfully did on the campaign, and making an end run around lobbyists and interest groups.

But if you are part of the Old Guard—part of the pre-Obama DNC or a liberal interest group like the Center for American Progress or labor or the environmental lobby—which has spent years trying to figure out a way to rouse and organize the Democratic machine, then this new initiative might give you pause. Because if Plouffe runs it like he ran the campaign, unless you join the ticket and stay on message, you will be left on the bench, asking Sarah Palin for a light. It is a new Democratic take on the old Bush maxim: Either you will be with Organizing for America, or you will be against it.

"The outside groups are worried about being bulldozed," says one well-placed Democratic source. "The question is, is this shortsighted on behalf of Team Obama? This is the strategy they adopted during their campaign, which was no independent expenditures, no 527's, no outside groups. They would be command central on messaging. And it was a strategy that paid off . . . [because] everything went Obama's way. You can't count on that going forward."

The fear is that the Obama machine will ignore any groups or messages not in sync with the administration. Or worse, that if for some reason Organizing for America falters, there will be a vacuum.

Perhaps it's a silly fear. Misplaced. I mean, just look at David Plouffe sitting there, courteously sipping his Diet Coke from a straw, talking about the right way to get a small white ball into a red cup. He just got Barack Obama elected president.

You can trust David Plouffe. The president sure as hell does.

⤛ • ⤜

President Obama is in Hawaii. It's a few weeks before he's sworn in, and he is taking time from his family to confirm that Plouffe was not mostly lucky in getting him elected. "I don't buy it," he says. "If you just look at the mechanics of our campaign, how we raised money, how we turned out votes, how we managed the caucus process—all these pieces were incredibly complex, and we had to build it from scratch. . . . I'm not sure there's anybody [else] who could have done it."

An aide has just said that this is one of the only interviews the president has allowed during his last vacation before taking office. He wouldn't do this, they say, for anyone but David Plouffe.

This is why. People love other people when they are behind the scenes and precisely brilliant there.

"David is a very unassuming guy," says the president. "He's not flashy. He's not loud. He doesn't wear his brilliance on his sleeve. He's not trying to impress people. But what I think people miss with David is how tough he is—somebody who's very confident about what he knows, and he's able to stand his ground when he thinks he's right."

Fellow golden boy Axelrod was the professorial message. The Socratic dude with the uncombed hair and the rambling intelligence who oversaw the sound and the vision, what Obama stood for and how he presented himself. He was the David you knew, the one who pointed to the name on the side of the rocket and pointed to it again and read it to you backward.

Together the two winning Davids sit at a postelection symposium at Harvard in early December. Here, the brains behind the McCain and Obama campaigns are gathered before an audience of bright kids so that the future may learn from the past. They reconstruct what they did right while the losing side—McCain campaign manager Rick Davis and pollster Bill McInturff—defend what they did wrong to a crowd who cares only to hear from the winners.

Onstage Axelrod preens in tweed. In the bright lights, he says the presidential election is an MRI for the soul. He smiles when he uses the word *nostrums*. Axelrod is the floppier David, who almost missed a plane because he forgot his briefcase at Joe Biden's house, who got a glazed doughnut stuck in his BlackBerry's tracking ball.

Plouffe, meanwhile, sits boyishly. He's the meticulous David who charted the course for winning the electoral college from an unseen helm. Plouffe would rather be with his map. "I look at it on the computer all the time," he says later. "It's kind of like my North Star. They can never take that away from me. I don't think my wife would like it, but I'd put that map up in every room of our house if I could."

All day Plouffe chews carefully and entertains uninteresting bright-eyed questions. In his pink tie, sandwiched between Axelrod and McCain manager Rick Davis, Plouffe looks the least like he wants to be there.

On the campaign, he had the reputation of hanging back in meetings and on conference calls, keeping silent unless he had something significant to say. Spartan and purposeful. You can see it here at one of the Harvard debates. When the moderator says something about the gaucheness of the stage for Obama's convention speech, Plouffe jumps in quietly but aggressively. "It wasn't that bad," he says, and he does not smile and he uses the man's name, throws it back at him, along with his question.

It's his subtle justice. Correcting missteps, protecting territory with a whisper and a light but certain shove. It's how Plouffe operated on the campaign. If someone broke the hierarchy, if he disagreed with his supervisor and decided to take the matter straight to Plouffe, Plouffe would simply forward the e-mail back to the supervisor. No comment. No need. Now get back in line.

Near the end of the day, on his way to the bathroom, he hasn't walked five feet before he is webbed by the spindly arms of the political groupies, the shawled women law professors, and the puffy beat reporters, who piece together their meals from convention salads. They stop him in his steady course, they grab his small elbow, *Wait, wait, David Plouffe, David Plouffe. Hi, do you know who I am? We worked together back in . . .*

He slows, though he keeps his body in the direction it was going, so all he needs to do is turn his head a touch to deal with the interloper. He smiles friendly as the baker, he lets his hand get lost in the folds of bodies.

No, he doesn't know who you are, but he does remember working with you, because he's a man who remembers everything. He doesn't like to do the smiling, hand-shaking, dead-eyed nodding, but he'll do it. It's not what he was built for, but he does remember what it was like to knock on farm doors.

-+- • -+-

It was a grassroots fairy tale. The notion of farmers in overalls standing in voter-registration lines, holding straw hats in callused hands. It's tangible and hardworking and Plouffe loves it: "You have this farmer who never voted Democrat in his life, and suddenly he says, 'Hey, know what, I never thought I'd be voting for some black guy named Barack Obama from Chicago, but know what? I am.' You can't put a price on that."

Plouffe first met the farmers in the early nineties, when he would tool around Des Moines in his blue Dodge Colt with a cracked windshield. He'd been one of twenty-five guys whom field veteran Joe Hansen had hired to work on railroad heir Sam Beard's Delaware senatorial bid, and in two weeks Plouffe became the boss of them all. Hansen and Plouffe grew up there, in the sort of politics where you live off the land. They saved pins and looseleaf, nicked paper clips from the dentist's office. Old ladies dripping red paint onto homemade yard signs.

"Plouffe outperformed everybody, by every metric," says Hansen, a D.C.-based strategist and close friend who just came from breakfast at Plouffe's place. "In 1990, when I moved back to Iowa and managed field organization for Tom Harkin's [reelection] campaign, David got a job that was better than mine—so realize that in one cycle it went from me supervising him to him supervising me."

Plouffe never returned to school to finish his final semester. Instead and doggedly, he marked high-end territory across the nation, from facilitating an East Coast hard-nosed beat-down (New Jersey in 1996, where he managed Bob Torricelli's victory over Dick Zimmer—which Plouffe proudly refers to as brass-knuckle time) to Dick Gephardt's deputy chief of staff job to the executive-director gig at the DCCC in 1999, where he raised a record $95 million for House races. A year later, he accepted a job with Axelrod's consultancy firm (which would become AKP&D Message and Media) and went on to run Obama's successful 2004 Senate campaign.

Finally, as campaign manager of Obama for America in early 2007, Plouffe was charged with building an underdog campaign for president from virtually nothing—no money, one office, five staff members, and a few dreams from one's father. The main thing he knew was that there were no shortcuts. His focus was on 270, and every decision had to flow from there. You had to get the job done. He told Obama the same thing he told everyone who worked for him: You have to be all in. The president asked the manager, Are there shortcuts? And the manager said, No. You get to work, and you stay there.

⤙ • ⤚

David Plouffe orders his lunch neatly. He does not ask the waitress if his sandwich comes with fries or if his Diet Coke comes with lemon. "Elections are all about numbers," he says. "You have to get a certain number of votes, delegates, you have to raise a certain amount of money, your strategy and budget have to be married to how many votes and delegates you're trying to get."

To get the numbers right, Plouffe broke down the country into sixteen separate campaigns—a different strategy for each battleground state—and gave each its own ground crew and press office. His desk back in Chicago was the control center. On the walls there were electoral maps in reds, blues, deeper blues. But the helm and the center was the desk, a wood-laminate piece, neat and lap-topped and bolted to the floor. Every morning he sat at that desk with a large to-do list that he parsed out to the to-doers. He watched the scroll of e-mails—he says it was like a volcano, exploding in bold at the top.

"We'd get the clips overnight, and I'd read them all. Hundreds of them. That's basically what it was like. Wake up, reach for your BlackBerry, the way guys used to reach for their packs of cigarettes." He read everything and got on a call, then another, and another and another. A rolling two-year conference call. He looks tired when he tells you.

Because he came from a place where hard workers could barely afford the twenty-five-dollar donations they pushed across the hay bale, he immediately acquired the reputation of budget miser. There was an Axelrodism that claimed that if you went to the bathroom, pulled out a paper towel, then went to pull out a second one, it would actually be a note that said, "See Plouffe."

To find the voters and build a swarm of volunteers to help, he hired twenty-seven-year-old Joe Rospars and the rest of the former Howard Dean Web guys—now Blue State Digital—and made the most confident investment that a political campaign has ever made in the Internet. He brought them up from the basements and into top-line meetings. He told them, *We have to beat Clinton. She has the establishment support, she has this huge system of money-raisers, so we must create an alternative network.*

Beside the gray walls and atop the gray pattern carpets, they enacted Plouffe's vision. These were futuristic people building small revolutions in a humdrum place. They took the now-comparatively primitive Web-roots platform that Dean—along with his manager, Joe Trippi, and Web guru, Nicco Male—first unearthed in 2003 and extended it. There were more tools now. YouTube. Twitter. More potential inputs. They used them all and invented new ones.

Obama owned the Web because Plouffe believed in a few smart kids and let them go a little nuts. But the meticulous managerial thing, according to the Blue State Digital guys, is that Plouffe still held those nuts in the palm of his careful hand.

Plouffe maintains there was no forerunner to this strategy, not really. Not Dean or Trippi in terms of the Web, or Marshall Ganz, the famed Chavez farm-labor organizer turned Harvard professor, often (erroneously, according to Plouffe) cited as the brain behind the grassroots organization. Because he never tries to convince you, you are more apt to believe him. He says every situation was dynamic and that they got their plan from the people.

You talk to anyone who heard of David Plouffe before Election Day, and mostly it was because they got a few hundred e-mails from him, and they liked to see it as a personal thing. On e-mail, he was chatty. Conversationally, he asked for money. The college kid who wired ten bucks of twelve-pack cash to Plouffe felt like he was saving the country with a few fast keystrokes and Dad's AmEx.

And yet Plouffe insists that to focus too much on the netroots is to overlook the pure fieldwork, which was essential to winning. "You can't be too reliant on just technology in politics . . . knocking and phone calls is still the bread and butter." He smiles. He likes the notion. It's how he started. "It'll be a long time before those new apps replace the old ones."

The old application was a line of staffers and volunteers stretching down the fluorescent hall of Obama headquarters, past the great and daily newspaper wall in communications and out across America—each eager college kid, grandmother, and housewife, standing in their campaign T-shirt waiting for a "love note from David Plouffe," in their words, so they might deploy their democratic energy. He drew the most passionate, thousands of them, into two- or three-day Camp Obama training sessions. Each team leader had his own job: You are responsible for finding twenty volunteers. You: fifty, a hundred, two hundred voters. Call them. Write the plan and then we're going to track you.

Teams would report back with stats and the field directors would chart the cumulative info and they would know whether their "supervolunteers" were hitting their targets. Plouffe, back at his desk, sat at the top of the pyramid, checking the checkers, glancing at the North Star on his wall, believing deeply in the prize, in the red, white, and blue of mostly blue.

"Do you realize that more than half those volunteers had never been involved in politics before?" David Plouffe is wide-eyed now, and leaning in. "More than *half.*" He emphasizes the final word to let the incredulity settle. And then there is a moment—it's almost imperceptible, and you almost wish you hadn't noticed, because there is something agonizing about a private man showing public emotion. But it happens. His eyes tear up. The soft-spoken, indefatigable general is talking about his troops and his eyes glisten. Iowa, the grassroots effort, he says, rivaled election night. Then quickly he shakes the chaff from his hair and recomposes. Safely, he returns to his numbers.

This is the passion Plouffe rarely shows. But from top-floor, eventful offices, people will gush about it. The pep talks, for example. "They would, at the end, make you wanna go run off a cliff with the guy. He mixed a very hard edge with a sort of, *I'm imagining Barack Obama on Capitol Hill as the next leader* . . . a sort of inspirational rhetoric," says twenty-seven-year-old speechwriter Jon Favreau. It was a centaur blend, the gruff, focused mug of the football coach and the graceful neck and confident purr of the golden orator. The night they lost New Hampshire, Plouffe said to get everyone across the country on the phone. In his uneventful and sure voice, he promised that he'd never been more confident and proud of everyone, and he ended it by saying: "Let's go win this fucking thing."

As much as he likes to inspire, he loves to win. When Plouffe plays baseball, he is always the pitcher. Like Roger Clemens, he is turned on by the hectic pulse of unmanageable jurisdiction, the notion of controlling a field with runners on every base. The calm during the storm. But the calm is only on the outside. There is a deeper sense of competition and passion, and Plouffe takes it and he uses it, but he doesn't show it, not even after the win.

Obama saw this in the lead-up to the Iowa caucus. It's when he realized he could trust Plouffe fully, and in the muck: "Plouffe was getting calls and e-mails all across the country, the newspaper reports saying that the campaign was over, and he was able to just keep us on a steady course and instill calm, and it showed me the kind of leader he could be in difficult times. It's always easy to be a campaign manager when things are going well, but when things aren't, that's the real test. He was, in his quiet way, able to maintain focus and confidence."

"I'm a competitive person," Plouffe says, without pride but forcefully. His eyes and chin rise. "Elections are nothing about doing well. You win or lose, and I love to win, and it feels absolutely terrible when you lose. We built something from scratch," he continues, "and we beat Hillary Clinton and John McCain. That's like, uh, beating the L.A. Lakers and the Boston Celtics to win the championship." If he had lost, "I'd have felt like I let the country down."

To win the country, the manager took the risks. "We always seemed to be better when we were up in the high water," says Plouffe. "Whenever we got safe, we stagnated. We liked rolling the dice." This meant bleeding $25 million in North Carolina, $10 million in Indiana, $15 million in Virginia, just to keep McCain off balance. It meant convincing Obama to move his convention speech outdoors, though Obama worried it might rain. It meant convincing Obama to do a thirty-minute advertorial, even though Obama thought it was too risky so close to Election Day.

"Yes, it was high risk," Plouffe says of the advertorial. It's hard to convince the man you work for to do something he's unsure about. Obama argued that the undecideds were already decided. But Plouffe explained the statistics to him. "Obama was not someone who understood numbers and states. He wasn't a political creature," he says. This wasn't about undecided voters. This was about the soft supporters who had recently swung.

"We have to hold them," the manager told the candidate. And the candidate relented.

Obama trusted Plouffe and Plouffe trusted himself, and Plouffe's instinct was to look serene on the outside, while shrewdly gaming for angles within. Yes, David Plouffe is a numbers genius and his round, blinking eyes dissected a country into a few rounds of Battleship, but he is more, even, than the man Obama calls his "most valuable player." He is Roger Clemens in the rain, down by two in the bottom half, stripping the ball hard and sure and a little to the left, knowing that even if this batter hits a homer, he will regroup and strike out the next twenty.

◄◄ ● ►►

It is now early January. There are Christmas trees on the curbs. It's cold and the end of a season and David Plouffe is in an airport. He's one of those men in the security line who has his shoes off ahead of time and in his hands, five people before he needs to. He's walking in thin black dress socks, and nobody knows he is important, only that he is not a pain in the ass.

David Plouffe is in an airport, three days after the president he got elected flew to Washington, D.C., to take office. But Plouffe is not going to Washington. He's leaving for a speaking engagement in Arizona. It's one of those things he's been doing since he turned down Obama's invitation to join the administration. Obama pushed him, because, he says, "There is nobody I trust more." But Plouffe declined. "He understood that I would need to spend some time on the outside," says Plouffe. "He also knew there was some value in having friends on the outside."

For weeks, rumors of Obama 2.0 have been trickling out on the Internet. The talk is of the next Obama-powered revolution. Everyone in Washington knows that this slight man owns the e-mail addresses, but nobody is quite sure what he will do with them. For the most part, he's kept his head low and spent time with his family, his new daughter born two days after the election, and he has slowed down to half civilian. There's a book on the way about his campaign strategy, and he's open to the possibility of corporate consulting. He's had dozens of offers.

But now, as the airplanes taxi outside, Plouffe starts to talk about another story. A story about endless phone calls and meetings, some taken between diaper changes. Plouffe couldn't talk much about it, he says, because they were still working out the legal details. And they needed to select who would be heading the DNC. But Tim Kaine's appointment became public three days ago, and so in a few weeks Plouffe will be sending out another one of his famous folksy e-mails and posting an announcement on YouTube, in which he'll formally announce the new initiative.

Organizing for America, he says, was six weeks in the making. In that time he spoke daily with Tim Kaine. They studied how the Obama campaign machine functioned and read briefings on how it could be transformed into Obama's governing machine. Obama, he says, made clear that the mandate of Organizing for America was to push forward his agenda for change, not for reelection. "I can assure you it isn't that way with Obama. He sent that message out loud and clear, and I could not agree more strongly."

The model they came up with will be an independent entity under the umbrella of the DNC, with a separate staff in Washington, its own structure and Web site, and field offices with technical staff and fieldworkers across the country. Like the campaign operation. Also like the campaign, Organizing for America won't accept any outside PAC or lobbyist money. Instead, it will be funded solely from individual donors.

"Most of what this entity will be doing is building grassroots support for issues and politics," says Plouffe. "Let's say there's an energy effort, an energy plan, that the president and some of Congress would like to get passed. People would get out there and talk to their neighbors and try to build support." Petitions, canvassing, phone calls, house parties. David Plouffe will send out an e-mail or a video: *America, we need your help.* The state field offices will go into action. And the housewives will unsuckle themselves from Oprah and the college kids will put down their pong paddles, and together they will rise up and their voices will be heard.

The voice of David Plouffe rises now above the announcements and the suitcase wheels. You can tell he believes this could be bigger than the campaign he just led, won, and loved. This will be a direct link to the people who got Obama elected, a way to harness the grassroots power of thirteen million hopeful Americans who voted for change and have pledged to help Obama and Plouffe enact it.

Mitch Stewart, Obama's Iowa caucus director, will serve as executive director, with Plouffe overseeing from afar with the freedom to come and go as he pleases. But Plouffe will not be on the payroll. He says they wouldn't pay him that much, anyway, plus he sees it as a way of passing the torch. But also, "The DNC has a history of having people on contract, and our hope is that that tradition can come to an end." In other words, in the old DNC you could be a free agent, divide your time, come in as a pinch hitter.

Not anymore. In the new DNC—in Organizing for America—you will work full-time for the DNC and Obama's goals, or you will not work for them at all. Unless, of course, you are the unpaid architect of the whole initiative.

Plouffe insists the initiative has nothing to do with reelection. But by being part of the DNC, Organizing for America will be able to morph depending upon needs. "Some people will want to help out in a Senate race in 2010," says Plouffe. He means giving or asking for money on the Web site. "We needed to have some entity to be allowed to have all range of possibility." Options. David Plouffe, President Obama's inside man on the outside, is giving the president options.

Of course, some people are scared of these options, especially if Plouffe and his team do indeed run Organizing for America in the same hyper-controlling way they ran the campaign. To them, Obama's talk of a "new politics" that excludes them—the very progressive advocacy groups they've been building and nurturing since before David Plouffe cut his mullet—is a frightening affront.

They talk about an infamous finance-committee meeting last May, just as the long war with Hillary was winding down, when Obama's national finance chair, Penny Pritzker, delivered a message: Do not contribute to these groups. The word was that anyone who works for or contributes to any independent-expenditure efforts could forget about working in an Obama administration. Many such groups feared that Obama didn't have the stomach or the instinct to run a campaign against Republicans. But *they* did. They'd spent years building their own machines and were ready to get in on the action with funding from some of the very people Pritzker was now admonishing. And now the rookie and his Axelrod- and Plouffe-led posse was shutting them down. Oh, were they pissed. In the bars, they didn't hide it.

"It's not the Democratic Party anymore," one highly placed Democrat said. "It's the Obama party."

–←• •→–

The president says one last thing about the manager before his handlers pull him off the phone. He says he has no doubt of David Plouffe's truth and faith, of his love of country.

Even over a crackly phone line the president sounds like hope distilled into something gluttonously drinkable, peach iced tea for a hot-day hangover.

David Plouffe doesn't speak as eloquently as the president. He doesn't shine. But he does believe.

What that belief can become remains to be seen. The president's impact and the manager's execution, and the country's will and work. Even for Plouffe. He's the first to say that the real function and reach of Organizing for America won't be fully understood until it gets running. Like the campaign, it is a living organism that will be ever-changing depending upon circumstance. But the sketch is there. And its potential impact could be utter and complete.

As for what happens if the money runs dry and the grassroots enthusiasm follows, or what becomes of all the old-line interest groups that have spent years working to mobilize progressive voters, or what happens if you have a Democratic message or pitch you want disseminated but without Obama's approval—all that's a bit unclear.

Listen, says Plouffe, quietly and forcefully. Calm and competitive, wired together. "My wildest hope is that the debate will move out of Washington" and onto the porches of America.

He says it with the earnest sincerity of the old patriotic ideal to which we float our flags. He says it so you want to believe him. And perhaps you should, because as quiet and reserved and calm as David Plouffe is, as many secrets as he seems to hold onto for himself alone, there is no doubting his conviction. In Obama, in changing the way politics is conducted, in the potential to harness the power of the movement he built, and himself.

Somewhere, behind the face of a man who has never preened, you can be sure David Plouffe has already thought through the questions. And he believes he has the answers.

6

THE SPREADSHEET PSYCHIC: HOW NATE SILVER BUILT A BETTER CRYSTAL BALL

ADAM STERNBERGH
New York magazine   October 12, 2008

As each presidential campaign winds its way toward its quadrennial conclusion, any political aficionado worth his or her salt turns into an obsessive poll-follower. Just how valid all these polls are is another matter, of course. It took Nate Silver, founder of FiveThirtyEight.com (the name refers to the total number of votes in the U.S. Electoral College) to demystify this ritual reading of the tea leaves. Having made his bones in the statistics-mad world of major league baseball, Silver decided to apply his acumen to the ever-expanding universe of political pulse-taking. Silver's website, with its blend of poll parsing, number-crunching, and lucid exposition, has become a mandatory bookmark on the browsers of political junkies everywhere.

In this article, published shortly before Election Day 2008, New York *magazine's Adam Sternbergh profiles the baseball whiz kid–turned–political analyst. Meanwhile, Silver, like the visitors to his website, has admittedly gone through a bit of postelection withdrawal. But his site still has plenty of statistical grist to mill (a recent series of postings was devoted to an analysis of the swing vote and what the Republicans need to do to harness it for the next election). In his spare time, Silver has also begun a column called "The Data" for* Esquire, *in which he dissects American driving habits; why baseball teams overpay for free agents; and, yes, the real explanation behind Obama's victory last November.*

In a month when the Dow had its worst single-day plunge in over twenty years, when Lehman imploded, AIG faltered, and WaMu failed, when the word *crisis* became an everyday staple in newspaper headlines and the presidential race pulled close, then pulled apart, when the Chicago Cubs kicked off a playoff quest to win their first championship in 100 years (then got swept out in three straight games) and, for good measure, some scientists in an underground lab near the Swiss Alps fired up a Large Hadron Collider that some serious observers warned might create a black hole that would swallow up the Earth, it was comforting to sit down and have lunch in midtown with a man who can see the future. It's not that Nate Silver is psychic, or even that he's right all the time. He's just proved very good, especially of late, at looking at what's already happened and using that information to predict what will happen next.

Silver, who's 30, thin, and lives in Chicago, had been flown to New York at the invitation of a hedge fund to give a talk. "They just said, 'Why don't you come in, talk about your models,'" he said with a shrug. "I'll probably just take a lot of questions." Silver doesn't know all that much about high finance; these days, he's spending most of his energy on his political Web site, FiveThirtyEight (the total number of Electoral College votes), where he uses data analysis to track and interpret political polls and project the outcome of November's election. The site earned some national recognition back in May, during the Democratic primaries, when almost every other commentator was celebrating Hillary Clinton's resurgent momentum. Reading the polls, most pundits predicted she'd win Indiana by five points and noted she'd narrowed the gap with Obama in North Carolina to just eight.

Silver, who was writing anonymously as "Poblano" and receiving about 800 visits a day, disagreed with this consensus. He'd broken the numbers down demographically and come up with a much less encouraging outcome for Clinton: a two-point squeaker in Indiana, and a seventeen-point drubbing in North Carolina. On the night of the primaries, Clinton took Indiana by one and lost North Carolina by fifteen. The national pundits were doubly shocked: one, because the results were so divergent from the polls, and two, because some guy named after a chili pepper had predicted the outcome better than anyone else.

Silver's site now gets about 600,000 visits daily. And as more and more people started wondering who he was, in May, Silver decided to unmask himself. To most people, the fact that Poblano turned out to be a guy named Nate Silver meant nothing. But to anyone who follows baseball seriously, this was like finding out that a guy anonymously running a high-fashion Web site turned out to be Howard Cosell. At his day job, Silver works for Baseball Prospectus, a loosely organized think tank that, in the last ten years, has revolutionized the interpretation of baseball stats. Furthermore, Silver himself invented a system called PECOTA, an algorithm for predicting future performance by baseball players and teams. (It stands for "player empirical comparison and optimization test algorithm," but is named, with a wink, after the mediocre Kansas City Royals infielder Bill Pecota.) Baseball Prospectus has a reputation in sports-media circles for being unfailingly rigorous, occasionally arrogant, and almost always correct.

This season, for example, the PECOTA system predicted that the Tampa Bay Rays would win 90 games. This seemed bold, even amusing, given that the Rays were arguably the worst team in baseball. In 2007, they'd *lost* 96 games. They'd finished last in all but one season of their ten-year existence. (In 2004, they finished fourth.) They had some young talent, sure, but most people, even those in the Rays' front office, thought that if the team simply managed to win more games than it lost, that would represent a quantum leap.

PECOTA, however, saw it differently. PECOTA recognized that the past Rays weren't a hopelessly bad team so much as a good team hampered by a few fixable problems—which, thanks to some key off-season changes, had been largely remedied. Silver argued on the Baseball Prospectus Web site that the long-suffering team had finally "decided to transform themselves from a sort of hedge fund for undervalued assets into a real, functional baseball club."

PECOTA, as it turns out, wasn't exactly right. The Rays didn't win 90 games this year. They won 97 games and are currently playing the Red Sox for the American League championship. [Editor's note: The Rays won, 4 games to 3, then went on to lose the World Series to the Philadelphia Phillies, 4–1.]

So, Nate Silver: What happens next?

-<|- • -|>-

Sports and politics offer several obvious parallels. Both involve a competition, essentially between two teams. Both involve reams of statistical data available for devotees to sort through—or, more commonly, for intermediary experts to sort through, analyze, and then interpret for you. In baseball, these stats track player performance—how many hits a player gets, and when, and against what kind of pitchers—while in politics, the data tracks voter preferences. Who do you like and why? What kind of choice are you likely to make on Election Day? These stats, on their face, seem pretty straightforward. If a hitter hits .300, he's valuable. If Obama opens up a six-point national lead, he's in good shape.

And yet in both sports and politics, there's an industry built around studying this data, making up stories about it, and then trying to sell those stories to you. For example: A-Rod, for all his greatness, can't deliver in the clutch. Obama, for all his charisma, has struggled to connect with white working-class voters. The Mets are a bunch of chokers. This election, it's all about the hockey moms.

As a result, in baseball and, now, politics, there exists a small subculture of counterexperts: People who argue against these conventional story lines using new interpretations of the raw data to make their case. In baseball, this counterculture has been growing for roughly 30 years and can be traced, improbably, to one man: Bill James, a cranky Midwesterner who started writing articles about baseball while working the night shift as a security guard at a pork-and-beans factory in Lawrence, Kansas. In 1977, he published a photocopied newsletter called *Baseball Abstract*, which found a cult following that later blossomed into a national audience. By the late eighties, he was hailed as the founder of "sabermetrics"—a new field dedicated to better analysis of baseball stats—and the father of a revolution. Once considered a Unabomber-style outcast, James now consults for the Red Sox.

And in the nineties, the study of sabermetrics exploded. For starters, the development of so-called fantasy baseball—a game in which fans draft a team of real players, then compete with each other based on the players' on-field success—created a huge new market for performance projections.

(If you want to win your fantasy league, you care a lot less about who hit 40 home runs last year than you do about who'll hit 40 next year.) And the advent of the Internet allowed fans unprecedented access to stats, both raw and packaged by various experts. Then, in 2003, Michael Lewis wrote *Moneyball*, a best-selling book that valorized Billy Beane, the general manager of the Oakland A's, for using some of these new insights to overcome the financial advantage of richer teams.

In the midst of all this, in 1996, Baseball Prospectus was born. Founded by five baseball fans who met each other online, the BP crew are like the bratty children of Bill James, adding a new level of analytical sophistication to his contrarian philosophy. "When he started, Bill James had to actually call up teams and ask for their information," says Joe Sheehan, one of BP's founders. "Now we're able to download databases. We can do things with one-tenth the effort and a hundred times the available data." Also, whereas James used stats to explain what a player had done, BP uses stats to predict what a player might do. As a result, BP has built a small but successful empire of smarty-pants, with a Web site, syndicated columns, and most prominently, a preseason annual full of player projections.

As an avid fantasy player, I've spent long hours combing through the pages of the Baseball Prospectus book. It arrives each season huge, heavy, and intimidatingly dense. ("It's longer than *Moby-Dick* and heavier than *War and Peace*," jokes Steven Goldman, one of the editors.) Last year's edition weighed in at 605 oversize pages and offered essays like "Expanding the Cannon: Quantifying the Impact of Outfield Throwing Arms." The writing is lively and funny, nerd-nip for baseball obsessives. But the book, with its extensive charts and graphs, its talk of VORP (value over replacement player) and SNLVAR (support-neutral lineup adjusted value added above replacement), its SAC percent and EqH9 (oh, never mind), can also make you feel like you're reading a Ph.D. dissertation in statistics or a book by Dr. Seuss—or both, at the same time.

In fact, the work of stat hounds in general, and of Baseball Prospectus in particular, is so obviously the product of high-wattage brainpower and creativity that you can't help but occasionally wonder: *What if someone applied all this energy to something that actually mattered, like, I don't know, politics?*

Last year, at the start of an unusually unpredictable election season, Nate Silver began to wonder the same thing.

-<+-   •   ->->-

As stats are to baseball, polls are to politics; i.e., the basic numeric measurement of how things have gone in the past and how they might go in the future. Ask any pollster, though, and he will tell you that polls aren't meant to be used as predictive tools—they're simply a rough measure of where the electorate stands at a given moment. As pollster John Zogby put it to me, "We take snapshots. And when you take many snapshots in a row, you get motion pictures."

But unlike baseball stats, polls are a notoriously imprecise measurement. In baseball, at least, a hit is a hit. With polls, a yes isn't always a yes. Sometimes it's more like a "maybe," or a "yes, until I change my mind," or an "I don't know, but I'll say yes anyway to get you off the phone." Poll results can vary dramatically based on what you're asking, who you're asking, how you're asking, and how many people decide to answer you. Three different polls were conducted recently asking Americans how they felt about the federal $700 billion bailout. They all asked the question in slightly different ways and the results were essentially useless: One poll had people in favor of the bailout 57 to 30 percent, one had them against it 55 to 31, and one was basically split down the middle. In other words, polls are, at best, educated guesses. But if there's one thing Nate Silver loves to make, it's an educated guess.

In this year's Democratic primary, for example, the polls were all over the place. Before the Iowa caucuses on January 3, one poll had Clinton winning by nine, one had Clinton by two, and one had Obama by one. Obama won by seven. In the New Hampshire primary, five days later, one poll had Obama by thirteen and most others had him winning by eight or nine. Clinton won by three. Primaries are notoriously difficult to poll, because unlike in a general election, turnout is very unpredictable and people are much more likely to switch their choice at the last minute. As the primaries went on, however, Silver, who had been writing an anonymous diary for the liberal Web site Daily Kos, made an observation about this year's voters: While

the polls were wobbling wildly state-to-state, the demographic groups supporting each candidate, and especially Clinton and Obama, were remarkably static. He wasn't the only one who noticed this, of course—it was a major
narrative theme of the campaign. One pundit summed it up by saying that
Clinton had "the beer track"—blue-collar whites, Latinos, and seniors—
while Barack had African-Americans and "the wine track": young voters
and educated whites.

Every other pundit, though, was doing what they've always done, i.e.,
following the polls. Silver decided to ignore the polls. Instead, he used this
observation about demographics to create a model that took voting patterns from previous primaries and applied them to upcoming contests. No
phone calls, no sample sizes, no guesswork. His crucial assumption, of
course, was that each demographic group would vote in the same way, in the
same percentages, as they had in other states in the past.

Like many of the so-called *Moneyball* breakthroughs in baseball, this
was both a fairly intuitive conclusion and a radical break from conventional
thinking. (In *Moneyball*, for example, the idea that players who get on base
most often are the most valuable—which now seems kind of obvious—
was a major breakthrough in strategy.) After all, political pundits love to
talk about states as voting blocs—New Hampshire's leaning this way, North
Carolinians care about this, etc.—as though residency is the single most
important factor in someone's vote. Silver's model more or less ignored residency. But his hunch about demographics proved correct: It's how he called
the Indiana and North Carolina results so accurately when the polls got
them so wrong.

The model didn't always work throughout the primaries: Silver missed
on Kentucky and South Dakota. But the model proved that the kind of creative swashbuckling that exemplifies Baseball Prospectus—the institutional
obsession with questioning assumptions, even your own, even (or especially) to the point of heresy—could work when applied to politics as well.
When I asked Joe Sheehan to sum up the Baseball Prospectus philosophy,
he said simply, "Back up your argument. Because too many people are
telling stories, as opposed to actually looking for the truth."

Meanwhile, even as his primary model attracted attention, Silver was
cooking up another idea. He figured there must be a better way to use the
daily tracking polls to predict a candidate's future, just as he'd once found a

better way to use baseball stats to predict how many home runs a player might hit. His simple goal, as he explained on Daily Kos in late February, was to "assess state-by-state general-election polls in a probabilistic manner." In other words, he wanted to find a way to use all those occasionally erratic, occasionally unreliable, occasionally misleading polls to tell him who would win the election in November, which at that point was over 250 days away.

⋘ • ⋙

It's a tough business, being an oracle. Everyone cheers when you hit a bull's-eye, but no one's arrows fly true all the time. "Sometimes being more accurate means you're getting things right 52 percent of the time instead of 50," says Silver. "PECOTA is the most accurate projection system in baseball, but it's the most accurate by half a percent." That half-percent, though, makes all the difference. Silver's work, in both baseball and politics, is about finding that slim advantage. "I hate the first 90 percent [of a solution]," he says. "What I want is that last 10 percent."

As a kid, Silver was not a dork in a plastic bubble, as you might expect, gobbling stats and spouting figures. He grew up in East Lansing, Michigan, a typical baseball fan with a Tigers pennant on his bedroom wall. In person, talking baseball, he hardly comes off as a human computer; rather, he talks with the same bursts of enthusiasm familiar to any engaged fan in a sports bar. (And it's been a rough year for Silver, fanwise: His home team, the Tigers, were an underperforming disaster, and his two adopted teams, the Cubs and the White Sox, were both quickly and tragically dispatched from the playoffs this year.)

His approach to politics is similar—he's an engaged fan. He unapologetically roots for Obama. One of his early posts as a contributor to Daily Kos, titled "I Got Dinner with Barack Obama," recounts with gee-whiz wonder a chance sighting of Obama during Silver's birthday outing at a Mexican restaurant. ("At first I was pissed off with my friend for not doing more to alert me," he wrote, "but if I'd had more advance warning, I'd probably have done something stupid like scream 'Fired up!,' which would have been embarrassing in retrospect.") But he doesn't try to pummel you with numbers to prove his argument, like a typical hot-blooded partisan. Instead, on his site, he exhibits the cool confidence of someone who's simply used to knowing his stuff better than anyone else in the room.

Not that he can't pick, and win, a good fight. In a post on Daily Kos last December titled "Is a Bad Poll Better Than No Poll at All?" Silver singled out a few pollsters, particularly American Research Group, to show that their consistently off-base numbers will skew polling averages so severely that they harm one's results. Of ARG he wrote, "They have a track record of rolling out some polls that are completely different from anybody else in the race, and when they do, they are almost always wrong."

Dick Bennett, the pollster for ARG, responded by posting items on his Web site such as "Nate Silver Is Wrong Again," and mocking FiveThirtyEight's slogan ("Electoral Projections Done Right") in a tone that echoed current political attack ads. ("So much for electoral projections done right.") Then, in June, Silver posted an open letter to Bennett, which read, "It has been a long and hard-fought primary campaign. We've both had our share of successes, and made our share of mistakes. Granted, you made a few more than I did"—and in that last sentence, every word but "Granted" was a separate link to an ARG polling misfire. Then Silver challenged Bennett to a contest, in which each site would call the elections results, state-by-state, with a $1,000 bounty per state. Bennett never took him up on it, and this is what he has to say about Silver now: "What he does is different than what I do. There's a market for that. There's also a lady down the street who will read your palm."

As a high-schooler, Silver was a state-champion debater, though he claims to be only a so-so public speaker. I asked if he ever thought of becoming a baseball G.M., like the 34-year-old boy wonder (and sabermetrics proponent) Theo Epstein, who took the Red Sox to two championships (and counting). Silver said, "The people who do that are very talented. They're very smart, very polished. And I'm not much of a schmoozer. With Baseball Prospectus, you still have a voice and it's influential. I prefer shaping public opinion, I suppose."

After earning a degree in economics from the University of Chicago, Silver took a corporate job at a consulting firm but found it boring. He seems endlessly distractable; for example, in 2007, he started a Web site, The Burrito Bracket, that rated Mexican restaurants in Wicker Park. ("Each week, I will be visiting two restaurants and having the same item of food

[carne asada burritos, for example] at each one. The restaurant that provides the superior experience advances to the next round of the bracket.")
For a while, he was supplementing his income playing online poker, and
even earned six figures one year, but eventually he quit. "For a while, there
was a lot of money to be made, but you kind of eliminate one sucker at a
time," he says, "until finally you're the sucker." After he developed PECOTA
and joined Baseball Prospectus, he turned his eye to political analyses, thus
finding another field in which to identify suckers and eliminate them one
at a time.

⊰⊱ • ⊰⊱

In concocting FiveThirtyEight, Silver decided the best way to read the polls
was to put them all together, with the idea that averaging ten polls would
give you a better result than trying to pick out the best one. Again, he wasn't
the first person to do this—other sites like RealClearPolitics and Pollster
offer the same service. But, as Silver told me, "Sometimes the answer is in
looking at other alternatives that exist in the market and saying, 'They have
the right idea, but they're not doing it quite the right way.'"

Silver wanted to average the polls, but he wanted the polls that were
more accurate to count for more, while the bad polls would be discounted.
Other sites, like RealClearPolitics, treat every poll as equal. Silver knows
that some polls are simply better than others. Yet it's hard to know how accurate a general-election poll is before the actual election.

So he came up with a system that predicts a pollster's future performance
based on how good it's been in the past. In finding his average, Silver
weights each poll differently—ranking them according to his own statistic,
PIE (pollster-introduced error)—based on a number of factors, including
its track record and its methodology. One advantage of this system is that,
during the primaries, the system actually got smarter. Because each time a
poll performed well in a primary, its ranking improved.

For the general election, this gets trickier, since you have polls coming
out every single day and you can't know which ones are getting it right until
Election Day. You can, however, weigh these new polls based on the pollster's history, the poll's sample size, and how recently the poll was conducted.
You can also track trends over time and use these trend lines to forecast

where things will end up on November 4. You can also, as Silver has done, analyze all the presidential polling data back to 1952, looking for information as to what is likely to happen next. (For example, how much the polls are likely to tighten in the last month of the race, which they traditionally do.) You can also run 10,000 computer simulations of the election every day based on your poll projections. (Think of this as sort of like that scene at the end of *WarGames,* where the computer blurs through every possible nuclear-war scenario.) As of October 8, the day after the town-hall debate, Silver's simulations had Obama winning the election 90 percent of the time.

All of which is very seductive (and heartening to Obamaphiles), especially when you see it laid out on Silver's site, with its pleasing graphs, compelling charts, and graphically vibrant electoral maps. But in essence, Silver's whole undertaking is premised on breaking the first rule of reading polls: He's assuming—in his complex, elegant, partially proprietary and yet-to-be-entirely-validated way—that today's polls can predict tomorrow's election. Rival statisticians, in particular Sam Wang at Princeton (who runs his own poll-aggregation blog), have criticized Silver, arguing that polls can't and shouldn't be used as a crystal ball. Other critics have argued that the idea of a projection model is inherently flawed because it can't predict the unpredictable—for example, before the financial meltdown and McCain's campaign-suspension stunt, the polls were much tighter and Silver's electoral map had McCain on top.

Silver agrees, to a point, comparing daily polls, especially ones that come out months before the election, to "a 162-game baseball season, where one individual win or loss doesn't really tell you that much about the ultimate outcome." But for him, you have to use polls to predict the future—that's the whole point. Unlike other electoral projection maps, Silver calls each state for one candidate or the other—there are no undecideds—because the goal is to approximate what the map will look like after Election Day. "I think the entire value of the exercise is in predicting the outcome in November," Silver says, in a response to Wang. "What would happen in an election held today is a largely meaningless question."

And Silver is right. The truth is that everyone reads polls this way. When you pick up the paper and see McCain up by three or Obama up by six, you assume that means that candidate is on his way to a win. Silver's goal with FiveThirtyEight, then, is to simply do what everyone does, but do it better—

to read the polls in such a way that those assumptions we all naturally make will actually turn out to be true.

-‹- • -›-

For all the numbers and nuance, the adjustments and algorithms, there's really only one stark, looming, unambiguous test for the political prognosticator. "Pretty soon, there's going to be an Election Day," says pollster J. Ann Selzer of Selzer & Co. "And you're either going to be golden or a goat." (Selzer, this season, has consistently been golden, calling the Iowa caucus flawlessly, which is partly why Selzer & Co. is Silver's top-ranked pollster on FiveThirtyEight.)

Like everyone else calling this election, Silver's day of reckoning will come on November 4. In the meantime, he's become an increasingly confident commentator, growing into a national role as a calming anti-pundit among the white noise of partisan spin. FiveThirtyEight not only tracks numbers, but features field reports from the 50 states by Silver's colleague, Sean Quinn, and the documentary photographer Brett Marty. And Silver posts to his blog several times daily, spotting and dissecting surprising trends or aberrations, such as a recent poll in Minnesota that handed McCain a sudden one-point lead. Normally, you'd expect a liberal-leaning commentator to read such a result and blame bias, or error, or voodoo. Silver, however, poked around and determined that McCain had been recently outspending Obama three-to-one in Minnesota, making it the only state in the country where he was out-advertising Obama. "So McCain may literally have bought his way into a competitive race," Silver wrote. "So, yes, you can beat a state into submission if you really want to. . . . But whether it's been a *good* use of resources, we'll have to see."

I caught up with Silver on the phone recently, on a day when he'd just arrived back in Chicago from New York, having appeared the night before on *The Colbert Report*. We talked about Obama's widening lead over McCain, and the remaining undecideds—a group, he says, that's "mostly older rather than younger, more religious than not, and a lot of Independents, which is typical"—and how a lot of formerly solid red states now look like good bets to turn blue. "My pet theory is that these states along the Atlantic coast, like Virginia and North Carolina, are growing so fast that you have a lot of newly registered Democrats. That universe now contains people that it didn't a month ago. Literally, the composition of the North Carolina electorate is different than it was six months ago. They update their registration figures on a weekly basis, and last week the Democrats registered about 16,000 new voters—which would represent 1 percent of their turnout from 2004." And this year, at least, for all the surprises and *Sturm und Drang*, the electorate appears to be acting rationally. "The conventional punditry underestimates voters. The voters are pretty smart. They picked two very strong candidates. Even if McCain's in trouble now, if it had been Fred Thompson, he might have conceded already."

Even as he updates his projections and runs his 10,000 simulations a day, Silver wonders if maybe we don't yet know what the narrative of this election will be. In September, he wrote a post on Obama's extensive "ground game"—his efforts to set up outposts and register new voters, which have far outstripped McCain's—and suggested, "Suppose that, because of their ground efforts, the Obama campaign is 5 percent more efficient at turning out its vote than the McCain campaign on Election Day.... The implications of this would be enormous—a net of two to three points in each and every swing state—but we know zip, zilch, nada at this stage about their ultimate effect."

This is the paradoxical spirit of the stat-heads: They can be arrogant, sure, and even bullying as they charge forward, brandishing their spreadsheets. But they are just as happy to prove themselves wrong as they are to debunk anyone else. This, I think, is at the heart of Silver's appeal. (From a recent random Facebook status update: "I am an empiricist and I trust Nate Silver. Read it and chill.") "Nate's medium-term goal is to accomplish what we've accomplished at Prospectus—to change the conversation," says Sheehan. "And Nate's growth curve has been much sharper than ours ever was. He's crammed about five years' of BP's growth into five months. And if you get good enough arguments out there, if you do your work well enough, then other people have to do their work better. Nate's watched that at Prospectus. But FiveThirtyEight can do things for America that Baseball Prospectus never could."

FiveThirtyEight is the product of a movement, but also of a moment. The political media is polarized. Cable anchors choke on their own spin. The red states and blue states act like the Jets versus the Sharks—they don't trust us and we don't trust them. So we all rail against the enemy in the echo chambers of comment boards, retreating to the bomb-shelter safety of partisan blogs.

It's not that Silver is objective or impartial—he's not. He's still that young guy who almost yelled "Fired up!" across a crowded Mexican restaurant. But his ultimate goal is simple and nonpartisan: to build a better expert. Sure, he'll be disappointed if Obama loses. But he also says, "If Obama does lose, I think it's healthy to try and understand why, rather than just kicking and throwing things." If he ever decides to run for office, that wouldn't make for a bad slogan. Nate Silver: More understanding. Less kicking and throwing things.

ECONOMY IN CRISIS: POSTCARDS FROM THE EDGE

GEITHNER'S CRAP GAME

Illustration by Steve Brodner;
first appeared in *Business Week*.

7

CAPITALIST FOOLS

JOSEPH E. STIGLITZ

Vanity Fair   January 2009

The overriding political topic during the presidential campaign and Obama's first days in office was, of course, the Great Recession. Fueled by the collapse of the housing market and the subsequent implosion of the financial sector, the U.S. gross domestic product underwent bone-crunching contractions of 6.3 percent in the fourth quarter of 2008 and another 5.7 percent in the first quarter of 2009, pushing the nation's unemployment rate to nearly 9 percent.

As 2009 crept to its halfway point, however, there were finally signs of an impending recovery. Projections called for a second-quarter contraction of "only" 1 to 3 percent, while the 539,000 jobs lost in May 2009 represented the best employment report since the previous October. American construction spending also posted its biggest gain in eight months, and, perhaps most important, the Consumer Confidence Index jumped sharply for the second straight month, rebounding from the winter's record lows. Meanwhile, the stock market, hit by huge losses in 2008 and early 2009, managed to stage a spring rally that left the major indexes more or less even for the year.

Still, the economy is hardly out of the woods: With one out of five homeowners owing more on their mortgages than their homes are worth, foreclosure rates continue to rise, and economists are predicting that unemployment will also keep climbing well into 2010. At the same time, our banking system appears to have stabilized, but credit remains tight, and two of America's Big Three car manufacturers have filed for bankruptcy. Wondering who to blame for the mess? In this essay, Nobel laureate Joseph Stiglitz explains how the political decisions of the past three decades set the stage for the most severe economic downturn since the Great Depression.

There will come a moment when the most urgent threats posed by the credit crisis have eased and the larger task before us will be to chart a direction for the economic steps ahead. This will be a dangerous moment. Behind the debates over future policy is a debate over history—a debate over the causes of our current situation. The battle for the past will determine the battle for the present. So it's crucial to get the history straight.

What were the critical decisions that led to the crisis? Mistakes were made at every fork in the road—we had what engineers call a "system failure," when not a single decision but a cascade of decisions produce a tragic result. Let's look at five key moments.

NO. 1: FIRING THE CHAIRMAN

In 1987 the Reagan administration decided to remove Paul Volcker as chairman of the Federal Reserve Board and appoint Alan Greenspan in his place. Volcker had done what central bankers are supposed to do. On his watch, inflation had been brought down from more than 11 percent to under 4 percent. In the world of central banking, that should have earned him a grade of A+++ and assured his reappointment. But Volcker also understood that financial markets need to be regulated. Reagan wanted someone who did not believe any such thing, and he found him in a devotee of the objectivist philosopher and free-market zealot Ayn Rand.

Greenspan played a double role. The Fed controls the money spigot, and in the early years of this decade, he turned it on full force. But the Fed is also a regulator. If you appoint an anti-regulator as your enforcer, you know what kind of enforcement you'll get. A flood of liquidity combined with the failed levees of regulation proved disastrous.

Greenspan presided over not one but two financial bubbles. After the high-tech bubble popped, in 2000–2001, he helped inflate the housing bubble. The first responsibility of a central bank should be to maintain the stability of the financial system. If banks lend on the basis of artificially high asset prices, the result can be a meltdown—as we are seeing now, and as Greenspan should have known. He had many of the tools he needed to cope with the situation. To deal with the high-tech bubble, he could have increased margin requirements (the amount of cash people need to put down to buy stock). To deflate the housing bubble, he could have curbed predatory lending to low-income households and prohibited other insidious practices (the no-documentation—or "liar"—loans, the interest-only loans, and so on). This would have gone a long way toward protecting us. If he didn't have the tools, he could have gone to Congress and asked for them.

Of course, the current problems with our financial system are not solely the result of bad lending. The banks have made mega-bets with one another through complicated instruments such as derivatives, credit-default swaps, and so forth. With these, one party pays another if certain events happen—for instance, if Bear Stearns goes bankrupt, or if the dollar soars. These instruments were originally created to help manage risk—but they can also be used to gamble. Thus, if you felt confident that the dollar was going to fall, you could make a big bet accordingly, and if the dollar indeed fell, your profits would soar. The problem is that, with this complicated intertwining of bets of great magnitude, no one could be sure of the financial position of anyone else—or even of one's own position. Not surprisingly, the credit markets froze.

Here too Greenspan played a role. When I was chairman of the Council of Economic Advisers, during the Clinton administration, I served on a committee of all the major federal financial regulators, a group that included Greenspan and Treasury Secretary Robert Rubin. Even then, it was clear that derivatives posed a danger. We didn't put it as memorably as Warren Buffett—who saw derivatives as "financial weapons of mass destruction"—but we took his point. And yet, for all the risk, the deregulators in charge of the financial system—at the Fed, at the Securities and Exchange Commission, and elsewhere—decided to do nothing, worried that any action might interfere with "innovation" in the financial system. But innovation, like "change," has no inherent value. It can be bad (the "liar" loans are a good example) as well as good.

NO. 2: TEARING DOWN THE WALLS

The deregulation philosophy would pay unwelcome dividends for years to come. In November 1999, Congress repealed the Glass-Steagall Act—the culmination of a $300 million lobbying effort by the banking and financial-services industries, and spearheaded in Congress by Senator Phil Gramm. Glass-Steagall had long separated commercial banks (which lend money) and investment banks (which organize the sale of bonds and equities); it had been enacted in the aftermath of the Great Depression and was meant to curb the excesses of that era, including grave conflicts of interest. For instance, without separation, if a company whose shares had been issued by an investment bank, with its strong endorsement, got into trouble, wouldn't its commercial arm, if it had one, feel pressure to lend it money, perhaps unwisely? An ensuing spiral of bad judgment is not hard to foresee. I had opposed repeal of Glass-Steagall. The proponents said, in effect, Trust us: we will create Chinese walls to make sure that the problems of the past do not recur. As an economist, I certainly possessed a healthy degree of trust, trust in the power of economic incentives to bend human behavior toward self-interest—toward short-term self-interest, at any rate, rather than Tocqueville's "self interest rightly understood."

The most important consequence of the repeal of Glass-Steagall was indirect—it lay in the way repeal changed an entire culture. Commercial banks are not supposed to be high-risk ventures; they are supposed to manage other people's money very conservatively. It is with this understanding that the government agrees to pick up the tab should they fail. Investment banks, on the other hand, have traditionally managed rich people's money—people who can take bigger risks in order to get bigger returns. When repeal of Glass-Steagall brought investment and commercial banks together, the investment-bank culture came out on top. There was a demand for the kind of high returns that could be obtained only through high leverage and big risk taking.

There were other important steps down the deregulatory path. One was the decision in April 2004 by the Securities and Exchange Commission, at a meeting attended by virtually no one and largely overlooked at the time, to allow big investment banks to increase their debt-to-capital ratio (from 12:1 to 30:1, or higher) so that they could buy more mortgage-backed securities, inflating the housing bubble in the process. In agreeing to this measure, the S.E.C. argued for the virtues of self-regulation: the peculiar notion that banks can effectively police themselves. Self-regulation is preposterous, as even Alan Greenspan now concedes, and as a practical matter it can't, in any case, identify systemic risks—the kinds of risks that arise when, for instance, the models used by each of the banks to manage their portfolios tell all the banks to sell some security all at once.

As we stripped back the old regulations, we did nothing to address the new challenges posed by 21st-century markets. The most important challenge was that posed by derivatives. In 1998 the head of the Commodity Futures Trading Commission, Brooksley Born, had called for such regulation—a concern that took on urgency after the Fed, in that same year, engineered the bailout of Long-Term Capital Management, a hedge fund whose trillion-dollar-plus failure threatened global financial markets. But Secretary of the Treasury Robert Rubin, his deputy, Larry Summers, and Greenspan were adamant—and successful—in their opposition. Nothing was done.

NO. 3: APPLYING THE LEECHES

Then along came the Bush tax cuts, enacted first on June 7, 2001, with a follow-on installment two years later. The president and his advisers seemed to believe that tax cuts, especially for upper-income Americans and corporations, were a cure-all for any economic disease—the modern-day equivalent of leeches. The tax cuts played a pivotal role in shaping the background conditions of the current crisis. Because they did very little to stimulate the economy, real stimulation was left to the Fed, which took up the task with unprecedented low-interest rates and liquidity. The war in Iraq made matters worse, because it led to soaring oil prices. With America so dependent on oil imports, we had to spend several hundred billion more to purchase oil—money that otherwise would have been spent on American goods. Normally this would have led to an economic slowdown, as it had in the 1970s. But the Fed met the challenge in the most myopic way imaginable. The flood of liquidity made money readily available in mortgage markets, even to those who would normally not be able to borrow. And, yes, this succeeded in forestalling an economic downturn; America's household saving rate plummeted to zero. But it should have been clear that we were living on borrowed money and borrowed time.

The cut in the tax rate on capital gains contributed to the crisis in another way. It was a decision that turned on values: those who speculated (read: gambled) and won were taxed more lightly than wage earners who simply worked hard. But more than that, the decision encouraged leveraging, because interest was tax-deductible. If, for instance, you borrowed a million to buy a home or took a $100,000 home-equity loan to buy stock, the interest would be fully deductible every year. Any capital gains you made were taxed lightly—and at some possibly remote day in the future. The Bush administration was providing an open invitation to excessive borrowing and lending—not that American consumers needed any more encouragement.

NO. 4: FAKING THE NUMBERS

Meanwhile, on July 30, 2002, in the wake of a series of major scandals—notably the collapse of WorldCom and Enron—Congress passed the Sarbanes-Oxley Act. The scandals had involved every major American accounting firm, most of our banks, and some of our premier companies, and made it clear that we had serious problems with our accounting system. Accounting is a sleep-inducing topic for most people, but if you can't have faith in a company's numbers, then you can't have faith in anything about a company at all. Unfortunately, in the negotiations over what became Sarbanes-Oxley a decision was made not to deal with what many, including the respected former head of the S.E.C. Arthur Levitt, believed to be a fundamental underlying problem: stock options. Stock options have been defended as providing healthy incentives toward good management, but in fact they are "incentive pay" in name only. If a company does well, the CEO gets great rewards in the form of stock options; if a company does poorly, the compensation is almost as substantial but is bestowed in other ways. This is bad enough. But a collateral problem with stock options is that they provide incentives for bad accounting: top management has every incentive to provide distorted information in order to pump up share prices.

The incentive structure of the rating agencies also proved perverse. Agencies such as Moody's and Standard & Poor's are paid by the very people they are supposed to grade. As a result, they've had every reason to give companies high ratings, in a financial version of what college professors know as grade inflation. The rating agencies, like the investment banks that were paying them, believed in financial alchemy—that F-rated toxic mortgages could be converted into products that were safe enough to be held by commercial banks and pension funds. We had seen this same failure of the rating agencies during the East Asia crisis of the 1990s: high ratings facilitated a rush of money into the region, and then a sudden reversal in the ratings brought devastation. But the financial overseers paid no attention.

NO. 5: LETTING IT BLEED

The final turning point came with the passage of a bailout package on October 3, 2008—that is, with the administration's response to the crisis itself. We will be feeling the consequences for years to come. Both the administration and the Fed had long been driven by wishful thinking, hoping that the bad news was just a blip, and that a return to growth was just around the corner. As America's banks faced collapse, the administration veered from one course of action to another. Some institutions (Bear Stearns, A.I.G., Fannie Mae, Freddie Mac) were bailed out. Lehman Brothers was not. Some shareholders got something back. Others did not.

The original proposal by Treasury Secretary Henry Paulson, a three-page document that would have provided $700 billion for the secretary to spend at his sole discretion, without oversight or judicial review, was an act of extraordinary arrogance. He sold the program as necessary to restore confidence. But it didn't address the underlying reasons for the loss of confidence. The banks had made too many bad loans. There were big holes in their balance sheets. No one knew what was truth and what was fiction. The bailout package was like a massive transfusion to a patient suffering from internal bleeding—and nothing was being done about the source of the problem, namely all those foreclosures. Valuable time was wasted as Paulson pushed his own plan, "cash for trash," buying up the bad assets and putting the risk onto American taxpayers. When he finally abandoned it, providing banks with money they needed, he did it in a way that not only cheated America's taxpayers but failed to ensure that the banks would use the money to re-start lending. He even allowed the banks to pour out money to their shareholders as taxpayers were pouring money into the banks.

The other problem not addressed involved the looming weaknesses in the economy. The economy had been sustained by excessive borrowing. That game was up. As consumption contracted, exports kept the economy going, but with the dollar strengthening and Europe and the rest of the world declining, it was hard to see how that could continue. Meanwhile, states faced massive drop-offs in revenues—they would have to cut back on expenditures. Without quick action by government, the economy faced a downturn. And even if banks had lent wisely—which they hadn't—the downturn was sure to mean an increase in bad debts, further weakening the struggling financial sector.

The administration talked about confidence building, but what it delivered was actually a confidence trick. If the administration had really wanted to restore confidence in the financial system, it would have begun by addressing the underlying problems—the flawed incentive structures and the inadequate regulatory system.

⤙ • ⤚

Was there any single decision which, had it been reversed, would have changed the course of history? Every decision—including decisions not to do something, as many of our bad economic decisions have been—is a consequence of prior decisions, an interlinked web stretching from the distant past into the future. You'll hear some on the right point to certain actions by the government itself—such as the Community Reinvestment Act, which requires banks to make mortgage money available in low-income neighborhoods. (Defaults on C.R.A. lending were actually much lower than on other lending.) There has been much finger-pointing at Fannie Mae and Freddie Mac, the two huge mortgage lenders, which were originally government-owned. But in fact they came late to the subprime game, and their problem was similar to that of the private sector: their CEO's had the same perverse incentive to indulge in gambling.

The truth is most of the individual mistakes boil down to just one: a belief that markets are self-adjusting and that the role of government should be minimal. Looking back at that belief during hearings this fall on Capitol Hill, Alan Greenspan said out loud, "I have found a flaw." Congressman Henry Waxman pushed him, responding, "In other words, you found that your view of the world, your ideology, was not right; it was not working." "Absolutely, precisely," Greenspan said. The embrace by America—and much of the rest of the world—of this flawed economic philosophy made it inevitable that we would eventually arrive at the place we are today.

8

OBAMA'S BAILOUT

PAUL KRUGMAN
Rolling Stone   March 19, 2009

Economist and New York Times columnist Paul Krugman, who received the 2008 Nobel Prize in economics for his work on trade theory, has been right about a lot of things. He was one of the first to raise an alarm in the media about the housing bubble and the threat it posed to our economy, and he has also been an early and persistent advocate of strong government action in response to the current economic crisis. In this essay, Krugman analyzes the Obama administration's bailout package and comes up with a couple of disquieting conclusions: first, that the $787 billion stimulus bill—passed by a straight party-line vote in the House, and with the support of just three moderate Republicans in the Senate—may be big, but it isn't big enough. And second, that the reluctance of Treasury Secretary Tim Geithner and Obama's other economic advisers to temporarily nationalize Citigroup, Bank of America, and other at-risk banks is seriously jeopardizing our prospects for a vigorous and timely economic recovery. In Krugman's words, "We're staring into the abyss: Without an effective response by the government, there's no telling how deep this slump might go."

If these were normal times, it would be ludicrous to issue a report card on the Obama administration's economic policies. Only a few weeks have passed since the new president was sworn in, and many important economic positions have yet to be filled. As some wags put it, we're still at the stage when officials are trying to find their way to the bathroom.

But these aren't normal times. Barack Obama took office in the midst of the worst economic crisis since the Great Depression, a crisis requiring immediate action. Indeed, some people, myself included, had hoped that the outgoing Bush administration would work with the incoming team, allowing Obama to take action *before* moving into the White House. But it soon became clear that as Obama tries to deal with the crisis, he will get no help from Republican leaders. Instead, he'll face obstruction and lies.

So our new president is on his own, scrambling to meet a crisis that is far worse now than it was when he won the 2008 election. How's he doing?

The short answer is, very well by any normal standard—especially when you compare it with what a McCain-Palin administration would have done. Indeed, not since F.D.R. has a new president moved so aggressively on the economic front.

But the current economic disaster demands even more aggressive action than Obama has taken so far. What's truly scary is the breadth of the crisis. What began as a housing bust mutated into an implosion of the entire financial system. What began as a recession centered in the United States has gone global, with industrial production plummeting from Ukraine to Japan. Falling home and stock prices have wiped out a decade of savings, and consumers have slashed spending in a way they didn't in previous recessions. Losses from the housing bust and debt defaults have crippled the banking system; the resulting credit squeeze, in turn, has worsened the housing bust and fueled a sharp fall in business investment. And exports are plunging too, as the slump spreads around the world.

As a result, we're staring into the abyss: Without an effective response by the government, there's no telling how deep this slump might go. To promote more spending, the Federal Reserve has cut interest rates to almost zero and has vastly expanded its activities, financing everything from assets backed by credit-card debt to the operations of insurance companies. But while these efforts may have eased the credit crunch somewhat, they have been nowhere near enough to turn the economy around.

So now it's up to the Obama administration.

THE STIMULUS

There are, broadly speaking, three things the federal government can do to address this kind of economic crisis.

First, the government can offer help to victims of the crisis, with the goal of diminishing the suffering. This help can take a number of forms, from expanding unemployment benefits to rewriting mortgage terms.

Second, the government can act to support the overall level of spending in the economy, either by spending money itself or by giving money to individuals or businesses and hoping that they'll spend it.

Third, the government can step in to rescue and sustain key institutions crippled by the crisis—especially banks, whose continuing ability to lend is crucial to the economy.

These aren't mutually exclusive categories: To an important extent, the government can do well by doing good, and vice versa. Helping the unemployed can prop up consumer spending, helping homeowners can strengthen the banks, and a stronger economy reduces the number of victims.

The Obama administration has moved on two of these fronts. But it hasn't moved enough on either and has so far balked at the third.

The best of the policies announced so far is the homeowner-relief package. To reduce foreclosures, the administration will offer reduced rates on millions of mortgage loans made by Fannie Mae and Freddie Mac, the government-sponsored (and, since they were nationalized last year, government-owned) lenders. It will also offer subsidies and guarantees to private lenders who restructure mortgages.

Overall, this plan should help large numbers of people. But the arithmetic of the situation suggests that it will make only a minor dent in the overall economic problem.

The stimulus bill that was signed into law on February 17th is a much bigger deal: $787 billion in economic support, most of it over two years—a huge measure by normal standards. In addition to helping support the economy, the bill will do a lot to aid the slump's victims: increasing unemployment benefits, helping unemployed workers maintain their health insurance and assisting state governments in paying for Medicaid and education—which will in turn help them avoid painful cuts in services that tend to fall hardest on the most vulnerable members of society.

Yet impressive as the stimulus bill is by normal standards, it's smaller than many economists were recommending. In my own pre-inauguration letter to the President ("What Obama Must Do," *Rolling Stone*, January 22, 2009), I called for a stimulus of $800 billion in the first year alone—more than twice as large as Obama's plan, which amounts to less than $400 billion a year. Furthermore, a relatively large share of the plan—almost 40 percent—consists of tax cuts. And cutting taxes yields much less bang for the buck than government spending, because a substantial fraction of tax cuts will be saved rather than spent.

Here's one way to see the trouble with the stimulus: The Congressional Budget Office predicts an "output gap," the difference between what the economy could produce and what it will actually produce, of $2.9 trillion over the next three years. A $787 billion stimulus just isn't big enough to bridge that large a gap; even when you account for indirect effects, such as the fact that higher employment will lead to higher consumer spending, we'll be lucky if the plan closes a third of the gap.

Or think of it in terms of jobs: The administration says that the stimulus will, at its peak late next year, create or save around 3.5 million jobs, which is nothing to sneeze at. But as of last January, the number of unemployed Americans had already risen by 4.1 million since the official start of the recession, and the economy was continuing to lose jobs at the rate of 600,000 a month. So while the bill will significantly reduce the eventual rise in unemployment, it won't even be enough to make up for the damage that has already happened, let alone the further damage to come.

Why wasn't the plan bigger, and why does it contain such a large proportion of tax cuts? Part of the explanation lies in the economics: Obama officials wanted public spending to focus on "shovel-ready" projects—that is, projects that could start employing workers and boosting the economy fairly quickly. But there is a limited supply of such projects: We can all think of major public investment projects that should be undertaken, but most of these would take years to get under way. As it is, more than half the "discretionary spending" in the bill (which means things like infrastructure projects) is expected to take place after September 2010.

But that's not as much of a problem as it may seem, because almost everyone expects the economy to remain depressed for years. The minutes of the latest Fed meeting, for example, tell us that "all participants anticipated that unemployment would remain substantially above its longer-run sustainable rate at the end of 2011."

And it would also have been possible to provide a lot more aid, both to distressed individuals and to hard-pressed state and local governments.

Before the bill was passed, state governments were projecting deficits of $350 billion over the next two and half years—deficits that will have to be closed with spending cuts and tax increases, which in turn will reduce vital services and further depress the economy. The stimulus bill makes up about 40 percent of this shortfall—a significant help, but it could have done more.

The fact that the bill doesn't do more reflects politics—and, arguably, some important misjudgments on the part of the president and his advisers.

THE GOP ATTACKS

From the start, the Obama administration proposed a stimulus that was at the low end of what independent economists thought was necessary and was relatively heavy on tax cuts. This seems to have been done in the hope of gaining broad bipartisan support: According to news reports from early January, Obama aides hoped they might get as many as 80 votes in the Senate.

Instead, Republicans rejected Obama's overtures en masse. Not a single Republican in the House voted for the plan. In the Senate, 36 out of 41 Republicans voted for the DeMint amendment, which would have scrapped all of the spending provisions and replaced the whole thing with permanent tax cuts.

To listen to critics on the right, the stimulus was a terrible idea. First, they claimed that it was filled with pork—but in order to make that claim, they had to denounce things that were not, in fact, in the bill. An aide to John Boehner, the House minority leader, claimed the stimulus would spend $30 million protecting a marsh mouse near Nancy Pelosi's district; no such provision was in the bill. Boehner and other Republicans insisted it would spend $8 billion on a high-speed rail link between Los Angeles and Las Vegas; no, it wouldn't. In a way, the apparent need of Republicans to invent wasteful spending out of thin air was a demonstration of how clean the bill really is: They obviously couldn't find enough real waste to complain about.

Second, Republicans claimed that the bill will impose huge costs on future generations—that it's "generational theft," as Sen. John McCain put it. Now, the U.S. government does indeed have a long-term fiscal problem. Recent estimates by the nonpartisan Tax Policy Center put the long-run "fiscal gap"—the difference between spending and revenue under current policy—at between 4 and 6 percent of GDP. But the cost of the stimulus will add only slightly to that gap—around 0.12 percent of GDP. That's nothing compared to policy initiatives that Republicans in Congress enthusiastically supported over the past eight years. The Bush tax cuts will ultimately cost at least $2 trillion; the Iraq War at least $1 trillion. The stimulus will be a much smaller burden, especially when you bear in mind that by helping the economy, it will also raise tax receipts, offsetting at least a third of the measure's cost.

But anyway, all the stuff about burdening future generations is pure hypocrisy. The tax cuts in the DeMint amendment, which was supported by 36 Republicans—including McCain, the self-proclaimed opponent of "generational theft"—would have cost $3.1 trillion over the next 10 years. That's four times as much as the Obama stimulus.

One last line of attack was the claim that fiscal stimulus, in principle, simply can't work. You hear this from conservative "experts" like Brian Riedl of the Heritage Foundation, who declares, "Every dollar Congress injects into the economy must first be taxed or borrowed out of the economy. You're not creating new demand, you're just transferring it from one group of people to another." Borrowing from domestic lenders, the argument goes, cuts into the money available for investments; borrowing from foreigners curbs exports.

What's wrong with this claim? The answer lies in the very nature of our economic crisis. When the economy is at or near full employment, government spending does indeed come at the expense of private spending. But right now, we're suffering from a problem known as the "paradox of thrift"—everyone is trying to save more at the same time, even as investment demand is falling. Those vast quantities of potential savings—from consumers, corporations and institutional investors—have nowhere to go. By borrowing that excess money and using it to finance temporary budget deficits, the government can put it to good use, helping to sustain the economy. In a crisis like this, government spending is actually a way of getting unemployed resources working again.

So given all the objections to the stimulus, was Obama wrong to seek broad bipartisan support? That depends on how you interpret the endgame. To get the 60 Senate votes needed to override a filibuster, Obama had to make concessions to a few Republican "moderates"—and those concessions made a somewhat weak plan significantly weaker, stripping out spending, especially aid to states, and replacing it with tax cuts. Obama aides, notably Rahm Emanuel, claim that this showed that the Obama plan was the strongest possible. But I'd argue that the moderates would have demanded a pound of flesh from whatever Obama proposed, and that he guaranteed a too-weak bill by aiming low.

Whatever your interpretation of what happened, however, the result was a stimulus bill that is much better than nothing but one that will at best mitigate the slump, not cure it.

THE BANK BAILOUT

So far, Obama has taken sensible action on homeowner relief, and sensible but probably inadequate action on fiscal stimulus. What about the third type of action, rescuing financial institutions? At the time of writing, the Obama administration had announced what it said was a plan—but nobody knew what it meant. And thereby hangs a tale. Banks, broadly defined—which include many institutions that don't have big marble buildings and rows of tellers but nonetheless fulfill banking functions—play a crucial role in the economy. Yet major U.S. banks have suffered heavy losses in this crisis, leaving them severely undercapitalized if not insolvent. What that means, in English, is that big banks don't have enough assets to be sure of paying their debts—which in turn means that nobody wants to deal with them, for fear that they won't be repaid. As a result, our financial system is half-crippled.

To help the economy, the government needs to get the banks back on their feet. But how should that be done? Some proposals call for having the government buy troubled assets, like mortgage-backed securities, from the banks—but this only helps the banks if the government pays much higher prices for these assets than private investors are willing to offer, which means that taxpayers get a raw deal and the banks get a huge windfall. Or the government could guarantee the banks against large losses—but this, again, is a raw deal for taxpayers and a gift to the banks. And we're talking about a lot of money here: Some estimates put the losses of U.S. banks in this crisis at more than $1.5 trillion.

There is one more option, however. The government could put money into the banks in return for a commensurate share of ownership. What that would mean in practice, for at least some of the biggest banks, would be nationalization. Think of it this way: Citigroup and Bank of America probably need hundreds of billions of dollars in additional capital, yet as of February 26th, their combined stock-market value was less than $40 billion—and even that figure was inflated by the lingering hope of receiving a government handout. There's really no way for the government to inject the capital these banks need without either providing that handout, on a grand scale, or taking ownership itself.

A number of people have followed this line of thought to its natural conclusion—including some people whose names might surprise you. Maybe it's no big deal that Sen. Chris Dodd of Connecticut has said that temporary nationalization may be necessary, but so has Sen. Charles Schumer of New York, usually a defender of the investment industry—and so has none other than Alan Greenspan.

At the time of this writing, however, the Obama administration still wasn't willing to go there. On February 10th, Tim Geithner, the Treasury secretary, purportedly laid out the administration's bank plan—but nobody understood what, exactly, he was proposing, probably because the administration itself hadn't decided what to do. Even Obama has been cagey about the matter, praising the "Swedish model" (Sweden nationalized some major banks in the early 1990s) but suggesting that the United States is different.

Why the hesitation? The bankers themselves, not surprisingly, insist that a government takeover would be a terrible idea. And then there are the cries of "socialism" coming from the usual suspects, along with assertions that governments do a very bad job of running banks. Actually, as many of us have pointed out, the lesson of the past few years is that bankers do a very bad job of running banks—it was the private sector, not the government, that lost all that money. And in an important sense, the banks are already socialized: They're getting lots of government money, and the government has made it clear that they won't be allowed to fail. In effect, the government already owns their possible losses; why shouldn't it own their possible gains?

But anyway, talk of socialism deliberately misses the point. Nobody involved in the rescue plan wants the government running banks on a permanent basis. The idea, instead, is to do what is routinely done with smaller banks when they go bust and are seized by the FDIC: The government takes them into temporary receivership and cleans up their balance sheets—taking over their bad assets and paying off enough of their debts so that what's left is a viable enterprise. Then the bank is re-privatized, and the government gets the best price it can for the troubled assets. That's what Sweden did in the early 1990s, in what is widely regarded as a success story. It's also what we ourselves did with failed savings-and-loan institutions at the end of the 1980s; the Resolution Trust Corporation, which took over the troubled assets, is almost always cited as a good example of how to resolve a banking crisis while getting the best possible deal for the taxpayers.

Maybe it's a problem with words: Some have suggested, in fact, that we stop talking about "nationalization" and call the process "pre-privatization." Yet, whatever you call it, the Obama administration is still hesitating. Why?

It may be the same kind of political caution that led to a too-weak stimulus, although it's hard to see why that caution persists now that so many mainstream figures have accepted the possible need for nationalization. (Who would have expected to find Alan Greenspan taking a position to Obama's left?)

It may also reflect the character of Obama's economic team, which is smart but perhaps too conventionally minded. I had no problem when Obama chose familiar faces like Larry Summers and Tim Geithner to be in charge: The urgency of the crisis means that there's no time for a learning curve, so you have to appoint people who know where the bodies are buried (but preferably people who weren't personally responsible for any of the burials). But perhaps the very familiarity of the economic team with Wall Street is making it reluctant to lower the boom on bankers, even when they deserve it.

This could all change quickly. One part of Geithner's plan that seems comprehensible is his call for a "stress test" on major banks: Government auditors would study their books to determine whether they are viable. This could be turned into a Claude Rains moment, in which the Obama administration declares itself shocked—shocked!—to find that several giant banks are insolvent, leaving no choice except temporary government receivership.

But so far, at least, Obama is trying to finesse the crisis; he's looking for solutions that are less radical than temporary nationalization. On February 23rd, the administration floated a complex plan to convert some of the $45 billion in preferred shares it currently holds in Citigroup into common shares, while avoiding taking a controlling interest. Nobody outside the administration seems to think this would make much difference—it sounds as if Geithner is rearranging the deck chairs on the *Titanic*, while hoping the iceberg melts.

The truth is that there aren't any non-radical solutions to the banking crisis. The only way to resolve the crisis without nationalization would be a huge giveaway of taxpayer money, and that's impossible both fiscally and politically.

So the result of the Obama administration's caution is that the banking crisis remains unresolved. As long as government aid is perceived as a handout to bankers (because it is), that aid will be deeply unpopular. The result will be a banking system that, while being kept by government aid from outright collapse, has too little capital to provide the economy with the credit it needs. That's what people mean when they talk about "zombie banks"—they're still walking around, but they're too crippled to fulfill their proper role. And we know from Japan's experience in the "lost decade" of the 1990s that zombie banks can stifle economic recovery, even if the government spends heavily on fiscal stimulus.

LOOKING AHEAD

So far, at least, the administration's recovery plans seem to be based on the belief that the economy will somehow heal itself within five years. The official projections for the stimulus bill assume that even without it, the unemployment rate, after peaking at 9 percent next year, would begin a steady decline back to 5 percent by 2014. Because the effects of the stimulus plan will fade out over time, this long-term return to normal levels of unemployment depends on unspecified natural forces of recovery.

In reality, however, it's hard to see where that recovery is supposed to come from.

The closest parallel in modern times to our current crisis is Japan's "lost decade." As the name suggests, this slump went on for much longer than the slump assumed in the administration's projections. And when Japan finally did recover, the revival was led by booming exports to China. With the whole world now caught up in economic crisis, the United States can't count on that kind of economic rescue.

Our own Great Depression, of course, also lasted more than a decade and was brought to an end only by a gigantic war—not something we want to emulate. Now, it would be wrong to suggest that there are no forces that will lead to recovery, given enough time. The revival of private saving will, gradually, boost consumer wealth. Home construction is now running at its slowest rate in half a century, which will create a pent-up demand for new homes. Auto sales are so low that at current rates it would take 27 years to replace the existing fleet; as cars wear out, sales will surge. In the long run, the U.S. economy will indeed recover even without government support.

But as John Maynard Keynes famously declared, in the long run we are all dead.

Here's what I think will happen: At some point, probably later this year, the Obama administration will realize that what it has done is not enough. (The economic team is very smart and intellectually flexible; if they were on the outside, they would probably offer an analysis quite similar to the one you're reading now.) At that point, the administration will devise a more ambitious plan, one designed not just to provide a cushion against the slump, but to lead the way to full recovery. That will almost surely involve nationalizing several major banks on a temporary basis and pumping in a lot of cash to get them running effectively.

Can such a plan be passed, when the administration was barely able to scrape up enough Senate votes to get the original stimulus through? I think so, for three reasons. First, as the economy deteriorates, more Republicans may see the need to do something sensible. Second, Al Franken will eventually be seated, meaning Obama will only need to win over one Republican to avoid a filibuster. And third, the next phase of the stimulus won't necessarily need 60 votes: The administration can use the budget process to increase spending or reduce revenues by a simple majority—something Obama can easily obtain.

Whatever the legislative maneuvering required, much more must be done. Right now, there's a strong chance that the unemployment rate will go into double digits—which means 15 million or more Americans seeking jobs but unable to find them. Millions more could lose their homes, even with the new housing plan. And worst of all, this could last for a long time: At this point, America is following right in the tracks of Japan's "lost decade."

When it comes to fixing the economy, President Obama has only begun his work.

9

NO RETURN TO NORMAL

JAMES K. GALBRAITH
Washington Monthly   March/April 2009

In this essay, economist James Galbraith (whose father, economist John Kenneth Galbraith, served in the administrations of four presidents) strikes some of the same notes sounded by Paul Krugman in the preceding selection—warning that the recently passed federal stimulus bill may be inadequate for dealing with the crisis at hand and that not enough is being done to support the banking system. Galbraith then goes a step further, arguing that the collapse of the financial system has had a more profound effect than Obama's team realizes—and that if private banks and the credit they supply take as long to recover as he suspects they will, the U.S. government will have to play a far more active role in running the economy than most experts imagine.

Barack Obama's presidency began in hope and goodwill, but its test will be its success or failure on the economics. Did the president and his team correctly diagnose the problem? Did they act with sufficient imagination and force? And did they prevail against the political obstacles—and not only that, but also against the procedures and the habits of thought to which official Washington is addicted?

The president has an economic program. But there is, so far, no clear statement of the thinking behind that program, and there may not be one, until the first report of the new Council of Economic Advisers appears next year. We therefore resort to what we know about the economists: the chair of the National Economic Council, Lawrence Summers; the CEA chair, Christina Romer; the budget director, Peter Orszag; and their titular head,

Treasury Secretary Timothy Geithner. This is plainly a capable, close-knit group, acting with energy and commitment. Deficiencies of their program cannot, therefore, be blamed on incompetence. Rather, if deficiencies exist, they probably result from their shared background and creed—in short, from the limitations of their ideas.

The deepest belief of the modern economist is that the economy is a self-stabilizing system. This means that, even if nothing is done, normal rates of employment and production will someday return. Practically all modern economists believe this, often without thinking much about it. (Federal Reserve Chairman Ben Bernanke said it reflexively in a major speech in London in January: "The global economy will recover." He did not say how he knew.) The difference between conservatives and liberals is over whether policy can usefully speed things up. Conservatives say no, liberals say yes, and on this point Obama's economists lean left. Hence the priority they gave, in their first days, to the stimulus package.

But did they get the scale right? Was the plan big enough? Policies are based on models; in a slump, plans for spending depend on a forecast of how deep and long the slump would otherwise be. The program will only be correctly sized if the forecast is accurate. And the forecast depends on the underlying belief. If recovery is not built into the genes of the system, then the forecast will be too optimistic, and the stimulus based on it will be too small.

⤙ • ⤚

Consider the baseline economic forecast of the Congressional Budget Office, the nonpartisan agency lawmakers rely on to evaluate the economy and their budget plans. In its early-January forecast, the CBO measured and projected the difference between actual economic performance and "normal" economic performance—the so-called GDP gap. The forecast has two astonishing features. First, the CBO did not expect the present recession to be any worse than that of 1981–82, our deepest postwar recession. Second, the CBO expected a turnaround beginning late this year, with the economy returning to normal around 2015, even if Congress had taken no action at all.

With this projection in mind, the recovery bill pours a bit less than 2 percent of GDP into new spending per year, plus some tax cuts, for two years, into a GDP gap estimated to average 6 percent for three years. The stimulus does not need to fill the whole gap, because the CBO expects a "multiplier effect," as first-round spending on bridges and roads, for example, is followed by second-round spending by steelworkers and road crews. The CBO estimates that because of the multiplier effect, two dollars of new public spending produces about three dollars of new output. (For tax cuts the numbers are lower, since some of the cuts will be saved in the first round.) And with this help, the recession becomes fairly mild. After two years, growth would be solidly established and Congress's work would be done. In this way, the duration as well as the scale of action was driven, behind the scenes, by the CBO's baseline forecast.

Why did the CBO reach this conclusion? On depth, CBO's model is based on the postwar experience, and such models cannot predict outcomes more serious than anything already seen. If we are facing a downturn worse than 1982, our computers won't tell us; we will be surprised. And if the slump is destined to drag on, the computers won't tell us that either. Baked into the CBO model we find a "natural rate of unemployment" of 4.8 percent; the model moves the economy back toward that value no matter what. In the real world, however, there is no reason to believe this will happen. Some alternative forecasts, freed of the mystical return to "normal," now project a GDP gap twice as large as the CBO model predicts, and with no near-term recovery at all.

Considerations of timing also influenced the choice of line items. The bill tilted toward "shovel-ready" projects like refurbishing schools and fixing roads, and away from projects requiring planning and long construction lead times, like urban mass transit. The push for speed also influenced the bill in another way. Drafting new legislative authority takes time. In an emergency, it was sensible for Chairman David Obey of the House Appropriations Committee to mine the legislative docket for ideas already commanding broad support (especially within the Democratic caucus). In this way he produced a bill that was a triumph of fast drafting, practical politics, and progressive principle—a good bill which the Republicans hated. But the scale of action possible by such means is unrelated, except by coincidence, to what the economy needs.

Three further considerations limited the plan. There was, to begin with, the desire for political consensus; President Obama chose to start his administration with a bill that might win bipartisan support and pass in Congress by wide margins. (He was, of course, spurned by the Republicans.)

Second, the new team also sought consensus of another type. Christina Romer polled a bipartisan group of professional economists, and Larry Summers told *Meet the Press* that the final package reflected a "balance" of their views. This procedure guarantees a result near the middle of the professional mind-set. The method would be useful if the errors of economists were unsystematic. But they are not. Economists are a cautious group, and in *any* extreme situation the midpoint of professional opinion is bound to be wrong.

Third, the initial package was affected by the new team's desire to get past this crisis and to return to the familiar problems of their past lives. For these protégés of Robert Rubin, veterans in several cases of Rubin's Hamilton Project, a key preconception has always been the budget deficit and what they call the "entitlement problem." This is D.C.-speak for rolling back Social Security and Medicare, opening new markets for fund managers and private insurers, behind a wave of budget babble about "long-term deficits" and "unfunded liabilities." To this our new president is not immune. Even before the inauguration Obama was moved to commit to "entitlement reform," and on February 23 he convened what he called a "fiscal responsibility summit." The idea took hold that after two years or so of big spending, the return to normal would be under way, and the costs of fiscal relief and infrastructure improvement might be recouped, in part by taking a pound of flesh from the incomes and health care of the old.

◄◄ • ►►

The chance of a return to normal depends, in turn, on the banking strategy. To Obama's economists a "normal" economy is led and guided by private banks. When domestic credit booms are under way, they tend to generate high employment and low inflation; this makes the public budget look good, and spares the president and Congress many hard decisions. For this reason the new team instinctively seeks to return the bankers to their normal position at the top of the economic hill. Secretary Geithner told CNBC, "We have a financial system that is run by private shareholders, managed by private institutions, and we'd like to do our best to preserve that system."

But, is this a realistic hope? Is it even a possibility? The normal mechanics of a credit cycle do involve interludes when asset values crash and credit relations collapse. In 1981, Paul Volcker's campaign against inflation caused such a crash. But, though they came close, the big banks did not fail then. (I learned recently from William Isaac, Ronald Reagan's chair of the FDIC, that the government had contingency plans to nationalize the large banks in 1982, had Mexico, Argentina, or Brazil defaulted outright on their debts.) When monetary policy relaxed and the delayed tax cuts of 1981 kicked in, there was both pent-up demand for credit and the capacity to supply it. The final result was that the economy recovered quickly. Again in 1994, after a long period of credit crunch, banks and households were strong enough, even without a stimulus, to support a vast renewal of lending which propelled the economy forward for six years.

The Bush-era disasters guarantee that these happy patterns will not be repeated. For the first time since the 1930s, millions of American households are financially ruined. Families that two years ago enjoyed wealth in stocks and in their homes now have neither. Their 401(k)s have fallen by half, their mortgages are a burden, and their homes are an albatross. For many the best strategy is to mail the keys to the bank. This practically assures that excess supply and collapsed prices in housing will continue for years. Apart from cash—protected by deposit insurance and now desperately being conserved—the American middle class finds today that its major source of wealth is the implicit value of Social Security and Medicare—illiquid and intangible but real and inalienable in a way that home and equity values are not. And so it will remain, as long as future benefits are not cut.

In addition, some of the biggest banks are bust, almost for certain. Having abandoned prudent risk management in a climate of regulatory negligence and complicity under Bush, these banks participated gleefully in a poisonous game of abusive mortgage originations followed by rounds of pass-the-bad-penny-to-the-greater-fool. But they could not pass them all. And when in August 2007 the music stopped, banks discovered that the markets for their toxic-mortgage-backed securities had collapsed, and found themselves insolvent. Only a dogged political refusal to admit this has since kept the banks from being taken into receivership by the Federal Deposit Insurance Corporation—something the FDIC has the power to do, and has done as recently as last year with IndyMac in California.

‹‹ • ››

Geithner's banking plan would prolong the state of denial. It involves government guarantees of the bad assets, keeping current management in place and attempting to attract new private capital. (Conversion of preferred shares to equity, which may happen with Citigroup, conveys no powers that the government, as regulator, does not already have.) The idea is that one can fix the banks from the top down, by reestablishing markets for their bad securities. If the idea seems familiar, it is: Henry Paulson also pressed for this, to the point of winning congressional approval. But then he abandoned the idea. Why? He learned it could not work.

Paulson faced two insuperable problems. One was quantity: there were too many bad assets. The project of buying them back could be likened to "filling the Pacific Ocean with basketballs," as one observer said to me at the time. (When I tried to find out where the original request for $700 billion in the Troubled Asset Relief Program came from, a senior Senate aide replied, "Well, it's a number between five hundred billion and one trillion.")

The other problem was price. The only price at which the assets could be disposed of, protecting the taxpayer, was of course the market price. In the collapse of the market for mortgage-backed securities and their associated credit default swaps, this price was too low to save the banks. But any higher price would have amounted to a gift of public funds, justifiable only if there was a good chance that the assets might recover value when "normal" conditions return.

That chance can be assessed, of course, only by doing what any reasonable private investor would do: due diligence, meaning a close inspection of the loan tapes. On the face of it, such inspections will reveal a very high proportion of missing documentation, inflated appraisals, and other evidence of fraud. (In late 2007 the ratings agency Fitch conducted this exercise on a small sample of loan files, and found indications of misrepresentation or fraud present in practically every one.) The reasonable inference would be that many more of the loans will default. Geithner's plan to guarantee these so-called assets, therefore, is almost sure to overstate their value; it is only a way of delaying the ultimate public recognition of loss, while keeping the perpetrators afloat.

Delay is not innocuous. When a bank's insolvency is ignored, the incentives for normal prudent banking collapse. Management has nothing to lose. It may take big new risks, in volatile markets like commodities, in the hope of salvation before the regulators close in. Or it may loot the institution—*nomenklatura privatization*, as the Russians would say—through unjustified bonuses, dividends, and options. It will never fully disclose the extent of insolvency on its own.

The most likely scenario, should the Geithner plan go through, is a combination of looting, fraud, and a renewed speculation in volatile commodity markets such as oil. Ultimately the losses fall on the public anyway, since deposits are largely insured. There is no chance that the banks will simply resume normal long-term lending. To whom would they lend? For what? Against what collateral? And if banks are recapitalized without changing their management, why should we expect them to change the behavior that caused the insolvency in the first place?

⊰⊹ • ⊹⊱

The oddest thing about the Geithner program is its failure to act as though the financial crisis is a true crisis—an integrated, long-term economic threat—rather than merely a couple of related but temporary problems, one in banking and the other in jobs. In banking, the dominant metaphor is of plumbing: there is a blockage to be cleared. Take a plunger to the toxic assets, it is said, and credit conditions will return to normal. This, then, will make the recession essentially normal, validating the stimulus package. Solve these two problems, and the crisis will end. That's the thinking.

But the plumbing metaphor is misleading. Credit is not a flow. It is not something that can be forced downstream by clearing a pipe. Credit is a contract. It requires a borrower as well as a lender, a customer as well as a bank. And the borrower must meet two conditions. One is creditworthiness, meaning a secure income and, usually, a house with equity in it. Asset prices therefore matter. With a chronic oversupply of houses, prices fall, collateral disappears, and even if borrowers are willing they can't qualify for loans. The other requirement is a willingness to borrow, motivated by what Keynes called the "animal spirits" of entrepreneurial enthusiasm. In a slump, such optimism is scarce. Even if people have collateral, they want the security of cash. And it is precisely because they want cash that they will not deplete their reserves by plunking down a payment on a new car.

The credit flow metaphor implies that people came flocking to the new-car showrooms last November and were turned away because there were no loans to be had. This is not true—what happened was that people stopped coming in. And they stopped coming in because, suddenly, they felt poor.

Strapped and afraid, people want to be in cash. This is what economists call the liquidity trap. And it gets worse: in these conditions, the normal estimates for multipliers—the bang for the buck—may be too high. Government spending on goods and services always increases total spending directly; a dollar of public spending is a dollar of GDP. But if the workers simply save their extra income, or use it to pay debt, that's the end of the line: there is no further effect. For tax cuts (especially for the middle class and up), the new funds are mostly saved or used to pay down debt. Debt reduction may help lay a foundation for better times later on, but it doesn't help now. With smaller multipliers, the public spending package would need to be even larger, in order to fill in all the holes in total demand. Thus financial crisis makes the real crisis worse, and the failure of the bank plan practically assures that the stimulus also will be too small.

-<- • -><-

In short, if we are in a true collapse of finance, our models will not serve. It is then appropriate to reach back, past the postwar years, to the experience of the Great Depression. And this can only be done by qualitative and historical analysis. Our modern numerical models just don't capture the key feature of that crisis—which is, precisely, the collapse of the financial system.

If the banking system is crippled, then to be effective the public sector must do much, much more. How much more? By how much can spending be raised in a real depression? And does this remedy work? Recent months have seen much debate over the economic effects of the New Deal, and much repetition of the commonplace that the effort was too small to end the Great Depression, something achieved, it is said, only by World War II. A new paper by the economist Marshall Auerback has usefully corrected this record. Auerback plainly illustrates by how much Roosevelt's ambition exceeded anything yet seen in this crisis:

> [Roosevelt's] government hired about 60 per cent of the unem-
> ployed in public works and conservation projects that planted a bil-
> lion trees, saved the whooping crane, modernized rural America,
> and built such diverse projects as the Cathedral of Learning in Pitts-
> burgh, the Montana state capitol, much of the Chicago lakefront,
> New York's Lincoln Tunnel and Triborough Bridge complex, the
> Tennessee Valley Authority [TVA] and the aircraft carriers *Enter-
> prise* and *Yorktown*. It also built or renovated 2,500 hospitals, 45,000
> schools, 13,000 parks and playgrounds, 7,800 bridges, 700,000 miles
> of roads, and a thousand airfields. And it employed 50,000 teachers,
> rebuilt the country's entire rural school system, and hired 3,000
> writers, musicians, sculptors and painters, including Willem de
> Kooning and Jackson Pollock.

In other words, Roosevelt employed Americans on a vast scale, bringing
the unemployment rates down to levels that were tolerable, even before the
war—from 25 percent in 1933 to below 10 percent in 1936, if you count
those employed by the government as employed, which they surely were. In
1937, Roosevelt tried to balance the budget, the economy relapsed again,
and in 1938 the New Deal was relaunched. This again brought unemployment down to about 10 percent, still before the war.

The New Deal rebuilt America physically, providing a foundation (the
TVA's power plants, for example) from which the mobilization of World
War II could be launched. But it also saved the country politically and
morally, providing jobs, hope, and confidence that in the end democracy
was worth preserving. There were many, in the 1930s, who did not think so.

What did *not* recover, under Roosevelt, was the private banking system.
Borrowing and lending—mortgages and home construction—contributed
far less to the growth of output in the 1930s and '40s than they had in the
1920s or would come to do after the war. If they had savings at all, people
stayed in Treasuries, and despite huge deficits interest rates for federal debt
remained near zero. The liquidity trap wasn't overcome until the war ended.

It was the war, and only the war, that restored (or, more accurately, created for the first time) the financial wealth of the American middle class.
During the 1930s public spending was large, but the incomes earned were
spent. And while that spending increased consumption, it did not jump-

start a cycle of investment and growth, because the idle factories left over from the 1920s were quite sufficient to meet the demand for new output. Only after 1940 did total demand outstrip the economy's capacity to produce civilian private goods—in part because private incomes soared, in part because the government ordered the production of some products, like cars, to halt.

All that extra demand would normally have driven up prices. But the federal government prevented this with price controls. (Disclosure: this writer's father, John Kenneth Galbraith, ran the controls during the first year of the war.) And so, with nowhere else for their extra dollars to go, the public bought and held government bonds. These provided claims to postwar purchasing power. After the war, the existence of those claims could, and did, establish creditworthiness for millions, making possible the revival of private banking, and on the broadly based, middle-class foundation that so distinguished the 1950s from the 1920s. But the relaunching of private finance took twenty years, and the war besides.

A brief reflection on this history and present circumstances drives a plain conclusion: the full restoration of private credit will take a long time. It will follow, not precede, the restoration of sound private household finances. There is no way the project of resurrecting the economy by stuffing the banks with cash will work. Effective policy can only work the other way around.

⤛ • ⤜

That being so, what must now be done? The first thing we need, in the wake of the recovery bill, is more recovery bills. The next efforts should be larger, reflecting the true scale of the emergency. There should be open-ended support for state and local governments, public utilities, transit authorities, public hospitals, schools, and universities for the duration, and generous support for public capital investment in the short and long term. To the extent possible, all the resources being released from the private residential and commercial construction industries should be absorbed into public building projects. There should be comprehensive foreclosure relief, through a moratorium followed by restructuring or by conversion-to-rental, except in cases of speculative investment and borrower fraud. The president's foreclosure-prevention plan is a useful step to relieve mortgage burdens on at-risk households, but it will not stop the downward spiral of home prices and correct the chronic oversupply of housing that is the cause of that.

Second, we should offset the violent drop in the wealth of the elderly population as a whole. The squeeze on the elderly has been little noted so far, but it hits in three separate ways: through the fall in the stock market; through the collapse of home values; and through the drop in interest rates, which reduces interest income on accumulated cash. For an increasing number of the elderly, Social Security and Medicare wealth are all they have.

That means that the entitlement reformers have it backward: instead of cutting Social Security benefits, we should increase them, especially for those at the bottom of the benefit scale. Indeed, in this crisis, precisely because it is universal and efficient, Social Security is an economic recovery ace in the hole. Increasing benefits is a simple, direct, progressive, and highly efficient way to prevent poverty and sustain purchasing power for this vulnerable population. I would also argue for lowering the age of eligibility for Medicare to (say) fifty-five, to permit workers to retire earlier and to free firms from the burden of managing health plans for older workers.

This suggestion is meant, in part, to call attention to the madness of talk about Social Security and Medicare cuts. The prospect of future cuts in this modest but vital source of retirement security can only prompt worried prime-age workers to spend less and save more today. And that will make the present economic crisis deeper. In reality, there is no Social Security "financing problem" at all. There is a health care problem, but that can be dealt with only by deciding what health services to provide, and how to pay for them, for the whole population. It cannot be dealt with, responsibly or ethically, by cutting care for the old.

Third, we will soon need a jobs program to put the unemployed to work quickly. Infrastructure spending can help, but major building projects can take years to gear up, and they can, for the most part, provide jobs only for those who have the requisite skills. So the federal government should sponsor projects that employ people to do what they do best, including art, letters, drama, dance, music, scientific research, teaching, conservation, and the nonprofit sector, including community organizing—why not?

Finally, a payroll tax holiday would help restore the purchasing power of working families, as well as make it easier for employers to keep them on the payroll. This is a particularly potent suggestion, because it is large and immediate. And if growth resumes rapidly, it can also be scaled back. There is no error in doing too much that cannot easily be repaired, by doing a bit less.

❅ • ❅

As these measures take effect, the government must take control of insolvent banks, however large, and get on with the business of reorganizing, re-regulating, decapitating, and recapitalizing them. Depositors should be insured fully to prevent runs, and private risk capital (common and preferred equity and subordinated debt) should take the first loss. Effective compensation limits should be enforced—it is a good thing that they will encourage those at the top to retire. As Senator Christopher Dodd of Connecticut correctly stated in the brouhaha following the discovery that Senate Democrats had put tough limits into the recovery bill, there are many competent replacements for those who leave.

Ultimately the big banks can be resold as smaller private institutions, run on a scale that permits prudent credit assessment and risk management by people close enough to their client communities to foster an effective revival, among other things, of household credit and of independent small business—another lost hallmark of the 1950s. No one should imagine that the swaggering, bank-driven world of high finance and credit bubbles should be made to reappear. Big banks should be run largely by men and women with the long-term perspective, outlook, and temperament of middle managers, and not by the transient, self-regarding plutocrats who run them now.

The chorus of deficit hawks and entitlement reformers are certain to regard this program with horror. What about the deficit? What about the debt? These questions are unavoidable, so let's answer them. First, the deficit and the public debt of the U.S. government can, should, must, and will increase in this crisis. They will increase whether the government acts or not. The choice is between an active program, running up debt while creating jobs and rebuilding America, or a passive program, running up debt because revenues collapse, because the population has to be maintained on the dole, and because the Treasury wishes, for no constructive reason, to rescue the big bankers and make them whole.

Second, so long as the economy is placed on a path to recovery, even a massive increase in public debt poses no risk that the U.S. government will find itself in the sort of situation known to Argentines and Indonesians. Why not? Because the rest of the world recognizes that the United States performs certain indispensable functions, including acting as the lynchpin of collective security and a principal source of new science and technology. So long as we meet those responsibilities, the rest of the world is likely to want to hold our debts.

Third, in the debt deflation, liquidity trap, and global crisis we are in, there is no risk of even a massive program generating inflation or higher long-term interest rates. That much is obvious from current financial conditions: interest rates on long-maturity Treasury bonds are amazingly low. Those rates also tell you that the markets are not worried about financing Social Security or Medicare. They are more worried, as I am, that the larger economic outlook will remain very bleak for a long time.

Finally, there is the big problem: How to recapitalize the household sector? How to restore the security and prosperity they've lost? How to build the productive economy for the next generation? Is there anything today that we might do that can compare with the transformation of World War II? Almost surely, there is not: World War II doubled production in five years.

Today the largest problems we face are energy security and climate change—massive issues because energy underpins everything we do, and because climate change threatens the survival of civilization. And here, obviously, we need a comprehensive national effort. Such a thing, if done right, combining planning and markets, could add 5 or even 10 percent of GDP to net investment. That's not the scale of wartime mobilization. But it probably could return the country to full employment and keep it there, for years.

Moreover, the work does resemble wartime mobilization in important financial respects. Weatherization, conservation, mass transit, renewable power, and the smart grid are public investments. As with the armaments in World War II, work on them would generate incomes not matched by the new production of consumer goods. If handled carefully—say, with a new program of deferred claims to future purchasing power like war bonds—the incomes earned by dealing with oil security and climate change have the potential to become a foundation of restored financial wealth for the middle class.

This cannot be made to happen over just three years, as we did in 1942–44. But we could manage it over, say, twenty years or a bit longer. What is required are careful, sustained planning, consistent policy, and the recognition now that there are no quick fixes, no easy return to "normal," no going back to a world run by bankers—and no alternative to taking the long view.

A paradox of the long view is that the time to embrace it is right now. We need to start down that path before disastrous policy errors, including fatal banker bailouts and cuts in Social Security and Medicare, are put into effect. It is therefore especially important that thought and learning move quickly. Does the Geithner team, forged and trained in normal times, have the range and the flexibility required? If not, everything finally will depend, as it did with Roosevelt, on the imagination and character of President Obama.

10

THE NEW LIBERALISM: HOW THE ECONOMIC CRISIS CAN HELP OBAMA REDEFINE THE DEMOCRATS

GEORGE PACKER

The New Yorker   November 17, 2008

In the following article, which ran in the same postelection issue of The New Yorker *(with its iconic cover drawing of the Lincoln Memorial lit up at night, and the "O" from the magazine's name shining luminescent above it) as this anthology's opening selection, George Packer places the current economic crisis in a political context. The essay—which is also featured in Packer's upcoming book,* Interesting Times: Writings from a Turbulent Decade—*draws a direct parallel between Barack Obama and Franklin D. Roosevelt, equating Obama's election with the end of a conservative era—"one that rose amid the ashes of the New Deal coalition in the late sixties, consolidated its power with the election of Ronald Reagan, in 1980, and immolated itself during the presidency of George W. Bush"—and the dawn of a new liberal epoch that "will be more about public good than private goods." "For the first time since the Johnson administration," he adds, "the idea that government should take bold action to create equal opportunity for all citizens doesn't have to explain itself in a defensive mumble."*

In September, 1932, Franklin Delano Roosevelt, the Democratic nominee for president, was asked by a reporter for his view of the job that he was seeking. "The presidency is not merely an administrative office," Roosevelt said. "That's the least of it. It is more than an engineering job, efficient or inefficient. It is preeminently a place of moral leadership. All our great presidents were leaders of thought at times when certain historic ideas in the life of the nation had to be clarified." He went down the list of what we would now call transformative presidents: Washington, Jefferson, Jackson, Lincoln, Theodore Roosevelt, Wilson. (He also included Grover Cleveland, who hasn't aged as well.) Then Roosevelt asked, "Isn't that what the office is, a superb opportunity for reapplying—applying in new conditions—the simple rules of human conduct we always go back to? I stress the modern application, because we are always moving on; the technical and economic environment changes, and never so quickly as now. Without leadership alert and sensitive to change, we are bogged up or lose our way, as we have lost it in the past decade."

When the reporter pressed Roosevelt to offer a vision of his own historical opportunity, he gave two answers. First, he said, America needed "someone whose interests are not special but general, someone who can understand and treat the country as a whole. For as much as anything it needs to be reaffirmed at this juncture that the United States is one organic entity, that no interest, no class, no section, is either separate or supreme above the interests of all." But Roosevelt didn't limit himself to the benign self-portrait of a unifying president. "Moral leadership" had a philosophical component: he was, he said, "a liberal." The election of 1932 arrived at one of those recurring moments when "the general problems of civilization change in such a way that new difficulties of adjustment are presented to government." As opposed to a conservative or a radical, Roosevelt concluded, a liberal "recognizes the need of new machinery" but also "works to control the processes of change, to the end that the break with the old pattern may not be too violent."

That November, Roosevelt defeated President Herbert Hoover in a landslide. His election ended an age of conservative Republican rule, created a Democratic coalition that endured for the next four decades, and fundamentally changed the American idea of the relationship between citizen and state. On March 4, 1933, Roosevelt was inaugurated under a bleak sky, at the darkest hour of the Great Depression, with banks across the country failing, hundreds of thousands of homes and farms foreclosed, and a quarter of Americans out of work.

In defining his idea of the presidency, Roosevelt had left himself considerable room for maneuvering. His campaign slogan of a "new deal" promised change, but to different observers this meant wildly different things, from a planned economy to a balanced budget. "Roosevelt arrived in Washington with no firm commitments, apart from his promise to 'try something,'" the *Times* editorialist Adam Cohen writes in his forthcoming book, *Nothing to Fear: FDR's Inner Circle and the Hundred Days That Created Modern America.* "At a time when Americans were drawn to ideologies of all sorts, he was not wedded to any overarching theory."

Barack Obama's decisive defeat of John McCain is the most important victory of a Democratic candidate since 1932. It brings to a close another conservative era, one that rose amid the ashes of the New Deal coalition in the late sixties, consolidated its power with the election of Ronald Reagan, in 1980, and immolated itself during the presidency of George W. Bush. Obama will enter the White House at a moment of economic crisis worse than anything the nation has seen since the Great Depression; the old assumptions of free-market fundamentalism have, like a charlatan's incantations, failed to work, and the need for some "new machinery" is painfully obvious. But what philosophy of government will characterize it?

The answer was given three days before the election by a soldier and memoirist of the Reagan revolution, Peggy Noonan, who wrote in the *Wall Street Journal*, "Something new is happening in America. It is the imminent arrival of a new liberal moment." The *Journal's* editorial page anticipated with dread "one of the most profound political and ideological shifts in U.S. history. Liberals would dominate the entire government in a way they haven't since 1965, or 1933. In other words, the election would mark the restoration of the activist government that fell out of public favor in the 1970s." The *Journal's* nightmare scenario of America under President Obama and a Democratic Congress included health care for all, a green revolution, expanded voting rights, due process for terror suspects, more powerful unions, financial regulation, and a shift of the tax burden upward. (If the editorial had had more space, full employment and the conquest of disease might have made the list.)

For the first time since the Johnson administration, the idea that government should take bold action to create equal opportunity for all citizens doesn't have to explain itself in a defensive mumble. That idea is ascendant in 2008 because it answers the times. These political circumstances, even more than the election of the first black American to the highest office, make Obama's victory historic. Whether his presidency will be transformative, in the manner of Roosevelt and the handful of predecessors named by F.D.R. in 1932, will depend, in part, on history—it's unclear whether today's financial troubles will offer a political challenge, and an opportunity, of the magnitude of the Great Depression. But the power of Obama's presidency will ultimately hinge on how he chooses to interpret the "modern application" of liberalism in the twenty-first century.

During the two years that he spent campaigning for the presidency, amid relentless media scrutiny, Obama made a greater commitment to specific plans than Roosevelt did. Yet he, too, represented different versions of moral leadership to different groups of voters, at various stages of the campaign. Roosevelt's answer to his interviewer reflected a belief that the presidency has both a political role and a philosophical role. Obama, using the language of the modern age, has reflected Roosevelt's belief: there is the "post-partisan" Obama and the "progressive" Obama. Some tension exists between these two approaches, but he will have to reconcile them if he is to fulfill his ambition of bringing profound change to the country.

Ask yourself what thinkers and ideas Reagan took with him to the White House and the answer comes pretty quickly: Milton Friedman, George Gilder, supply-side economics, anti-Communism. Bill Clinton's presidency was ushered in by a shelf of books and papers under the not entirely convincing rubric of the Third Way, espoused by policy wonks called New Democrats. I recently asked a number of people who know Obama, both within and outside the campaign, to name a few books and ideas that will help shape his presidency. None of them could give me an answer. It's strangely difficult to identify what the intellectual influences on this cerebral and literary politician have been.

David Axelrod, the chief strategist behind Obama's victory, described Obama's influences as "very eclectic." He went on, "He's a guy who reads very widely—he reads opinion on the right and left, and scholarly treatises of the right or left. I don't think he's in the left-wing or right-wing book club. I think he's willing to draw from everywhere." Unlike Reagan, Obama has no clear, simple ideology. People who have observed him in meetings describe a politician who solicits advice and information from a variety of sources, puts a high value on empirical evidence, and has the self-assurance to reach his own conclusions. A word that comes up again and again, from Obama himself and from people who know him, is "pragmatic."

Cass Sunstein, the Harvard law professor and author, was Obama's colleague for many years at the University of Chicago Law School. Sunstein's most recent book, *Nudge*, co-written with the behavioral economist Richard Thaler, tries to find a new path between governmental control and the unfettered free market. "*Nudge*," Sunstein said, is about "ways of helping people to make better choices without requiring anybody to do anything. It's a conception of government that is reluctant to impose mandates and bans but is kind of shrewd about enlisting what we know about human behavior in good directions." Sunstein added that the book is well known in Obama's circle; Obama's top economic adviser, Austan Goolsbee, also of the University of Chicago, has read it, and Sunstein has discussed its ideas with Obama. In *The Audacity of Hope*, Obama included a proposal from Sunstein and Thaler that would have employees automatically enrolled in retirement plans, with the option not to participate, because "evidence shows that by changing the default rule, employee participation rates go up dramatically"—a non-coercive "nudge" toward better decisions. "He knows an astonishing amount about cutting-edge economic thinking," Sunstein said.

Sunstein's Obama is the post-partisan one. He calls Obama a "visionary minimalist," meaning someone who wants to pursue large goals in a way that offends the deepest values of as few people as possible. Governing in this way would make him distinctly un-Rooseveltian. F.D.R. entered office with broad good will and a platform that offered almost all things to all people, but by the time he ran for reelection in 1936 his presidency had become aggressively partisan: he attacked "economic royalists" and said of them, "They are unanimous in their hate for me—and I welcome their hatred." In 2007, Paul Krugman, the *Times* columnist who recently won the Nobel Prize in Economics, commended these remarks to Obama, advising him to sharpen his ideological edge, and warning that his search for common ground with Republicans would be his undoing. But Sunstein said of Obama, "I think he believes—and this is his big split from Krugman—that if you take on board people's deepest commitments, or bracket them, show respect for them, then you make possible larger steps than would otherwise be imagined." It would not be Obama's way to trumpet the arrival of a

new era of liberalism—a word, Sunstein said, that is too laden with bag-
gage, and too much of a fighting word, for Obama's taste.

Instead, Sunstein suggested as the governing philosophy of an Obama
presidency the idea of "deliberative democracy." The phrase appears in *The
Audacity of Hope*, where it denotes a conversation among adults who listen
to one another, who attempt to persuade one another by means of argument and evidence, and who remain open to the possibility that they could
be wrong. Sunstein pointed out that "deliberative democracy" has certain
"preconditions": "It requires an educated citizenry, a virtuous and engaged
citizenry that has sufficient resources—and Madison sometimes spoke in
these terms—that they could actually be citizens, rather than subjects."
Obama links the concept with Lincoln, who was as consequential a president as Roosevelt but in ways that were less obviously partisan and ideological. In his first inaugural, just five weeks before Southern militiamen
fired on Fort Sumter, Lincoln urged his countrymen, "Think calmly and
well, upon this whole subject. Nothing valuable can be lost by taking time.
If there be an object to *hurry* any of you, in hot haste, to a step which you
would never take *deliberately*, that object will be frustrated by taking time;
but no good object can be frustrated by it."

The Audacity of Hope, written during Obama's first year in the Senate,
with the clear aim of laying the groundwork for his presidential candidacy,
has been criticized for burying the more revealing voice of his memoir
Dreams from My Father under a politician's blizzard of evenhanded, unob-
jectionable judgments. But, as campaign books go, it's a good deal more flu
ent and thoughtful than the genre requires. In it, Obama, who was born in
1961, presents himself as someone young enough not to be defined by the
terms and battles of the sixties. His political consciousness was shaped in
the eighties, and he opposed Reagan's agenda while nonetheless understanding its appeal, given the failure of liberal government to come
through for the middle class. Unlike the Clintons—iconic baby boomers—
Obama claims to have no dog in the culture wars; he doesn't feel compelled
to defend, or mend, or end every piece of legislation passed when he was
a toddler or decades before his birth. In *Hope*, he writes, "These efforts
seem exhausted, a constant game of defense, bereft of the energy and new
ideas needed to address the changing circumstances of globalization or a

stubbornly isolated inner city." Obama found his national voice at the 2004 Democratic Convention, in Boston, when his keynote address auguring the end of red-and-blue-state America made him an immediate presidential prospect.

After he declared his candidacy, in early 2007, the Obama who dominated his first year of campaigning was the post-partisan one. He won legions of followers through the sheer power of inspiration. At Dartmouth College in early January, on the night before the New Hampshire primary, a group of students expressed to me deep disenchantment with the Bush and the Clinton dynasties—the boomer War of the Roses. "Obama is the anti-Bush who could get us beyond Bush and all the polarization in Washington," one student said. Another put it this way: "He's one of us." The post-partisan Obama brought millions of young voters into his movement, and he began to peel away moderate Republicans who were sick of their party's being defined by Dick Cheney's autocratic style of governance and Karl Rove's cynical political tactics.

The real problem with partisanship, Obama believes, is that it's no longer pragmatic. After decades of bruising fights in Washington, it has become incompatible with effective government. "I believe any attempt by Democrats to pursue a more sharply partisan and ideological strategy misapprehends the moment we're in," he writes in *Hope*. "I am convinced that whenever we exaggerate or demonize, oversimplify or overstate our case, we lose. Whenever we dumb down the political debate, we lose. For it's precisely the pursuit of ideological purity, the rigid orthodoxy and the sheer predictability of our current political debate, that keeps us from finding new ways to meet the challenges we face as a country." Partisan politics, defined merely as demagoguery or stupidity, is easy to reject—but doing so doesn't take us very far. It's like calling on everyone to be decent. At its weakest, post-partisanship amounts to an aversion to fighting, a trait that some people who know Obama see in him. In the early months of the primary, Obama seemed almost physically to shrink from confrontation, and Hillary Clinton got the better of him in debate after debate.

Just before the Iowa caucus, Sidney Blumenthal, a friend and an adviser to both Bill and Hillary Clinton, told me, "It's not a question of transcending partisanship. It's a question of *fulfilling* it. If we can win and govern well while handling multiple crises at the same time and the Congress, then we can move the country out of this Republican era and into a progressive Democratic era, for a long period of time." Blumenthal found Obama's approach to be "ahistorical"—a simple hope that the past could be waved away. Should Obama win the nomination, members of the Clinton campaign cautioned, he would have no idea what was in store for him. At a Clinton event in Hampton, New Hampshire, a seventy-one-year-old woman named Ruth Keene told me that "the Republicans would chew Obama up."

They tried like hell. They called him an elitist, a radical, a socialist, a Marxist, a Muslim, an Arab, an appeaser, a danger to the republic, a threat to small children, a friend of terrorists, an enemy of Israel, a vote thief, a non-citizen, an anti-American, and a celebrity. Obama didn't defeat the Republicans simply by rising above partisanship, although his dignified manner served as a continual rebuke to his enemies and went a long way toward reassuring skeptical voters who weren't members of the cult of "Yes We Can." It turned out that the culture war, in spite of Sarah Palin's manic gunplay, was largely over. Obama won because he had a vastly superior organization, a steely resilience that became more evident in October than it was in January (for which he owes a debt to Hillary Clinton), and a willingness to fight back on ground on which the majority of Americans—looking to government for solutions—now stand.

≺≺ • ≻≻

According to David Axelrod, among the books that Obama has read recently is *Unequal Democracy*, by the Princeton political scientist Larry M. Bartels. It attributes the steep economic inequality of our time not to blind technological and market forces but to specific Republican policies. Bartels writes, "On average, the real incomes of middle-class families have grown twice as fast under Democrats as they have under Republicans, while the real income of working poor families have grown *six times* as fast under Democrats as they have under Republicans." For decades, rising inequality coincided with conservative electoral success, because voters were largely ignorant of the effects of tax-code changes and other economic policies, those in power were unresponsive to the concerns of working-class citizens, and broader income growth occurred in election years. In other words, the causes of inequality are essentially political—an insight that suggests that Obama might use economic policy to begin reversing a decades-long trend.

Unequal Democracy is decidedly a title from the left-wing book club, and it suits a candidate whose language became more ideological in the days after the markets crashed, in mid-September. Obama began to refer to the financial meltdown as "the final verdict" on a "failed economic philosophy"—words that one of his advisers called "the key line in the campaign narrative." Another adviser told me that, in the final months of the race, economic conditions pushed Obama to the left. "Barack is a progressive person but also cautious," the adviser wrote in an e-mail. "He understands politics and understands the limits it can create on progressive policy. But as the times have moved, he's moved quickly along with them." Early on, during the more vaporous and messianic phase of his candidacy, Obama took more cautious stands than Hillary Clinton did, but this fall he began to embrace some of Clinton's positions that he had once refused to support, such as a moratorium on foreclosures and a government buyout of mortgages.

Obama was able to make a powerful case for a break with conservative economics, in part, because he doesn't carry the scars of recent history. "He's not intimidated by the issue frames that have bedevilled Democrats for the last couple of decades," one of the advisers said. "There's never been a sense of having to triangulate." By the end of the campaign, Obama wasn't just running against broken politics, or even against the Bush presidency. He had the anti-government philosophy of the entire Age of Reagan in his sights.

So events in the homestretch crystallized Obama's economic liberalism. But anyone who has read *The Audacity of Hope* already knew that Obama is no moderate when it comes to the purpose of government. On social and legal issues—guns, abortion, the death penalty, same-sex marriage, the courts and the Constitution—Obama's instinct is usually to soften the left-right clash by reconciling opposites or by escaping them altogether, to find what he called, discussing abortion in his final debate with McCain, "common ground." The phrase is a perfect expression of what Sunstein says is Obama's determination to accommodate disagreement to the extent possible. On issues of culture and law, Obama's liberalism is more procedural than substantive: his most fervent belief is in rules and in standards of serious debate. Given the abuses of executive power and political discourse under George W. Bush, this trait will bring no insignificant cleansing. But Obama's personal caution and conservatism, his sense of rectitude, as well as his idea of politics as a mature calling, shouldn't be mistaken for split-the-difference centrism on every issue. On questions of social welfare—jobs, income, health care, energy—which don't immediately provoke a battle over irreconcilable values, he has given every indication of favoring activist government. When I asked Axelrod if the conservative era had just ended, he said, "From the standpoint of values, I wouldn't say that. But, from the standpoint of economics, yes—American history runs in epochs like this." He added, "That's what the theory of our race was—that this is one of those periods of change we encounter every once in a while in our history."

A chapter in *The Audacity of Hope* titled "Opportunity" describes why "the social compact F.D.R. helped construct is beginning to crumble," and begins to sketch a new social compact for a new century. Obama makes a point of incorporating some of the insights of the Reagan era—such as the importance of market incentives and efficiency—but his conclusion, which is unmistakably Rooseveltian, is a call for the renewal of "widespread economic security." Similarly, in a speech on the economy at New York's Cooper Union, last March, Obama said, "I do not believe that government should stand in the way of innovation or turn back the clock to an older era of regulation. But I do believe that government has a role to play in advancing our common prosperity, by providing stable macroeconomic and financial conditions for sustained growth, by demanding transparency, and by insuring fair competition in the marketplace. Our history should give us confidence that we don't have to choose between an oppressive government-run economy and a chaotic and unforgiving capitalism." Since then, Obama has made it even more clear that he wants to lay the ghost of Reagan to rest.

—‹+ ● +›—

In September, the John F. Kennedy Presidential Library, in Boston, held a forum on presidential leadership. Cass Sunstein was one of the participants; another was Robert Kuttner, the co-founder of *The American Prospect* and a liberal economics journalist. The two argued over what it would take for Obama to be a great president. In Kuttner's view, nothing short of a return to New Deal–style government intervention will be enough to prevent the dire economy from dooming Obama's presidency. This summer, Kuttner published a short book titled *Obama's Challenge*, which he described to me as "an open letter" to the candidate. "Obama will need to be a more radical president than he was a presidential candidate," Kuttner writes. "Obama, in his books and speeches, has been almost obsessed with the idea that people are sick of partisan bickering. Yet he also has claimed the identity of a resolute progressive. Can he be both? History suggests that it is possible both to govern as a radical reformer *and* to be a unifier, and thereby move the political center to the left." According to Kuttner, the next president must be willing to spend at least six hundred billion dollars—a Keynesian outpouring—on public works, health care, energy independence, unemployment benefits, mortgage refinancing, aid to state and local governments, and other programs. Otherwise, the country will slide into a depression that will rival the one Roosevelt inherited. (When I ran the six-hundred-billion figure by Paul Krugman, he agreed.)

"Sunstein's minimalism is exactly what's *not* called for," Kuttner told me, and he later added, "We're on the verge of Great Depression Two. All bets are off. The people who talk about post-liberal, post-ideological, they have been completely overtaken by events. It's the same abuses, the same scenario, that led to the crash of '29. It's the same dynamics of the financial economy dragging down the real economy—these are enduring lessons. Everybody who was talking about being in a kind of post-liberal world, they're the ones who don't have much purchase on what's going on. The question is whether Obama will come to this." The answer will depend in part on the advisers he chooses. In Kuttner's mind, the deficit hawks and deregulators of the Clinton administration—Robert Rubin, Lawrence Summers—have been discredited by the financial crisis, and he thinks that it would be a big mistake for Obama to give them powerful roles in his administration. (Summers is considered a likely candidate for Treasury Secretary [Editor's note: He was named director of Obama's National Economic Council instead], and his top economic advisers are connected with the Hamilton Project, a center-left affiliate of the Brookings Institution.) But, beyond macroeconomics, Kuttner, who plans to hold a conference in Washington called "Thinking Big," shortly before Obama's inauguration, thinks that the Democrats have a clear political agenda: "the reclamation of an ideology."

This is not an ambition that Obama has ever publicly embraced. In *The Audacity of Hope*, he specifically rejects such talk. "That's not Obama," Robert B. Reich, who was Bill Clinton's first Labor Secretary and now teaches at the University of California at Berkeley, said. "Obama is not about the restoration of government as a progressive force per se." He added, "Were Obama to approach this in an ideological way, talking about this as 'We are now going to affirm the importance and centrality of government in the future of the nation,' I think the public would walk away."

Reich, who holds Obama in high regard—he supported his candidacy over that of his old friend Hillary Clinton—bears his share of scars from the Clinton years, many of them inflicted by other members of the administration. He fought and lost a number of first-term battles against Rubin and other centrists, who persuaded Clinton to balance the budget rather than spend more on public investments. Obama will take office with a number of advantages that were unavailable to the last Democratic president. The party is more united, the Democrats in Congress energized by their recent return to a majority. As stagnant wages and pressing public needs have become the focus of Democratic domestic policy, the old line between deficit hawks and economic liberals has dissolved—last week, the *Times* published an op-ed piece co-written by a leading representative of each group: Rubin and the economist Jared Bernstein, respectively. (They met somewhere around the forty-yard line on Bernstein's half of the field.) Bill Clinton began his presidency as the country was coming out of a recession, and Alan Greenspan, the semi-divine chairman of the Federal Reserve, could hold the new president hostage to Wall Street. Now Greenspan, in retirement, has confessed to Congress that his free-market world view was flawed; Wall Street lies prostrate after suffering something like a paralyzing stroke; and, with the country entering a deep recession, both deficit spending and financial regulation are givens. More profoundly, the conservative tide was still high when Clinton entered the White House, and it quickly swamped him. Obama will take power at its lowest ebb. It is for all these reasons that 2009 will be more like 1933 than like 1993.

Nonetheless, in our conversation Reich kept returning to the many ways in which President Obama's ability to act quickly will be compromised. "We are not in Hundred Days territory," Reich said. "We may be, if the economy goes into free fall—the public may demand dramatic action. But there are

so many constraints on dramatic action." New presidents make mistakes—
in Clinton's case, Reich said, they included the push to integrate gays into
the military, the botched effort to reform health care, and a failure to establish priorities. Even with a solid majority in Congress, Obama will have
to deal with the Blue Dog Democrats, who represent states and districts
that are more conservative. Reich recently met with one Blue Dog, in the
Southwest, who "felt that it was going to be very difficult politically to make
the case" that increasing the deficit during a recession was the right thing
to do. On the other hand, unions will likely pressure the administration to
curtail trade agreements, in the interest of preventing the further loss of industrial jobs to other countries.

Finally, there will be a Republican opposition. Given the widespread
sense of national emergency, David Axelrod said, "I don't know that Republicans can afford to take a laissez-faire kind of approach. I think there
are going to be a fair number of Republicans who are going to want to cooperate because they're not going to be on the wrong side of the debate."
Kuttner implied that Obama can govern without them. Reich regarded
them with the wariness of a crime victim whose assailant is still at large.
"They are weaker," he said. "They're not dead by any stretch of the imagination. They're in disarray and discredited, but that's partly because they've
not had a clear target, and, undoubtedly, an Obama administration and a
Democratic Congress will give them a very clear target." In Washington, the
establishment is already beginning to warn that Obama shouldn't "overreach" by moving too far to the left. But the question isn't whether he tacks
left or center; it's whether he demonstrates early on that government can
begin to improve people's lives.

⤙ • ⤚

The tremendous expectations that will accompany Obama to the White
House practically guarantee that some of his supporters will be disappointed by the all-too-normal incapacities of a government founded as a
system of checks and balances, and lately choked with lobbyists and corporate money. This disappointment will only feed what Reich called the
"deep cynicism in the public about the capacity of government to do anything big and well."

Obama, in order to break through the inherent constraints of Washington, will need, above all, a mobilized public beyond Washington. Transformative presidents—those who changed the country's sense of itself in some fundamental way—have usually had great social movements supporting and pushing them. Lincoln had the abolitionists, Roosevelt the labor unions, Johnson the civil-rights leaders, Reagan the conservative movement. Clinton didn't have one, and after his election, Reich said, "everyone went home."

Obama has his own grass-roots organization, on the Internet and in hundreds of field offices. This is new territory, because those earlier movements had independent identities apart from any president, whereas Obama's movement didn't exist before his candidacy; its purpose was to get him elected. Even so, it has the breadth, the organization, and the generational energy of other movements, and it can be converted into a political coalition if its leader knows how to harness it.

Obama's advisers haven't yet worked out the mechanics of this conversion. The Internet could be used to insure transparency; almost every activity of the federal government could be documented online, as some state governments have begun to do. The White House could use the vast Obama e-mail list to convey information about key issues and bills, and to mobilize pressure on Congress. Just as F.D.R. used radio and Reagan television to speak to the public without going through the press, Obama could do the same with the Web.

It's hard to imagine, though, how an electronic "social-network platform" would constitute a movement with the clarity and the coherence of the religious right, or the freedom marchers, or the Congress of Industrial Organizations. The agenda of Obama's candidacy is a list of issues that have different constituencies rather than a single, overarching struggle for freedom or justice. Throughout the campaign, Obama spoke of change coming from the bottom up rather than from the top down, but every time I heard him tell a crowd, "This has never been about me; it's about you," he seemed to be saying just the opposite. The Obama movement was born in the meeting between a man and a historical moment; if he had died in the middle of the campaign, that movement would have died with him—proof that, whatever passions it has stirred, it remains something less than a durable social force.

With a movement behind him, Obama would have the latitude to begin to overcome the tremendous resistance to change that prevails in Washington. Without one, he will soon find himself simply cutting deals. And here is where the two aspects of his vision of the presidency—the post-partisan Obama and the progressive Obama—converge. "Changing politics and making government work are complementary, not opposed," Reich said. "Otherwise, it's the same old Washington. It's a morass."

Does "changing politics" mean finding a bipartisan consensus before moving on to major reforms? Or inspiring a new generation of public-spirited activists? Or simply using a language and a tone that reject divisiveness and respect the intelligence of the citizenry? A more idealistic and engaged politics would be a profoundly welcome departure from an age of disenchantment and venom. Consensus seems less likely. As Paul Krugman told me, post-partisan rhetoric will be the means. Solving problems through progressive government will be the end.

-+- • -+-

Last month, Charlie Rose asked Krugman what he would like to hear from Obama's Inaugural Address. "'The only thing we have to fear is fear itself,'" Krugman said. "I want him to call for something like a new New Deal, saying, 'Look, we've gone off the rails. Not everything's been bad these past couple of decades, but we lost sight of having a society that works for everybody, we lost sight of a society that provides some basic security, we lost sight of a society that provides some basic insurance against chaos in the financial markets, and we need to recapture some of those values that have made us successful.'" Krugman didn't say what a "new New Deal" would be.

There is a mysterious cycle in human events, but it doesn't swing back and forth like a pendulum. Arthur Schlesinger, Jr., building on his father's work, observed that American politics alternates between thirty-year periods of conservatism and reform—between the idea that we're on our own and the idea that we're all in this together. But the movement of history incorporates everything that went before, always inching ahead even as it oscillates, and anyone who governs as if the experience of entire eras could be reversed is bound to fail. (The Gingrich Congress, driven solely by a desire to dismantle government programs, comes to mind.) "It would be a mistake to surmise that the new era is somehow a return to the New Deal," Axelrod said. "The one theme that I think travels is the notion that there is a role for government to play. It may be just as a catalyst; it may be using the bully pulpit. But I think the progressive idea that government has a role to play in making sure there are rules of the road, that people get a fair shake, and so on—I think that is very much what people are looking for today."

If you dip into the literature of the New Deal, what immediately strikes you is its desperate radicalism. Next January, no one will use the kind of apocalyptic language with which Arthur Krock, of the *Times*, described Roosevelt's inauguration: "The atmosphere which surrounded the change of government in the United States was comparable to that which might be found in a beleaguered capital in war time." In his Inaugural Address, with the Depression in its fourth year, F.D.R. demanded wartime powers. He took office amid protests by military veterans clamoring for their bonuses, and not long after his inauguration he came up with the idea of sending many of them, along with a couple of hundred thousand other unemployed men, to clear firebreaks in the country's national parks. After a century and a half of American individualism, his Brain Trust—an advisory group of economists and lawyers—put the government in charge of organizing the economy. Vast programs costing millions of dollars and requiring entirely new agencies took shape overnight while Americans starved to death. Critics, including some Democrats, compared Roosevelt to Hitler, Mussolini, and Stalin. Demagogues and mobs sprang up around the country, calling for Communism, for Fascism, for old-age pensions. Out of this churn came the mixed economy, and Social Security.

Reagan couldn't cancel Roosevelt's legacy; Obama won't be able to obliterate Reagan's. The past few decades have generated a great surge of private energy and private pursuits, and for some Americans they have been years of dizzying abundance and creativity. Laptop computers and microbrews are just as characteristic of the Age of Reagan as financial derivatives and outsourcing. Next January, legions of earnest, overworked, slightly underfed young men and women won't flock to Washington to map out new government bureaucracies; instead, legions of healthy, casually ironic, extremely nice young men and women will flock to Washington to map out the green revolution. When it comes, it will look more like Google than like the Tennessee Valley Authority.

But November 4, 2008, is one of those infrequent dates when one historical age and one generation, with a distinct political and economic and cultural character, gave way to another age, another generation. The new era that is about to begin under President Obama will be more about public good than about private goods. The meal will be smaller, and have less interesting flavors, but it will be shared more fairly. The great American improvisation called democracy still bends along the curve of history. It has not yet finished astounding the world.

THE NEW NEW PRESIDENCY

100 DAYS

Illustration by Steve Brodner;
first appeared in the *Los Angeles Times*.

11

THE COOL PRESIDENCY

MICHELLE COTTLE

The New Republic   March 4, 2009

It's an inescapable truth of human psychology that, in addition to their policy and personnel decisions and their dealings with Congress and world leaders, America's presidents also influence the nation's mood and direction through the nature of their personalities. In this respect, Barack Obama couldn't be more different than his predecessor: nonconfrontational where George W. Bush was combative, deliberative where Bush reacted from the gut, the self-made offspring of an itinerant Kansan mother and absentee Kenyan father whereas Bush was the well-heeled son of a president and grandson of a U.S. senator.

As many observers have noted, our new chief executive also has an air of almost preternatural calm. Some credit this unflappable demeanor to being raised in laid-back Hawaii, others to his youthful struggle to find himself. But for whatever reason, "no drama Obama" is a consistently even-tempered presence in a political world prone to hyperventilation. In this New Republic *essay, Michelle Cottle takes a look at what it means to have a president who's cooler than you are.*

If one were to gather together a dozen of our society's key arbiters of cool—ad execs, movie stars, fashion designers, music critics, pollsters, suburban tweens—and instruct them to generate the profile of a "cool" politician, what are the odds that their efforts would result in a gangly, jug-eared, overeducated, workaholic with a fondness for Scrabble? Not to denigrate our freshly minted president, but, when you tick through some of the basics, Barack Obama comes across as an inveterate dork. It's not just that the guy is a double-Ivied academic; he is painfully wonky with hard-core professorial tendencies. If what we've witnessed thus far of his dancing is any indication, he is somewhat rhythmically challenged. His favorite book is *Moby-Dick*. His favorite TV program growing up was *MASH*, though *The Dick Van Dyke Show* was right up there. He has read at least six Harry Potter tomes. Perhaps most damning, he is a collector of comics—Spider-Man and Conan the Barbarian—a tidbit that prompted the editor-in-chief of Marvel to publicly enthuse: "This has got to be the coolest thing on Planet Earth for us. The commander-in-chief is actually a nerd-in-chief."

And yet, somehow, this nerd-in-chief has ascended to a level of global cool uninhabited by any of his political forebears. The opening spread of a recent *Entertainment Weekly* cover story, titled "President Rock Star," neatly summarized the situation: "He's bigger than Brangelina, bigger than Beyoncé: See how our new president has become the biggest celebrity in the world." Indeed, the entire First Family has transfixed the popular culture: How about that four-year-old footage *Entertainment Tonight* obtained of Sasha and Malia? Or the *Us Weekly* cover of Michelle and Barack? (Not to be confused with the one of Barack and the girls.) At this point, the conversation has moved beyond whether Obama himself possesses that special magic—when *Saturday Night Live* constructs a skit around your chronic coolness, the conventional wisdom is pretty much set—to how expansive his cool coattails will prove. Post-election, there has been contemplation of such questions as whether Obama can make public service cool (possibly), whether he can redefine cool in a way that will be uplifting for young black men (God willing), and whether he can make Washington cool (fat chance).

But, when an individual is propelled to supernova status at such astonishing speed, there are a couple of even more basic questions to consider: How did this happen? Where did this man's cool come from? And what can its roots tell us about how Obama will lead?

⤙ • ⤚

Glancing back over the president's life, you notice that he is a latecomer to cool. Far from growing up a smooth, charismatic, or cocky alpha male, "Barry" Obama spent much of his youth conflicted about his mixed-race heritage, confused about where he fit in, and insecure about who he was. In high school and college, he dabbled with some of cool's commonplace talismans—alcohol, cigarettes, drugs—as well as a few more culturally charged ones. In *Dreams from My Father*, Obama details his search for self, in part a struggle with racial identity and in part a more generic flirtation with angst and disaffection:

> To avoid being mistaken for a sellout, I chose my friends carefully. The more politically active black students. The foreign students. The Chicanos. The Marxist professors and structural feminists and punk-rock performance poets. We smoked cigarettes and wore leather jackets. At night, in the dorms, we discussed neocolonialism, Franz Fanon, Eurocentrism, and patriarchy. When we ground out our cigarettes in the hallway carpet or set our stereos so loud that the walls began to shake, we were resisting bourgeois society's stifling constraints. We weren't indifferent or careless or insecure. We were alienated.

Ultimately, Obama discarded this model of self. He changed his name from Barry to Barack and traveled from the projects of South Chicago to the villages of Western Kenya in pursuit of a more fulfilling identity. He emerged from this quest with a mellower vibe characterized by easy smiles and a thoughtful, unflappable demeanor. Barry fretted about being cool and therefore wasn't; Barack knew who he was and therefore didn't have to try to be anything. This is the cornerstone of a classic, old-school kind of cool—one based on confidence, nonchalance, and the ability to radiate that you are far too cool to care if others recognize your coolness.

This last quality is a key reason why cool is such a rare commodity in politics. The very nature of the game compels its practitioners to be petitioners, ever bowing and scraping for votes, legislative support, and money. And it is hard to be cool when you are constantly begging. Consider the field's premier pre-Obama phenom of recent times, Bill Clinton. Clinton too was a rock star, a legendary charmer with formidable gifts of persuasion who, through the power and profile of high office, achieved an impressive level of charisma. But Bill was never cool. Despite (or because of) all the sax-playing, underwear chatter, and schmoozing with Hollywood celebs, our forty-second president was too emotive, too eager, too *needy*. Part of what made him such a devastating retail politician was the sense, telegraphed with every broad grin and elbow clasp, that Clinton craved our love and approval. Similarly, no matter how famous he became, he always presented himself as the starstruck kid from Arkansas who could not believe his great fortune to be mingling with the likes of Barbra Streisand and David Geffen. It was charming. But it was deeply uncool.

Obama, by contrast, displays no such awe or hunger, even when hobnobbing with the shiniest A-listers (Jay-Z, George Clooney, Oprah). Whether it's Scarlett Johansson's gushing support being waved away by Candidate Obama or Beyoncé getting weepy at the Neighborhood Ball over the sheer awesomeness of President Obama, the upper hand rests always with the gangly guy with jug ears. As Obama assured *Us Weekly* last February, "I don't really get starstruck."

Far more vitally, Obama convinced millions of regular Americans that supporting him was all about fulfilling *our* needs, not his. (He also wisely rejected inquiries into his underwear preference.) Now, as he transitions to governing, Obama is aiming to communicate something similar: Fighting for his policies isn't about proving he's right or flexing his political muscle; it's about serving the public. When others don't share his urgency to get "the people's business" done, Obama might show some teeth, as he did at a February 5 speech hawking his stimulus package. (The brow furrowed, the finger wagged, the voice hardened, and there were mocking jabs at Republicans: "Then you get the argument, 'Well, this is not a stimulus bill. This is a *spending* bill.'" Pause. Look of total exasperation. "What do you think a stimulus *is*?!") But his is a controlled fire, one that seeks to convey that he does not take the battle personally—that it isn't, ultimately, about him. At a January stimulus meeting with Hill Republicans, the president sanguinely assured those assembled that he knew many of them would beat him up over the bill: "I understand that, and I will watch you on Fox News and feel bad about myself." With that bit of low-key sarcasm, Obama let everyone in the room—and beyond—know that he wouldn't feel bad about himself for one minute. Whatever partisan barbs fly his way, the president intends to remain cool.

It is fitting that much of Barry's journey toward Barack focused on questions of race, because much of Obama's cool has to do with color. Biracial heritage aside, Obama is a black man. And, in this country, black men have long had the edge on cool. As *The Washington Post*'s Donna Britt noted in her December 2006 contribution to the paper's "Being a Black Man" series, "there's cool—and then there's *brother* cool. . . . No other group's identity is as steeped in the *necessity* of appearing cool, or in the expectation that they instinctively bring coolness to the table." The phenomenon goes beyond the concrete trappings of black culture: the music, the style, the vernacular, the gestures. (Fist bump, anyone?) There is a broader, less tangible aura that black men have long possessed (and that white guys, from Elvis Presley to hip-hop obsessed suburban teens, have long imitated). And, for all the early-campaign debate about whether Obama was "black enough," he channels some of the basic elements of brothercool. He's got the walk. (The swagger is subtle, but it's there.) He's got the talk (more about cadence than lingo—though he has a touch of that too). And, of course, he oozes that fluid self-assurance. ("Confidence is cool's most essential element," Britt observes. "Perhaps that's why black men—for whom the appearance of assurance can be a matter of life or death—so often radiate it.") When *Ebony* magazine declared Obama one of "The 25 Coolest Brothers of All Time," he joined the exalted ranks of legends such as Malcolm X, Muhammad Ali, Tupac, and Michael Jordan. Obama clearly revels in his brothercool image and, just as clearly, recognizes its political appeal. At public events, he has demonstrated his ease with the fist bump, the shoulder brush, and the occasional bit of slang. "We straight," he told a D.C. waitress when settling a recent bill.

Black men, to be sure, do not have a monopoly on cool. But, just as a thought exercise, imagine Obama as a white politician. Wonky, overeducated, idealistic, unflappable, reform-minded, big into basketball, articulate but without the lyrical echoes of the African American pulpit—far from being brothercool, Obama would be ex-senator turned failed presidential candidate Bill Bradley.

Also fueling Obama's cool is the snap, crackle, and pop of youth—particularly noticeable in a field dominated by starchy gray-hairs. The new president may be a middle-aged wonk, but we are frequently reminded that he stays in sync with the younger generation. For starters, there is his endlessly discussed fitness and sports obsession, with an emphasis on hoops—a hip, urban, young man's game if ever there was one. (So much cooler than golf or tennis or even football.) Since the early primary days, we have been treated to a steady stream of stories about the candidate's workouts, pickup games, and scrimmages. (Now and again, he even played with reporters.) The cover of next month's *Men's Journal* proclaims Obama "jock-in-chief" and promises an insider look at "his moves, his trash talk, & his weekly power basketball game."

As for his pop-cult cred, we have been told repeatedly that *The Godfather* I and II (but *definitely* not III) are Obama's top movie picks of all time. His favorite TV show of recent years was HBO's gritty, Baltimore-based epic *The Wire*, on which his favorite character was a stickup man named Omar, who made his living ripping off local drug lords. And how many times have we heard that hip-hop mogul Jay-Z is on Obama's iPod? This tidbit is an especially valuable twofer, emphasizing both the president's familiarity with a musical genre anathema to most pols and his love of tech toys. Speaking of tech savvy, Obama has made much of his BlackBerry addiction, and his pioneering Facebook page was but one piece of the social-networking machine credited with mobilizing young voters. It didn't hurt, of course, that Team Obama tapped Chris Hughes, the 25-year-old co-founder of Facebook, to help run its online outreach.

Which brings us to Obama's posse of young 'uns—most notably his chief scribe, 27-year-old Jon Favreau; 24-year-old Eugene Kang, special assistant to the president; and 27-year-old Reggie Love, who, in addition to hovering at Obama's elbow as his "body man," also serves as his morning workout partner and preferred hoops mate. This is not to suggest that Obama favors certain staffers with an eye toward burnishing his image. He is clearly drawn to young people by their energy and idealism—and by his own desire not to feel like a fuddy-duddy. But there can be little doubt that inviting Favreau, Kang, and Love into his inner circle has helped to augment his cool. Press coverage of Favreau (including a spread in *The New York Times* Sunday Styles section) invariably draws attention to youthful quirks such as his preference for working at Starbucks, his tendency to prank e-mail fellow staffers, and his love of the video game "Rock Band." Even Favreau's worst moment—the Facebook party pic showing him groping a cardboard cutout of Hillary Clinton—had a frat-like quality that served to remind everyone just how young he is. Kang, who periodically pops up in pics with Obama—chatting on the plane, golfing in Hawaii—is now so tight with the president that he's referred to as "Reggie Jr." In *The New York Times Magazine*'s January photo survey of "Obama's People," Kang, dewy-faced and with a long gray scarf swallowing his slight frame, looked to have stepped straight out of a Banana Republic ad.

And what is there left to say about Love? A former basketball and football player for Duke who was signed (then cut) by both the Green Bay Packers and the Dallas Cowboys, Obama's hunky personal aide has developed his own cult following. *People* magazine named Love one of the most eligible bachelors of 2008, *Vanity Fair* included him on its "In" list, and ESPN did a minidocumentary on him titled "Chief of Stuff." Obama himself started cracking jokes on the trail about having an aide so much "cooler than the candidate."

But as Obama is surely aware, hanging with Love only boosts his own cool quotient. Every story about Obama banging in the paint alongside Love—not to mention some of Love's pals and former teammates, at least one of whom is now in the NBA—is a feather in the 47-year-old president's virility cap. Shrewdly, Team Obama has been liberal with its media access to Love. In multiple profiles of the infamously hip body man (he received A-1 treatment in the *Times*), we have learned, among other things, about Love's romantic preferences (a basic knowledge of sports is required), his late-night socializing (on the trail, he was the guy everyone wanted to party with), his tattoo ("MY WORD, MY BOND, MY BOYZ, MY BLOOD"), his enduring affinity for beer pong, and, of course, his role in helping his boss keep up with the hip kids. (It was Love who introduced Obama to the fist bump, Love who gave Obama an iPod for his forty-sixth birthday, and Love who loaded said iPod with Jay-Z and Lil Wayne.)

≺≺ • ≻≻

With a quality as elusive as cool, there is the temptation to assume that it must come naturally—that it cannot be forced or forged. But the dirty little secret of our new president's cool is that no element of it came with ease. Obama achieved his laid-back, too-cool-to-care persona by being a committed grind: He spent years working through his insecurities, learning to control his emotions, and sanding down the rough edges of his personality. Even figuring out whether and how to fully embrace his identity as a black man required effort. As a politician, Obama has taken the cultivation still further, with his cultural savvy and band of young *compadres*. He is Jay

Gatsby minus the criminal history—an unpolished youth who constructed a smoother, more glittering version of himself out of sweat, vision, and force of will.

In that sense, the key attribute that enabled Obama to become cool—his meticulous resolve—is the same one that also makes him kind of a dork. This should provide some measure of comfort to those who now and again wonder whether Obama is in fact too cool to lead, whether his steady reserve signals a chilly detachment from the problems facing the country. His calm charisma may put Obama on the cover of *People*—but it is still his striving that defines him, and will likely define his administration as well. The upshot is that wonks and intellectuals and other assorted Type-A obsessives across the country can rest easy: Having elected the coolest president in recent memory, we are almost certainly going to get four years of government by nerd.

12

REGARDING MICHELLE OBAMA

JENNIFER SENIOR

New York magazine   March 23, 2009

If Barack Obama is a breath of fresh air in the White House, his wife Michelle is a veritable sea breeze. Raised in a working-class neighborhood of Chicago; educated at Princeton (where she followed her older brother, Craig Robinson, who captained the basketball team there and now coaches at Oregon State University) and Harvard; a lawyer, hospital administrator, affectionate spouse, and hands-on mother, she embodies a combination of warmth and reserve that has stood her in good stead both on the campaign trail and as First Lady. She also has an appealing personal style (love that White House garden!) and unerring fashion sense (notwithstanding David Brooks's suggestion to fellow New York Times *columnist Maureen Dowd that it was time she covered up her bared biceps). But Michelle Obama's greatest political strength, as Jennifer Senior points out in this* New York *magazine essay, may be her ability to recalibrate her public image according the demands of the moment—a talent she'll undoubtedly have plenty of occasion to call on during the next four years.*

Until fairly recently, it looked like Michelle Obama was destined for the same public drubbing as Hillary Clinton, the only other First Lady to enter the White House with a law degree. It's hard to remember this now, but the two have an awful lot in common. Michelle grew up just 25 miles from where Hillary did, also in a modest home with a homemaker mother. In high school, she too was ambitious and straitlaced, working hard enough to attend both a fancy college and law school (Princeton followed by Harvard, rather than Wellesley followed by Yale). She too became known as the family hard-ass (Michelle's friends nicknamed her "the Taskmaster"). She too drew a higher salary in the private sector than her husband did in the public.

And like Hillary, Michelle discovered that any frank expression of her opinions on the campaign trail would instantly boomerang. When she ribbed her husband for his morning breath and all-around hopelessness when it came to putting away the perishables, Maureen Dowd wrote that some found her jokes "emasculating." When Michelle told an audience in Milwaukee, "For the first time in my adult life, I am proud of my country," the observation was regarded as only a shade less apple pie than Hillary's "I suppose I could have stayed home and baked cookies," and with the added valence of racial suspicion: Michelle was an "angry black woman," in the words of syndicated columnist Cal Thomas; "Mrs. Grievance" according to the cover of the *National Review*.

Yet by the time Michelle declared that her primary role in the Obama administration would be "mom-in-chief," it had the ring of total plausibility, drawing far less contempt than Hillary received when she offered America her chocolate-chip-cookie recipe. The question is: Why?

Some of the differences, surely, can be chalked up to temperament and upbringing: Michelle's campaign speeches teemed with warm anecdotes about her own stay-at-home mother, recently prompting *The Atlantic*'s Ta-Nehisi Coates to muse, "In all my years of watching black public figures, I'd never heard one recall such an idyllic youth." (Hillary's father, on the other hand, made minor sport of humiliating his wife, according to Carl Bernstein's *A Woman in Charge*.) Hillary generally framed her role as mother in policy terms (*It Takes a Village*), while Michelle tended to discuss hers in a more immediate, emotional vocabulary. One thinks of the moment in her convention speech when she described Barack driving home, white-knuckled, with their first child, "inching along at a snail's pace, peering at us anxiously through the rearview mirror." In one spare and true image, she managed to connect with her audience in a way that Hillary never did.

But perhaps an even bigger reason that Michelle's East Wing ambitions seem authentic to us is a generational one. Hillary graduated from college in 1969, that extraordinary cusp year for boomer women, when it seemed that half the nation's female graduates chose child-rearing as their main occupation while the other half marched boldly into the workplace, keeping custody of their last names and wearing the pants. (At her best friend's wedding, Hillary wore a tux.) Working was a politicized choice, made against a politicized backdrop (the women's movement, the civil-rights movement, Vietnam), with politics itself beckoning as a vocation. Yet many of the women who chose to work were still forced to make radical compromises. Just after law school, for instance, Hillary had a wealth of professional possibilities to choose from up north. But instead she followed Bill Clinton down to Arkansas, a virtual swampland for career women. She was savaged for keeping her last name and forced to pour tea for the ladies in the front rooms of the Governor's Mansion while the men talked politics in the back. ("This," one of Hillary's friends told her, according to Bernstein, "is like mind Jell-O.") It was a recipe for lifelong resentment.

By the time Michelle Obama came along, however, the age was both more and less progressive. Banking and corporate law were more appealing to her college cohort than political activism, but far more women were joining the workforce. They'd seen the generation before them attempt— imperfectly, but still—to balance work and family. If anything, Barack helped Michelle expand her professional horizons, encouraging her to leave her banal job at a big Chicago law firm for the more self-determining work of community outreach (for which she made as much as $315,000 annually, as a hospital executive). She, in turn, introduced Barack to a number of figures who'd prove influential to him, including Valerie Jarrett, his public liaison. When he won his Senate seat, Michelle wouldn't so much as follow him to Washington, D.C., let alone Arkansas. The balance she and Barack have struck over the years has by no means been ideal. Her husband wrote about it with bracing honesty in *The Audacity of Hope*: "'You only think about yourself,' she would tell me. 'I never thought I'd have to raise a family alone.'" But Michelle could at least talk with Barack about his absences. And her career didn't seem to suffer much in spite of her choices.

Of course, Michelle was never interested in running for elected office. Perhaps that, in the end, is the simplest explanation for why we believe her when she says she's content to take up residence in the East Wing. She's not depending on the White House to supply her with a vocation. Nor is she craving the spotlight. For all her practice on the hustings, Michelle still races through her public remarks too quickly, her voice quavering. Her case of nerves is precisely what gave her convention speech its extra power. We felt for her. We'd be the same up there. Who'd want to do this, anyway? Whereas Hillary . . . well, most of us are familiar with that story. At law school, those who knew both her and Bill always assumed it was she who'd make the better presidential candidate. By the time she got to 1600 Pennsylvania Avenue, in 1993, her thwarted executive self was desperate to come out.

Many working women have expressed disappointment over Michelle's choice to be mom-in-chief. But being a stay-at-home mother at the White House is hardly the same as being a stay-at-home mom in Hyde Park. It's a more peculiar job, for starters—how do you negotiate a normal life for your kids when the Secret Service trails them to slumber parties? Second, there may be a race-and-class-based cast to the complaint. "Most African-American women I know are thrilled she's in a position to make that choice," noted Allison Samuels in the December 1 issue of *Newsweek*. "The average African-American family can't survive without two incomes." Let's also remember that Michelle may be the only woman in the United States who can drop out of the workforce for four or eight years with no worries about losing her professional momentum.

But I also suspect that Michelle's professional skills will not lie fallow in the East Wing. She's a quick study, becoming an expert politician in a stunningly short period of time. People think she's too brassy? Fine, she'll stop teasing Barack about his failure to put his socks in the hamper. ("If the joke is clouding the point," she explained to *Vogue*, "then let's just get to the point.") People think she's an Ivy League elitist? Fine, she'll retool her stump speech to emphasize her modest roots. People think she's unpatriotic? Fine, she'll be as American as apple pie, declaring herself "mom-in-chief." Like her husband, she is a shrewd and inspiring communicator, better than any First Lady most of us can remember. And like her husband, she's well rounded, in touch with both her maternal and professional sides. (Did you know her Secret Service code name is Renaissance? True story.)

We have, in our minds, a false dichotomy: that First Ladies are either Hillary Clinton or Laura Bush. But that is, of course, a totally crude notion. It's just that we don't know what a third way of First Lady–dom looks like. Michelle, though perhaps the ideal kind of woman to show us, is also a complicated one. She's a private person in a public role, a black woman in a costume drama played previously only by whites, an outspoken professional with a traditional sense of hearth and home. We all feel like we know her, but we don't really. She has learned to dole herself out with extreme care. All we can rely on is what we've seen and heard. Much of that is more material than intellectual—her fashion sense, her arms, her kitchen, her kids, her awesome height. But we've recently gotten a glimpse of the opinionated, professional Michelle, too, when she spoke to government workers last month, cheering the stimulus and their morale. What kind of First Lady she'll ultimately be, we don't know. People often project more onto the role than First Ladies themselves project outward. But it's the ability to take advantage of those projections that separates a political wife from a political icon.

13

PRESIDENT OF EVERYTHING

BRIAN DOHERTY

The American Conservative   April 20, 2009

One aspect of U.S. politics that would be amusing if the stakes weren't so high is the tendency for both major political parties to attack presidents from the opposing party for amassing too much power—though usually for different reasons. The Democrats, for instance, decried George W. Bush's penchant for keeping government documents secret, his habit of penning signing statements—memos affirming his prerogative to ignore unwanted portions of a given congressional bill—and his administration's assertion of the right to suspend habeas corpus for suspected terrorists.

In this essay, Brian Doherty, offering a critique from the other side of the aisle, points out that even though Barack Obama campaigned against Bush's expansive view of presidential privilege, he's managed to assert his own fair share of executive power during his first months in office, especially in his dealings with American business—leading Doherty to suggest that "[Obama's] administration is as cynical about federalism as Bush's, if not more so."

In December 2007, Sen. Barack Obama's reassurances to the *Boston Globe* suggested that he understood constitutional limits on executive and government power. He knew that there were things the "president does not have power under the Constitution" to do, including unilaterally authorizing military action and surveilling citizens without warrants. He said he would "reject the Bush administration's claim that the president has plenary authority under the Constitution to detain U.S. citizens without charges as unlawful enemy combatants."

That thoughtful skeptic of executive power now sits in the Oval Office. Isolating random bits of his presidential rhetoric, you can almost believe that he understands how a society really thrives. Obama said in his pseudo–State of the Union Address, "The answers to our problems don't lie beyond our reach. They exist in our laboratories and universities; in our fields and our factories; in the imaginations of our entrepreneurs and the pride of the hardest-working people on Earth."

But in just three months, we have seen what Obama means when he talks about "reach." He doesn't mean "our reach" but his own. His sense of that reach, and the abrupt and scary speed with which he's used it, marks him as an executive with a tentacled grip—multiple, crushing, inescapable. No longer the cautious critic of presidential power of the campaign trail, he now sees nothing as beyond his grasp.

Less than a hundred days in, the fully articulated ideological contours of his vision remain unclear—just as he wishes. It suits Obama's self-image as a mere pragmatic problem solver to never explain, to float from power grab to usurpation as if nothing but thoughtful reaction to the exigencies of the moment guides him. But it's already obvious that those actions veer strongly toward expansive government, limiting our options in every aspect of national life.

Budget: The government fiscal game works as well as it does politically because most people don't think of government spending in terms of control over their lives. Most see it as a benefit, a graceful solution to a perceived lack. Healthcare? Obama's approximated buy-in is $600 billion over a decade—a figure sure to come up grossly short if history is any guide. But most think, well, I'm not the one with $600 billion to toss, so why not?

That money, plus all the many other nonexistent trillions Obama is planning to spend, gets paid back either in debt service down the line—funneling a larger percentage of the lifeblood, time, and effort of our children to Washington and thence to whoever's brave enough to hold U.S. debt by then—or in inflation that eats away at any attempt on our part to save or invest profitably.

When, according to the Congressional Budget Office's analysis of Obama's spending plans, the U.S. government deficit-spends $9.3 trillion over the next decade, that's more than an absurd abstraction. It's enslavement: the hours and days of our lives.

Business and the economy: Here Obama's grip is far less subtle. He's clear and decisive: the financial and industrial economy is his, and he'll do with it as he pleases. What's decided for the U.S. is what's decided for General Motors, as presidential pressure pushes out GM chief Rick Wagoner. Obama and his man at Treasury, Timothy Geithner, want the power to confiscate any company whose failure they claim threatens the larger economy.

Now that he occupies the White House, the new president—who justly pilloried Bush for asserting that national security excused any executive ukase—seems to believe that his own vision of economic security empowers him to take whatever he wants and make any decision he deems necessary, from curtailing CEO compensation to renegotiating mortgage terms. What private sector? This is economic war!

And lest one think this is all about being faithful stewards of the public wealth, as Obama and Geithner like to play it, the *Wall Street Journal* reported that an unnamed bank was not allowed to return money the Feds had stuck it with in the first bailout wave. The strings attached to those bailout funds gave the federal government effective ownership over the bank; evidently the Obama administration values an excuse for control more than it values taxpayer money.

It also seems primed to use more traditional means of throwing weight around the national economy. The president's pick for antitrust chief, Christine Varney, has already cast a stink eye at Google, expressing concern at a conference last year about the company's "monopoly in Internet online advertising." And Obama's pick to head the Department of Agriculture, former Iowa governor Tom Vilsack, is an enthusiastic supporter of one of the most foolish and damaging federal economic manipulations around, endless ethanol subsidies. Any noises about damping down agricultural subsidies in general, supposedly part of the "fiscally responsible" Obama agenda, are dying in Congress.

State secrets: Even Obama's most ardent supporters are disillusioned by his close adherence to the Bush model when it comes to executive privilege. Obama's Department of Justice has openly agreed that lawsuits challenging rendition and warrantless-wiretapping programs should be dismissed because trying them would expose state secrets. His legal team declares that the president—and only the president—has the right to make such classified decisions, with neither courts nor Congress, and of course no one as inconsequential as an aggrieved citizen, able to second guess.

That's troubling enough, but it's not all. While Attorney General Eric Holder has released some Bush-era documents relating to torture policy, the Obama administration as a whole is, as this article went to press, agonizing over whether to release a further set said to be even more heinous. (Even if they eventually release them, that this wasn't a no-brainer shows executive secrecy is still far too robust in the administration.) Even an international intellectual-property treaty being actively considered by 27 countries had its contents declared a national-security secret in an Obama Department of Justice filing in March.

Healthcare: We don't yet know what combination of mandates, subsidies, government-supplied insurance, and controls will arise. But we do know that the cornerstone of the cost containment Obama seeks will be decisions about what gets covered by the insurance that the government will be guaranteeing, regulating, and demanding. This means rationing and a potentially fatal blow to one of the last markets where expensive and experimental new treatments can be developed and, if found worthwhile, thrive.

Given how Obama has shown such a scrupulous sense of pipers and their right to call the tune in the financial and automotive markets, he is apt to be more explicit than past politicians in insisting that any behavior by companies or individuals that costs the public money must be stringently controlled. That means your health will no longer be your own business but Barack Obama's.

Environment: The president did not immediately get the cap-and-trade carbon program he wanted. But he is using the powers of the stimulus package and bailout legislation to establish that he can push out corporate execs and take over any company he wants in other fields, so why not in this one, too? His executive branch seems to believe that it can legitimately claim whatever power it says it needs to achieve a goal it can halfway connect to a legitimate congressional mandate.

It is quite possible that Obama's EPA will claim authority for sweeping action under the Clean Air Act. The president of Clean Air Watch, Frank O'Donnell, told *Rolling Stone* that an EPA ruling that global warming is a public health danger "gives Obama added leverage in going to Congress. . . . He can say, 'I've got this authority in my back pocket. If you torpedo cap-and-trade, I'll have no choice but to deal with this administratively.'"

Foreign policy: Obama claims to be on schedule to wind down our involvement in Iraq. His rosy projections of declining deficits in the out-years— the ones he doesn't have to worry about now as he tries to keep the plates of an overextended economy spinning for one more month—depend on it. But if a rising insurgency ramps up the killings of U.S. troops or other Iraqis in the last months before the supposed pullout at the end of 2011, who believes that Obama will make good on his pledge?

He has no intention of ending the Bush-era policy of imperial overreach. He's just shifting the theater in which we act out this timeless drama of collapse, with 21,000 more troops promised to Afghanistan for the potentially eternal mission of ending the Taliban insurgency there.

This survey only scratches the surface of bad actions and ominous portents for President Obama's exercise of power. His administration is as cynical about federalism as Bush's, if not more so.

Indeed, he has such a yen for creating independent centers of executive power in the form of policy "czars" that even Democratic Senator Robert Byrd, no advocate of restrained government, recently complained that Obama is threatening "the constitutional system of checks and balances" by giving too much independent authority to the White House outside of Senate-approved department heads. But many other Democrats in Congress are looking to extend presidential reach still further, plumping to give Obama power over the entire food production and distribution system (the proposed "Food Safety Modernization Act") and to shut down the Internet in a "cybersecurity emergency" (the proposed "Cybersecurity Act of 2009").

Given the realities of Obama's practice of presidential power, his official vision seems less important. His team hasn't yet spelled out anything as sinister as the loopholes John Yoo devised for Bush from his Office of Legal Counsel, if only because Obama's pick for OLC, Dawn Johnsen, has had her appointment held up in the Senate, largely over her abortion views. From her record, it's unlikely that she'll give her boss a formalized framework of power. That's not how Obama likes to sell himself. But just because Johnsen doesn't deliver some tortuous explanation for why the president can do whatever he wants doesn't mean that her boss will be any more constrained than his predecessor.

For example, the Obama Justice Department's filings in the *habeas* hearings before U.S. District Court Judge John Bates in the legal challenge by four Bagram detainees no longer relies, as Bush did, on bald declarations of inherent presidential power. But Obama's Department of Justice does not therefore conclude that the president does not have the power to keep "enemy combatants" locked up indefinitely without *habeas* rights, even as Obama moves to shut down the public-relations nightmare of Guantánamo and abandon the term "enemy combatants."

The power Obama's Justice Department claims might not be "inherent" any longer. But as explained by Duke Law School's Christopher Schroeder on the website Executive Watch, Obama's team still "argues there is ample authority to detain in the combination of the AUMF [Authorization for Use of Military Force] itself, the president's conceded central role in executing the country's war powers, and international law." Those poor bastards languishing at Bagram and other mystery detention centers aren't likely to be cheered by this supposed change in theories of executive power.

U.S. presidents have been acting outside the explicit bounds of their constitutional mandates from the Adams and Jefferson eras—Alien and Sedition Acts, Louisiana Purchase—through Lincoln, Wilson, Roosevelt, and Johnson to Bush and now Obama. The story of the decay and destruction of constitutional limits on power is as old as the Republic itself. And expansions of executive power—see Richard Nixon with his plethora of new regulatory agencies and wage and price controls—need not be combined with an explicitly developed theory that supports and encourages government metastasis.

Executive overstretch has dominated American government for so long that we usually only hear effective complaints from those fighting to oust the incumbents steamrolling our liberties at any given moment. That's why candidate Obama was so sharp about criticizing Bush's extraconstitutional power claims and was able to find the one war he could be unequivocally against: the one he could blame on his political opponents. Now he perpetuates the same policies, albeit under different names and with different excuses (secrecy and "enemy combatants") or with promises to stop them eventually (Iraq).

As predictable as out-party opposition is in-party realization that, as Obama's right-hand man Rahm Emanuel openly put it, there's no sense in letting a crisis go to waste. After all, the costs of classic, FDR-style "bold, persistent experimentation" are low in such crises. American presidential powerhouses have had various rationales for their abuses—from war for Lincoln, Wilson, and Bush to economic crisis for Roosevelt to playing on a wealthy society's sense of fairness and guilt for Johnson.

Obama's specialty is shaping up to be particularly dangerous because it's hard to dispute given the average American's sensibilities. No call for liberty and constitutional principle seems convincing when Obama is arguing that those relying on government giveaways should have to follow government-set rules. That is, once you've allowed them to go ahead with the handouts, the political game is almost over. Under the guise of "managing the taxpayers' money," Obama and his crew are rewriting mortgages, deciding executive compensation, tossing out CEOs. And note carefully that his plans for where taxpayers' money should go continue to swell, from healthcare to the environment to energy policy to expanded "national service" programs. When taxpayers' money is everywhere—and Obama is doing his best to make sure it is—then Obama's control is everywhere.

The Octo-potus is claiming his space and flexing his grip. As far as he's concerned, it's Barack Obama's country. We're just living in it.

14

JOE BIDEN, ADVISOR IN CHIEF

JOHN H. RICHARDSON

Esquire   February 2009

In retrospect, it's hard to see how Barack Obama could have made a better choice for his running mate than Joe Biden. The veteran U.S. senator from Delaware has all the policy chops you could ask for—particularly in the foreign policy arena. A consistent voice of reason in the Iraq conflict, he was also a major force in pushing the Clinton administration to intervene in Bosnia. But his greatest contribution to Obama's campaign and, hopefully, to his presidency may be his sheer humanness. While Obama can tend toward the professorial, Biden is never anything but down to earth. Even his well-known penchant for running off at the mouth has generally worked in the duo's favor, providing a humorous foil for the sometimes overly serious Obama. Most important, the two clearly like and respect each other. In this engaging portrait, John Richardson profiles the tragedies and triumphs of Biden's life journey and talks to the new vice president about the path that lies ahead.

Five weeks after the election, just as the press has started saying that the man who will soon ascend to the vice-presidency has been muzzled, or gone missing, Joe Biden sits behind the desk in his Senate office surrounded by framed pictures of his family. The white dome of the Capitol building shines through the window behind him.

"You can drop the vice-president-elect stuff," he says.

"Well, I'm not going to call you Joe."

"No, that's all right, you can call me Joe—matter of fact, funny story ..."

And he's off. A couple of days ago, he says, he was coming down from Wilmington on the Amtrak train with a new shift of Secret Service guards in tow. He caught the 8:29, his usual morning train, and hurried up the platform to the business car. "And I get to the conductor at the front end and he goes, '*Heeeey*, Joey baby!'"

Once he got inside the car, it was more of the same. "He goes, 'Hey, Joe-Joe, come here!'"

They fell instantly into Biden's favorite part of any game, the huddle. He's been taking this train for thirty-six years now, eighty minutes each way, and the longtime commuters and train employees know exactly how to treat him. "Hey, Joe, what are you going to do about this economy? We need some help!" Or "Hey, Joe, my boy's over in Iraq. You gotta bring the troops home."

In Washington, the train discharged him into a long day of formality and meetings, the routine of his stunning new life. But when the day was over, he was back on the seven o'clock for the ride home—and the same thing happened. "Hey, Joey!"

When they got off at Wilmington, the lead Secret Service guy came up to Biden. "Can I ask you a question?" he asked.

"Sure, anything," Biden answered.

"Do people talk to you that way all the time?"

⤙ • ⤚

The true artists of democracy are never cynical. They are what they are, full of the moment, and when they grow full to overflowing they make us quiver with that old impossible dream—that now is the time, that revelation is finally at hand, that we are about to crash into the end zone and steal home and unfurl all our great potential like the wings of angels. That's how it feels on the buses and planes this last headlong week before the election. And you may say that Joe Biden's moment has passed, that he is not the one to help us unfurl our wings. But there is one thing that he knows:

He is who he is, and he likes this shirt.

It's an unusually sporty shirt. It has vertical blue stripes on the body and horizontal stripes on the buttonhole strip and red stripes inside the collar. It's the shirt of a yachtsman or a playboy, the shirt of a man with an ascot and a collection of pocket squares in his dresser drawer, which may seem like an odd choice given his reputation as a champion of the working class. But that's the whole point. The shirt is a statement, and the statement is: I like this shirt.

He's not going to wear a suit either. He's going to wear the blue sport coat with the gold buttons, the elegant brown shoes, and the dark chocolate slacks. And he'll skip the tie too. He's going to wear the sporty shirt with an open collar and flash those red stripes.

When he checks himself in the mirror, he likes what he sees. He had less hair than he's got now back when he was a kid just starting out in the Senate. And back then he'd have Nixon's five-o'clock shadow by noon, and could look a little shady. But by now Joe Biden has grown into his features. He has a high forehead and silver hair, a strong chin and a long nose, gray eyes and blindingly white and regular teeth. If he were an actor, these would be his castable years. He could be the generic distinguished older man in a magazine ad from the '60s for a fine liqueur, standing next to a red leather chair with a snifter in his hand. But there is also something natural and decent in his eyes. There's something determined in the straightforward set of his mouth. You can see, just by looking at him, that he's inclined to be gracious but also likes to come out swinging—like the time George W. Bush asked him if he'd fire Donald Rumsfeld and Biden said that he would, and then turned to Dick Cheney and said, "I'd fire you, too." Put all that together and you have the contradiction that has followed him his whole political life, qualities that made some people dismiss him as a showboat and others trust him with their lives.

But now it's time to leave. It's funny to think that this could be his last Holiday Inn, not that he minds a Holiday Inn. He does love living in a beautiful house and even got kind of crazy with the real estate deals in his younger years, always trading up to something bigger and grander, giving each one a name like it was some kind of nobleman's manor. But the fact is, he's always been one of the poorest members of a rich man's club. Having been in the United States Senate for two-thirds of his life, he somehow forgot to get rich. With an income pretty much limited to his salary and his wife's salary as a community-college professor, his net worth is—in the odd poetic of a senator's reporting requirements—"somewhere between $59,000 and $366,000." He mortgaged his house to put his kids through college. He really does love the feeling of connecting to the average Joe. He's like Bill Clinton that way, sucking up the energy in some primal way that goes much deeper than politics. And you have to remember where he was a year ago, campaigning for president in a one-car caravan with a handful of loyalists and staying in the kind of traveling-salesman hotels that serve a free breakfast. At rallies, he could be found setting up the folding chairs himself. After thirty-six years of solid accomplishment in the Senate, after leading the fight to keep Robert Bork off the Supreme Court, and after the 1994 Crime Bill that put a hundred thousand cops on the street and the paradigm-changing Violence Against Women Act and the long lonely struggle to get George Bush Sr. and Bill Clinton off their asses to do something to stop the Serbian genocide in the middle of Europe—which all by itself saved tens of thousands of people from torture, mass murder, systematic rape, and ethnic cleansing—he dropped out after winning less than 1 percent in the Iowa Caucus, stuck in Dennis Kucinich territory, an unmitigated failure.

You also have to remember where he started, those early years in a scrappy Irish Catholic neighborhood in Scranton, the times he had to put cardboard in his shoes to block the holes, the embarrassing stutter he had to overcome. Remember that his father raced cars and flew in private planes until his business failed, then put his fancy suits in the back of the closet and went out to clean boilers for a living.

He knows what it is to have your life turned into a story for public consumption. All those years of urgent motion, pulling himself into that fancy private school, that championship year as a football star, juggling girls and football those first two years at the University of Delaware, haunting the student lounge to watch Kennedy finesse the Cuban missile crisis on TV, panicking about whether he'd get into law school, courting Neilia, three kids and four houses before he was thirty, plus two years as a county councilman and that dazzling race for the Senate when nobody thought he could win—

All that, they put on a thumbnail. Some of them said the Christmas tree was in the back of the car when the truck hit. Some of them said Neilia was shopping for a Christmas tree. That was the sweet detail wherein God was said to dwell, the tinsel of irony on the death of his wife and baby girl. And the scene in the hospital where he was sworn in to the Senate as he stood beside the beds of his wounded sons, so dazed and naive he let the media in to watch. So he avoided personal woolgathering, even with people who were close to him. When it all flooded back, he would put Neilia's ring on his finger and worry it like his own personal rosary of grief. That's how his staff knew he was having a bad day.

After that he became Amtrak Joe, the guy who was always rushing to catch the train to Wilmington. Eccentric but admirable, doing it for the kids. They didn't know how much he just wanted to give it all up and buy a house in Vermont. Or the nights he slipped into bed next to his sons, trying to comfort himself by comforting them. To this day, he calls his grown sons what his father called him. *Hi, honey, how are you? Hey, honey.* But the truth is, he's always been hard to pigeonhole. No on busing, yes on civil rights. No on the first Gulf war, yes on the 2003 invasion of Iraq. No on partial-birth abortions, yes on stem cells. No on the surge but yes to support for Israel, yes on the 1994 Crime Bill ($10 billion for prisons, $13 billion for cops, sixty new death-penalty crimes), yes on a whole host of harsh drug laws— the federal asset-forfeiture law, the RAVE anti-Ecstasy act, the drug czar.

How do you summarize that?

Now, today, as the campaign nears its end, everything is different. A squad of Secret Service men flank him as he walks down the hall, another squad of sharp young aides are already waiting downstairs. When he slips out the back door and gets onto his big black bus, the convoy pulls out right on schedule. A couple of police cars take the lead, followed by another black bus for the staff and another black bus for the press and then more police cars, the whole thing moving across the flatlands of Florida like one of those articulated wooden snakes you see on Chinese New Year. The police cars race ahead and park slantways across the crossroads, drop behind and speed forward again to block the next crossroad, drop behind and speed forward again, their flashing lights festive outside the tinted windows.

As they approach the rally site, citizens wave from the side of the road. It ain't over till it's over, that's what he always says to anyone who asks, but you'd have to be dead not to feel the excitement. You can hear the music from here, sweet soul music from the 1970s pumping out its bottomless yearning and courage at nightclub volume: *I know a place (I'll take you there), ain't nobody crying (I'll take you there).* Then the bus takes a hard right and bumps into a horse pasture and there it is, another small-town rally in a long string of small-town rallies, thirty-five hundred people squeezed up against a wooden reviewing stand usually used for riding competitions, stars-and-stripes bunting hanging in half circles, a line of live oak trees forming a border beautiful enough for a postcard.

This time it's a town called Ocala in Marion County, Florida. Marion went 58.2 percent for George Bush in the last election. That's the mission Barack Obama sent him on—the blue-collar towns in the battleground states.

When he steps off the bus onto the grass, the cool air envelops him. It's a gorgeous day. The invocation and pledge and introductory speeches are already done, so it doesn't take long to catch up with the local dignitaries. Then the music stops and the loudspeakers echo with the disembodied sound campaign workers call the voice of God: "Ladies and gentlemen, the next vice-president of the United States!"

He steps up on the stage and waits for the cheers to stop. This is the part he has always loved, when the energy of the crowd comes washing up at him like a physical sensation. In the old days, when he really got going, he would look down and see tears on their cheeks. One time, he got a standing ovation from a ballroom full of lawyers. The critics said he was infatuated with his own voice, but that was never how it felt to him. He had an ego, no doubt. But when the hope came washing up at him, he had no choice— he had to feed it.

But that isn't the task today. He's not the vessel of hope in this election, and the words don't really matter this late in the game. So he starts off low-key, straightforward, one guy to another. He's a real person, that's the important thing to convey. He's not a Machiavellian insider who wants to manipulate them into unnecessary wars. He tells them right out, it's time to choose, the choice is obvious, go out and vote. You don't need to be told. You know the reasons. Just go do it.

Now he's into the body of the speech, ten more minutes to go. It's hard not to make this part sound canned, and these short outdoor rallies aren't his best venue. He needs the intimacy of a closed room. "I'm a Senate man," he told Harry Reid not long ago. "I always will be." There are moments when he disappears behind his eyes and lets Senator Biden do the talking. And when he gets to the emotional heart of the speech, the part where he slows down and his voice goes soft, where he's supposed to tug at their heartstrings with a glimpse of his personal history, he's just not feeling it.

That's when you see who Joe Biden really is—not in the things he says or doesn't say, but in a place as private as his heart and as obvious as the stripes on his shirt. That is the measure of Barack Obama's first executive decision, an arrow pointing to the future.

⤛ • ⤜

In the public narrative that seeks to account for the complexities of that time, Biden was holding his tongue because Barack Obama had muzzled him. He wasn't giving press conferences. This was because of his propensity for gaffes. As evidence, the same handful of lines were endlessly repeated: Hillary Clinton is as qualified or more qualified than I am to be vice-president. . . . I mean, you got the first mainstream African-American who is articulate and bright and clean and a nice-looking guy. . . . You cannot go to a 7-Eleven or a Dunkin' Donuts unless you have a slight Indian accent. . . . Mark my words, it will not be six months before the world tests Barack Obama like they did John Kennedy.

But the real story is not so simple and far more interesting. It starts with the first time Barack Obama got Biden on the phone to talk about the vice-presidency. "When he called to ask me whether or not I would be willing to be vetted—and he was very specific, he said, 'I'm not fooling around, it's down to three or fewer people, I'm not asking you to jump into a mix of ten people—would you be willing?' And I said, 'I have to think about it,'" Biden says now.

Obama told him he needed to know soon. When could he get an answer?

"If you need an answer right now, the answer's no," Biden said. "But let me think about it. I won't keep you out there hanging."

The next day, he called Obama back. "I will submit to being vetted," he said. "But I want to make it clear to you the last thing I'm worried about is the vetting. What I'm worried about is the decision if you ask me. But if, after the vetting, you believe I'm clean as a whistle and you then determine I'm the guy, we got to talk again. I'm not saying I will accept it if you offer it, I want to talk to you about it, because I want to make sure what is the expectation, what is the role, what is the deal."

During the next few weeks, Obama interviewed Indiana senator Evan Bayh, a respected centrist from the heartland, and Virginia governor Tim Kaine, whose résumé included a degree from Harvard Law and a tour as a Roman Catholic missionary in Honduras. Biden was a decade older than either of them, a walking contradiction to the theme of change, and his failure in the primaries did not suggest a useful level of popularity.

But Obama called Biden.

The president-elect's senior advisor, David Axelrod, says that contrary to most news accounts, the deciding factor was not Biden's foreign-policy background. "I don't think Obama felt he needed to backstop himself there. He's pretty fluent in foreign policy." Rather, it was clear the election was going to center on the economic crisis, Axelrod says, so they needed someone who could "go out and hammer that middle-class message." Another factor was Biden's mastery of the Senate process and legendary ability to work with Republicans, which would come in handy when they were trying to push legislation. Finally, there was the personal equation—Obama stood across from Biden in the debates, took the measure of the man, and felt comfortable with him. "There's an affection between these people that I think is important for the long-term success of the venture," Axelrod says.

Biden flew to Minneapolis for a secret meeting with Obama. For three hours, they talked alone in Obama's hotel room. "We were very, very candid with one another," Biden says, "and the one thing I can tell you is we both said, 'This won't work unless we both agree in building a relationship that we'll be absolutely straightforward and candid.'"

At that point, Obama laughed. "I *know* you'll be candid," he said. "Are you prepared for me to be?"

"Absolutely," Biden answered.

Another point of agreement came when Biden told Obama he had no desire to be a "quasi-executive" like Dick Cheney. The country had had quite enough of that in the last eight years, thank you. "He made it very clear to Barack from the first time they spoke that he wasn't seeking any portfolio," Axelrod says. "All he wanted to do was be a valued counselor on the big decisions."

Biden left Minneapolis and told no one of his meeting, save his family. He went home and sat down with his wife, Jill, his two sons, and his daughter. Together they mulled over the pros and cons. He loved his job as chairman of the Senate Foreign Relations Committee, loved the independence he had. Vice-president was a very different job with different requirements. He had close relationships with Walter Mondale and Al Gore, so he knew what the job was. It could give him a lot of power, but it could also be severely limiting.

One thing for sure, it was a hell of a time to enter the White House. With the financial crash and two wars, the country was experiencing its biggest crisis since the 1930s.

"This is the worst of times to come into office," he would tell me later. "The responsibilities, the burdens, the crises exceed anything—and I said it during the campaign and I believe it even more now—that any president has faced since Franklin Roosevelt. In many ways it's more complicated than Roosevelt because of the foreign-policy piece of it. But the flip side of that is, if you're ever going to do this job, this is the time to do it. If you're a surgeon, do you want to do a tonsillectomy or a heart transplant?"

But the real question was, which job would give him more influence?

A few days later, Obama called for his answer.

"What do you think, Joe?" he asked.

"Yes," Biden said.

"Are you sure?"

They joked about it. Was the job too small? Was he too big?

Biden's response was unequivocal. "No. I know the role of a vice-president."

When they hung up, Obama called Axelrod. "He said, 'I'm going to go with Joe. They're all good, they all have virtues, but he's the best mix for me right now. And he'll be a good guy to have around in the next four or eight years.'"

Once the decision was made, they got their first glimpse of how it would work in practice. "I was in the SWAT team that went to Wilmington back in the days when we could actually keep secrets," Axelrod says. "We gave him basic information about how it was going to move forward and helped him work on his speech for the day—and he was very eager to get on the same page and make sure we were fully coordinating."

The supposed gaffe issue mattered not one bit, before or after the election. "Everybody's strength is their weakness. Joe Biden's strength is he speaks his mind, and every once in a while it may not come out the right way—a speed bump. But those things were minor, and frankly did not hurt us. When you take the few times when he may have said something that would make you kind of scratch your head and weigh it against the good he did us, it isn't even a close contest."

Of course, this could all be spin—there's no doubt the Obama people are spectacular control freaks. And none of it answers the difficult questions about what to do in Iraq or how to solve the economic crisis, where reasonable people can disagree and both Biden's and Obama's positions tend to range from center to left. But the best proof is in those intense final weeks, when history was in the balance and the pressure never stopped.

⤙ • ⤚

He was supposed to be dead. They killed him twenty-one years ago, which is why it's so ironic that he's going to be the vice-president right here at the dawn of a new era of Democratic government—because way back in 1987, he was supposed to be the dawn of a new era of Democratic government. After eight years of Ronald Reagan imploded in the Iran-Contra scandal, the country was ready for a change. All the polling showed it. Gary Hart had just crashed in the flaming wreckage of his personal life, victim of his insane challenge to the media: "Follow me around. I don't care. I'm serious. If anybody wants to put a tail on me, go ahead." That was the start of the world as we know it today, the beginning of the politics of personal destruction, and Biden was about to jump right into its ravenous maw.

He announced his candidacy on June 9, five weeks after Hart flamed out. He'd already raised more money than any of the other candidates, and he sure as hell had more charisma and purpose than Michael Dukakis. Ever since his first campaign, people had been telling him he was going to be president. And he had a secret weapon in Delaware, which was part of the liberal East up near Wilmington and more like Alabama in the south. From his very first campaign, he showed a remarkable ability to span the divide— "like Houdini," in the words of his old friend and longtime staffer Ted Kaufman. The Delaware Democrats were split on Vietnam and he managed to finesse that. He was fighting for the environment and civil liberties and unions—he often says that unions created the American middle class—but also won over the folks down south as a man of faith and a champion of fiscal responsibility. And that was in 1972, twenty years before Clinton led the Democrats to the center.

Now he was forty-four, a senator for nearly fifteen years. He joined the Foreign Relations Committee when he was thirty-two, negotiated the fine points of an arms-control pact with Alexei Kosygin when he was thirty-six, formed personal relationships with foreign leaders like Helmut Schmidt and Golda Meir—even Josip Tito, the strongman of Yugoslavia. He had a reputation as a truly decent person, popular with Republicans as well as Democrats. (When Strom Thurmond was called to his final reward, Biden was the only Democrat invited to give a eulogy.)

On the downside, he had a reputation for talking too much and for promoting himself a little too shamelessly. His official bio read like a piece of cheesy advertising copy, and he seemed to have an endless hunger for approval, a need to be liked that came close to compulsion. Not to mention his long-standing desire to be president, so intense it was almost comical—in *What It Takes*, Richard Ben Cramer suggests he bought one of his homes because it resembled the White House. And when he was just a junior in college and his future mother-in-law asked what he wanted to be, Biden said:

"President."

She just looked at him, not sure how to take it.

"Of the United States," he added helpfully.

The first sign of trouble came just a few weeks after the campaign started, when Lewis Powell retired from the Supreme Court and Reagan nominated Robert Bork to replace him. The stakes couldn't have been higher. Powell was the swing vote on the court and Bork was a hard-right conservative who took extreme stands against the right to privacy and even civil rights. As the new chairman of the Judiciary Committee, Biden would be responsible for leading the fight to keep him off the bench. If he succeeded, he'd become a liberal hero and probably win the presidency. If he failed, his campaign was over.

Biden threw himself into work, poring over Bork's judicial decisions and prepping day after day with constitutional scholars from Harvard and the University of Chicago. As the fight grew more and more vicious—liberals called Bork a racist, conservatives dismissed Biden as a hack and a loudmouth—he began cutting campaign appearances to prepare for the hearings. He also began suffering from the blinding headaches that would erupt just six months later in an aneurysm so serious, surgeons had to open his skull and lift his brain to save his life. All that led to the fatal mistake that has plagued him ever since.

Biden saw the speech on videotape. It was by Neil Kinnock, head of the British Labour party. "Why am I the first Kinnock in a thousand generations to be able to go to a public university?" Kinnock asked. "Why is Glenys the first woman in her family in a thousand generations to be able to get to a university? Was it because all our predecessors were thick?"

No, it was because of public education, state colleges like the ones Biden attended.

It was the perfect response to the mingy Reaganites who kept saying government was the root of all evil. So Biden started quoting the speech, always giving Kinnock credit—until the Sunday late in August when he was scheduled to appear at the Iowa State Fair in Des Moines but spent all day Saturday prepping for Bork. He sketched out his speech on the plane and got into a van with his Iowa campaign manager, David Wilhelm, who suggested that Biden close with the Kinnock story.

"I was thinking as I was coming over here, why is it that Joe Biden is the first in his family ever to go to a university? Why is it that my wife who is sitting out there in the audience is the first in her family ever to go to college? Is it because our fathers and mothers were not bright?"

This time, Biden neglected to give Kinnock credit. The local reporters didn't think much about it because they'd heard him credit Kinnock before, and Biden came out of Iowa with spectacular numbers—without a single TV or radio ad, he shot from 1 percent to 15 percent in the polls, tied for the lead. Then, two days before the Bork hearings were to begin, Maureen Dowd broke the story in *The New York Times*. Where Kinnock spoke of ancestors who "could sing and play and write poetry," Biden cited ancestors who "read poetry and wrote poetry and taught me how to sing." Where Kinnock said they worked eight hours underground and came up to play football, Biden said his ancestors worked twelve hours in the coal mines and came up to play football. But there weren't any poets or coal miners in Biden's family. He lifted the speech complete with "phrases, gestures, and lyrical Welsh syntax intact."

The next day, NBC ran the two speeches on a split screen. Dowd was right. Biden even shook his fist at the exact moment Kinnock shook his fist. The story exploded, another Gary Hart feeding frenzy. *The Philadelphia Inquirer* called to question his line about marching for civil rights. Did he ever really march? *Legal Times* dug out his law-school records and found out that he'd been forced to take a class over because he quoted a legal journal without a citation. *The Wall Street Journal* wanted to know if he was really a teetotaler or maybe did he sneak a drink once. And didn't he use a Bobby Kennedy quote without attribution? And what about that line from Hubert Humphrey? And what about the time he ripped into that snotty guy who questioned his academic credentials? Now that was a suicidal rant:

I think I probably have a much higher IQ than you do, I suspect. I went to law school on a full academic scholarship, the only one in my class to have a full academic scholarship. In the first year in the law, I decided I didn't want to be in law school and ended up in the bottom two-thirds of my class and then decided I wanted to stay, went back to law school, and, in fact, ended up in the top half of my class. I won the international moot-court competition. I was the outstanding student in the political-science department at the end of my year. I graduated with three degrees from undergraduate school and 165 credits—only needed 123 credits. And I would be delighted to sit down and compare my IQ to yours. All on videotape! Full of lies! He finished seventy-six out of eighty-five in law school! He only got one degree! He wasn't the outstanding student in his political-science class! And he didn't stop there! *It seems to me if you can speak, you're a liability in the Democratic party, it seems to me you've all become heartless technocrats, it seems to me—*

Later, nuances emerged. He did cite that paper in law school, just not in the right place. He'd gone to a sit-in but not a march. He did win the moot-court competition. A staffer slipped in the Kennedy quote without telling him. But the headlines were coming too fast—the "death by a thousand cuts," as Kaufman remembers it. The second day of the Bork hearings, his staff had to pull him into the hall to get a response for *The New York Times*. A crowd of reporters packed the hall, firing questions.

Biden was trapped. His transgressions were trivial, especially when weighed against his accomplishments, but the stream of stories was threatening Bork and if he failed at that, his campaign was over anyway. So he called a press conference right outside the Judiciary hearing and faced down a swarm of reporters. "I'm angry with myself for having been put in the position—for having put myself in the position—of having to make this choice." With those words, Biden stepped aside, all but guaranteeing the election of George H. W. Bush, and ushering in the beginning of the Bush era.

Then he went straight back into the hearing room, hungry for redemption.

⤛ • ⤜

On the day he was elected vice-president of the United States, the whole family came along. Valerie and Jim, Gerry and Ashley, John, Hallie, Natalie, Hunter, Kathleen, Naomi, Finnegan, Maisy, Jim, Sarah, Jamie, Caroline, Nick, Jack, Missy, Casey, Jan, Nealie, Chad, Bonny, Paul, Paul Jr., Jennifer, Kim, Zachary, Jacob, Rachel, Kelly, and Tim all pile onto the plane to Chicago. And his mother, Catherine Eugenia "Jean" Finnegan Biden, ninety-one years old and still marching along on her own two feet. And his wife, Jill, looking beautiful in a sharp red jacket and high spike heels, plus a few old friends like Ted Kaufman, who keeps talking about how surreal this whole thing is—after all those years and all that struggle and loss, all of a sudden, out of nowhere, without even trying. From a kid who used to buy penny candy at Simmey's, who used to pay twelve cents for a double feature at the Roosie Theatre and play on the toxic banks of the Lackawanna River. When people ask Kaufman who the unluckiest person in the world is, he says Joe Biden. And when they ask him who the luckiest person in the world is, he says Joe Biden.

Truly, it's a happy day. Just look at Finnegan, his granddaughter. She's the one who pushed hardest to get him to accept the vice-presidential nomination. Barack Obama needs you, she said. Standing there with the expression of an impish angel, twirling an orange ribbon in her fingers. She's in the fourth grade, her favorite subject is social studies, and, um. . . . What do you want to be when you grow up?

She grins. "I want to be president!"

Biden strolls up behind her. "Did you say anything nice?"

She gives him a mischievous smile.

"I have absolute confidence in my granddaughter," he says, endorsing her for president at some point on down the road.

Then they talk about the pool at the vice-president's mansion and the possibility of a puppy—the important things, as he puts it. The whole time, he strokes her hair and cups her chin, caresses her cheek and cups her chin again, not even aware of what he's doing. He's a person who loves with his hands, who gives affection without reserve. And Finnegan loves him back the same way, leaning against him with absolute trust and pride. Then little Natalie toddles up and wraps her arms around his leg.

-<- • ->-

The next morning, sixty-nine million Americans have decided to give him a new job, and there's no time to rest. He wakes up early next to Jill in his suite at the Fairmont Hotel, cozy under the thick white duvet, and slips on a pair of jeans as a small gesture of freedom after all the months of ceremony and scrutiny. But now just getting out of the hotel is a major operation requiring an advance team of Secret Service agents to map the route and another team to flank him every step of the way. The scale of everything has increased. His personal security detail has gone from fewer than ten to as many as thirty. The city of Chicago is assigning sixty officers just to guard the transition headquarters over at the Kluczynski Federal Building. He always liked to just hop into the pickup for a run to the dump or the hardware store. Those days are over. Now wherever he goes, bomb-sniffing dogs precede him. This is going to take some getting used to.

At today's meeting, it's just the core transition group—Obama, Rahm Emanuel, John Podesta, Valerie Jarrett, and a few others. "It started with Barack saying to me, 'Joe, can you submit to me names of the people you think we should be putting in this Cabinet?'" Biden says.

For the next month, this takes up 75 percent of their time. Biden's short list included many of the names that end up being chosen, among them Robert Gates, Hillary Clinton, and General James L. Jones. He likes Gates for the many improvements he's made in Iraq, for his early call to close Guantánamo, for being a straight shooter. And continuity seems essential in the middle of two wars. He's known Jones since the early 1980s, when he was the Marine Corps liaison to the Senate. In the nineties, Jones helped Biden goose Clinton and the Joint Chiefs into the Balkans. As for Hillary Clinton, he agrees with her on almost every issue.

Obama makes it very clear that he wants these personnel deliberations kept very private. There's also a consensus that Biden should keep a low profile for a while. The way Axelrod puts it, every time you stick your head up, people want answers you don't know yet. Better just to stay low-key.

Biden takes this to heart. He even shuts out longtime staffers like Tony Blinken, who flew by his side on eight trips to Iraq and is likely to sign on as his new foreign-policy advisor. They would fish for information, but Biden would just smile and say, "I'm not talking about it." Same with his plans to banish the Cheney era by installing new procedures and guidelines for accountability—for now, the push for transparency is going to have to be conducted in secret. He's so eager to play by Obama's rules, his wife teases him about it. "He's the president, man," he says in answer.

"What even my staff didn't quite understand is, I really thought this through," he tells me later. "I've been here for eight, nine vice-presidents. I've been intimately involved with at least four of those presidents and vice-presidents. I mean, I know how this job works. There's going to be really good days and lousy days but the truth of the matter is, I crossed that Rubicon, I made that judgment. And it's not been hard."

Two days later, still in Chicago, at the transition team's first economic conference, he's sitting in the chair next to Obama with some of the most consequential economic thinkers in the world arrayed around him—Larry Summers right across the table, Paul Volcker two seats to his left, Robert Rubin to his right, Warren Buffett on the speakerphone. After Robert Reich presents the morning's dismal jobs report, Biden speaks up. It's a mistake to focus on bailing out one side or the other, he says. America's economic policy can't turn into a competition between Wall Street and the workers. He's been thinking about this for a long time and he has lots of detailed ideas— infrastructure development, for example, which would lay the foundations for business success in the twenty-first century and generate tens of thousands of construction jobs.

"Here's the point I was making," he says. "If the middle class doesn't grow, America fails, and I just wanted to remind some of the intellectual powerhouses in that meeting.

"It wasn't so much that people weren't consciously aware of the perspective I articulated, but nobody specifically articulated it. I just wanted to make sure, 'We're all on the same page, right guys? This has to be done.' So I kept coming back to that—I don't think Wall Street can survive without Main Street doing well. Look, 70 percent of this economy is consumer driven. How can you not look at Main Street?"

Everyone at that meeting was sworn to secrecy, so none of this hits the press. Instead, the Obama team keeps the focus on the banal surface: Biden and wife get a tour of the vice-president's mansion from Lynne and Dick Cheney, Biden goes to Nantucket for his thirty-third annual Thanksgiving retreat, on his sixty-sixth birthday Obama presents him with cupcakes. The press starts referring to him as the "incredible shrinking vice-president." Politico.com says that he "generates less buzz than the nonexistent first puppy." Even Biden jokes about it, "Ever since the election, nobody pays any attention to me at all."

Behind the scenes, he goes about his business. He calls the president of Georgia, the president of Colombia, the three leading candidates for prime minister of Israel. He meets with Al Gore and Walter Mondale, quizzing them on their approach to the vice-presidency. He joins Obama for their daily CIA briefing. Deep into the practical issues of reorganizing the government, a key task that includes streamlining the bureaucracy and creating new offices to fight cyber attacks and weapons proliferation, he spends three days a week in Chicago with Obama.

"I've been impressed with this guy," he says. "I was impressed with him already or I wouldn't have joined the ticket, but watching him unravel a knot is an interesting phenomenon—the guy is really disciplined. He listens and then he asks the right question. And he goes, 'I don't need that, I need this,' and you can see these guys in the first couple of meetings— people who don't know him that well—going, 'Whoa.'"

As soon as the major positions are filled and the organizational issues are moving, the core team then prioritizes the top fifteen or twenty policy issues that they'll have to tackle on January 20, starting to review and refine the options.

And that's when things really start to heat up. December is no rest for anybody. By 7:00 A.M. every day, he's on the phone with Ron Klain, his new chief of staff, with a list too long for one day. He'll meet with Secretary Gates, spend two hours with Hillary Clinton, interview a few candidates for his own office, spend some time with John Podesta reviewing the latest on where they are with Cabinet selections, meet with a potential Cabinet candidate that the president-elect wants him to interview, and report to him on that. Then he'll make some calls to the Hill to suss out the confirmability of one of the potential nominees. Then he'll be on the seven o'clock back to Wilmington, and after he gets home and has a bite to eat, he'll be back on the phone with Klain at 11:00 P.M.

In the swirl of activity and adjustment, he forgets to tell the Obama team that he's going to attend the ceremony for his son Beau's deployment to Iraq. Doesn't even occur to him that everything he does is now public and political. He doesn't realize that the new president could get questions like, you know, "By the way, what's your view about his son being deployed?" And there's that meeting that Biden's guys should have been invited to but aren't. Nothing intentional, but oh, Jesus. From now on, they have to clue each other in on every little thing.

"But there's been nothing so far, knock on wood here, but there's nothing that leads me to believe this won't be—as I said during the campaign and I meant it—I think we fit, I think our personalities complement one another."

Here, the personal and the political overlap. "The more I am with him as these decisions are made, the more I realize how philosophically in sync we are. It's not like what I've seen in other presidents and vice-presidents. We're in sync on almost every major issue. I mean, how we view everything in a personal sense, from how well and real the relationship is between Jill and Michelle and how we view family. For example, there was something coming up, I forget what the hell it was, some meeting he wanted me to be at, an important meeting, and I said, 'Well, look, Jill is having this procedure done'—she had been in an accident, she was getting this series of shots in the back of her neck to ease the—she's not big on needles. To other presidents, I'd have to say, 'Well, look guy. . . . ' It wasn't even a question. 'Of course, you gotta go with your wife.' I didn't have to call and say 'Can I?' It was just, 'I'm not coming.' And his response was, 'You *shouldn't* come.' It goes all the way from that level to choosing the Cabinet members. When I submitted my list, he didn't choose off my list. It turns out that his list was almost identical to mine."

But still, the truth is, standing there silently while another guy does all the talking doesn't come naturally to him. He looks like a man not entirely sure where he is as he accompanies the president-elect to announce the new government, as he stands meekly off Obama's right shoulder. It's like putting a boxer in the ring and telling him not to fight. He is not a man like Dick Cheney, who was determined to remain elusive and mysterious. Rather, Joe Biden likes to change the world and then brag about it. He has done so many times. And that was why he wouldn't give Obama a ready answer when they first began talking in earnest about the possibility of his joining the ticket in the middle of last summer. He already had an important job. What he didn't need was to be retired into a lesser job with a fancy title. Or some make-work assignment in the margins, like reinventing government. God, what a sentence that would be. No, Biden required and received Obama's assurances that he would be a partner in every major decision that issued forth from the White House—that would be his portfolio. He would not be shunted to the kiddie table, only to be propped up next to the Speaker once a year at the State of the Union.

He would not be John Nance Garner—a pillar of Congress just like Biden, the Speaker of the House become FDR's first vice-president, now remembered to history for describing the office as "not worth a bucket of warm piss." Or poor, emasculated Lyndon, another person uniquely unsuited to the role of attendant. After Gore, and especially Cheney, the vice-president has escaped that sorry fate, and he's likely never going back. But still, the sense of dislocation after thirty-six years of being his own man in the United States Senate was palpable. So when he finally broke his silence at the ceremony to introduce the new national-security team in early December, Biden couldn't resist a little bit of semaphore. After praising the new president for his appointments, he began to speak in the first person, in public, for the first time in weeks, and the color returned to his animated face as if he were breathing pure oxygen. "I have worked with and admired each of the members of this team. ..."

Biden gave his remarks a workmanlike brevity. Obama nodded his assent. Then the two men who will lead the country waved and walked from the stage. And so it was that Joe Biden, a man who had been given all the gifts except good timing, who had assumed that his moment would never come, took his place as the second most powerful man in the world.

"Here's the thing," Biden told me. "This is an historic moment. I started my career fighting for civil rights, and to be a part of what is both a moment in American history where the best people, the best ideas, the—how can I say it?—the single best reflection of the American people can be called upon—to be at that moment, with a guy who has such incredible talent and who is also a breakthrough figure in multiple ways—I genuinely find that exciting. It's a new America. It's the reflection of a new America."

Biden goes quiet for a moment. "And I think we got it right," he says. "We got it right, the president and vice-president. It's the right order."

15

MS. KENNEDY REGRETS (SHE'S UNABLE TO BE IN THE SENATE TODAY)

LARISSA MACFARQUHAR

The New Yorker   February 2, 2009

In the interconnected world of politics, every development affects everything else. When the newly elected Barack Obama tapped his defeated Democratic rival Hillary Clinton to be secretary of state, it left her New York Senate seat open. New York governor David Paterson eventually named upstate Congresswoman Kirsten Gillibrand to fill the vacancy—but not before Caroline Kennedy, daughter of the late President John Kennedy, ignited a media firestorm by publicly announcing she was interested in the job, only to abruptly withdraw her name from consideration a few weeks later. In this article, Larissa MacFarquhar (whose portrait of Barack Obama during the early stages of his presidential run appeared in Best American Political Writing 2007) *reports on the short, less-than-happy Senate campaign of the former First Daughter.*

Last Tuesday, Caroline Kennedy attended the Presidential Inauguration. The sun was shining on the Capitol, the sky was blue, the Marine Band was playing. Barack Obama, for whom she had campaigned ardently for nearly a year, believing him to be a leader who would inspire the country to greatness in the way that her father did, was about to become president. If ever there was a day to bolster a person's resolve to become a senator, this was it. And indeed Caroline Kennedy appeared stirred and happy and as determined as ever to become a part of the moment.

Then, on Wednesday, something happened to change her mind. That evening, she called Governor David Paterson—whose prerogative it was to appoint Hillary Clinton's successor to the Senate—to withdraw her name from consideration. What the something was, almost nobody knew. It was clearly not so serious as to be decisive, because she appeared to waver—people from the Kennedy circle at first denied that she was out of the running, and apparently people in Paterson's camp tried to persuade her to put herself back in again. But by midnight on Wednesday her decision was final: she was out.

The announcement took everybody by surprise. Even her closest friends had had no idea on Tuesday that it was coming. What could have happened? Nobody believed it was about Ted Kennedy's collapse, as the *Times* initially reported. That didn't make any sense—he'd been seriously ill for months. And his staff was said to be angry that his illness was being blamed. It was reported, on Thursday afternoon, that she had a household-employee problem and a tax problem, but even this, true or not, didn't answer all the questions: given that Paterson (according to some, contradicted by others, in a blizzard of claims and counterclaims) had apparently urged her to reconsider her decision, he evidently didn't regard the problem as disqualifying. By Friday morning, the situation had degenerated into open warfare, with some in Paterson's camp claiming that he hadn't meant to pick her anyway, and some in Kennedy's camp claiming that he had meant to pick her, that there was no nanny problem, and that the Governor was destroying an American icon out of pique. "This is a governor who lost his chief of staff a couple of months ago to the weirdest tax scandal imaginable, whose first day required him and his wife to discuss the affairs that they had during their marriage and whether or not government money was used for the hotel rooms, and he has people pushing vile comments about Caroline Kennedy?" Lawrence O'Donnell, a friend of hers and a political analyst for MSNBC, says. "And when they get into that phrase 'not ready for prime time'? This is the 'not ready for prime time' governor you're watching."

As for Caroline Kennedy's last-minute withdrawal, her friends were left to speculate. Had she suddenly panicked? Had she realized that she'd be signing on for more and more misery, of which the past few weeks had been just a foretaste? That her days would consist of drudgery—fund-raising phone calls, trudging up to frozen, decrepit towns she'd never heard of?

That there would be no more leisurely summers in the Hamptons, no more spontaneous long lunches with friends, no more undisclosed finances? Had she realized, in short, that she wanted her old life back?

A couple of weeks before Christmas, just before she declared her interest in the Senate, she went to the birthday party of a friend she'd known since high school. Several other of her oldest, most trusted friends were there. All of them thought she'd be a great senator; they were very supportive of her making a bid. But when they asked her about her decision to run she looked scared and panicky and couldn't talk about it. She folded her arms over her chest, a guest recalled, and disappeared into herself—a characteristic gesture. Even before things started to go sour, in other words, she was apprehensive about what lay ahead. Then, a week or two later, after the tabloids and the upstate papers had at her, she attended another friend's birthday party and looked as though she'd just disembarked from a very steep and terrifying roller coaster: shaken, startled, roughed up.

Her coming out had gone worse than even her detractors could have hoped. She gave a few interviews to the press and became famous for saying "you know" two hundred times in thirty minutes. An aide to Mayor Bloomberg tried to secure endorsements for her by telling people that she was going to be the next senator, so they'd better get on board early, but his aggressiveness backfired and turned people against her. Local politicians made snippy comments. Representative Gary Ackerman, of New York's Fifth District, in Queens and Long Island, compared her to J. Lo. "One of the things that we have to observe is that DNA in this business can take you just so far," Ackerman said, on *Face the Nation*. "You know, Rembrandt was a great artist. His brother Murray, on the other hand—Murray Rembrandt wouldn't paint a house."

In late December, New York voters preferred her for the Senate seat to Andrew Cuomo by thirty-three per cent to twenty-nine, but by early January, according to one poll, they preferred Cuomo by fifty-eight per cent to twenty-seven. Governor Paterson had clearly become irritated with the situation. "The notion that I have to take Caroline is not coming from me," he told the *Buffalo News*. "Why do you all pay so much attention to her? She's just another person. So what?" A Democratic Party consultant told the *News*, "He's not responding well to outside pressure. He's telling people, it would seem, that it's his decision and he doesn't like being pushed around." Even the favorable comments she received did not always redound to her benefit. "I somehow can't see her as being corrupt. It's not her legacy," Marie Owen, a sixty-nine-year-old flute player who lives on the Upper West Side, told the *Times*, when asked what she thought about the prospect of Caroline Kennedy's becoming a senator. "I kind of like the idea, maybe because I'm old."

Caroline Kennedy had many friends who had had ample experience with both the press and politicians, and many of them felt that the rollout had been handled stupidly. The public-relations firm she hired to advise her clearly didn't know what the hell they were doing, throwing her out there like that—they didn't understand her. "She's not glib, in the way that predictable politicians can be glib," Richard Plepler, a co-president at HBO and a friend, says. "She is thoughtful, articulate, fundamentally decent, and if you discussed any number of complicated issues with her currently part of the political dialogue she would be both informed and deeply thoughtful." When she met someone without a tape recorder running, she tended to make a good impression. "You always get a sense of entitlement or a sense of royalty, whether it's the Rockefellers or the Kennedys, and she never came off like that at all," Al Sharpton, who shared a photo-op lunch with her at Sylvia's, the restaurant in Harlem, soon after her announcement, says. "It was never like she felt like you were honored to meet her. She came off very studious, very sober, very serious. And I had that impression of her way before she ever thought about politics."

Why, the friends wondered, had she given those interviews without practicing first? The "you know"s should have been drilled out of her. Yes, under ordinary circumstances she was perfectly articulate, and she'd given lots of interviews before, but this wasn't chatting with Charlie Rose on a book tour. This was a shark tank. Everyone was always so careful around her—were they too afraid to tell her she needed help? She likely would not have minded some interview preparation. Having been around politics all her life, she must have been vividly aware of how a misplaced word could destroy a career. "She was really worried about doing something to screw up Obama on the campaign," a friend says. "She's very self-conscious. She's always like, 'I don't know what I think, don't ask me.'" Or maybe the mistake was talking to the press at all. Maybe it would have been better if she'd released a short, gracious statement submitting her name to the Governor and listing a belief or two, and then retreated into humble silence. Not, please not, this comedy with the upstate campaign tour that wasn't an upstate campaign tour, with her leaping in and out of her car every ten minutes like she was delivering pizza.

The basic problem, the friends felt, was that reporters had failed to see the smart and decent person behind the stammering. In fact, they believed, it was precisely because she was smart and decent that she had found herself in this mess. "Most people have never had the experience of selling themselves publicly with TV cameras on," O'Donnell, who worked for Senator Daniel Patrick Moynihan for many years, says. "Most of us have modesty impulses—you don't want to brag—and you have to learn to defy these basic human impulses and say, 'I am the greatest, and here is why you need me for this job,' and do it without any hesitation or any doubt. Which is inhuman." Her attempts at jokes somehow fell flat. When one of the *Times* reporters asked her at what point she decided to seek the Senate seat, she'd said, "Have you guys ever thought about writing for, like, a woman's magazine or something?" "That was an example of her wry sense of humor," a friend says. "She's always ready with a quip. It's disarming, it's meant to undermine the reverence that people sometimes attach to her."

As the weeks went by, people who were not her friends questioned whether she had the fluency or the toughness to fight for the Senate seat, as she'd have to in 2010. Could she handle the hot dogs and the fried dough? Was she ready for Utica? This sort of questioning drove the friends insane. It was so *irrelevant*. After all, she didn't have to campaign in the same way that an unknown person has to. People already knew who she was, she already had their attention. They even already knew more or less what she stood for: she was a Kennedy—she'd been born with a platform. "This is the part that I have found most absurd in the press coverage: a childish level of analysis of what's involved in campaigning in New York State, how many hands do you have to shake in state fairs and what kind of smile do you have to have, as though it's something extraordinarily difficult to master," Lawrence O'Donnell says. "The politics of campaigning are so simple: I'm going to beat you and leave you dead in a snowbank in New Hampshire and never look back. But in the Senate you can be trying to prevail over another senator on Tuesday afternoon whose vote you know you're going to need on Wednesday afternoon for something else. The ordinary work of the Senate never involves fighting. Virtually all the people who run for Senate seats lie and say they're going to fight, but what they're actually going to do—which they may not know when they go to Washington for the first time—is beg. And beg people like me, whom they've never heard of, the staff director of this or that committee, before they ever get to meet the chairman. So the personal qualities necessary for Senate work are politeness and charm and graciousness and generosity, which New York tabloids have no comprehension of. Why should they? The press is never allowed in the rooms where governance actually takes place."

⤙ • ⤚

Caroline Kennedy's friends are always saying how normal she is, and it appears that they are right. Normal people do not run for the Senate. Normal people with lots of money and families that they like tend to want to enjoy the money and the families. They do not spend their winters on the phone grovelling for support, or their summers at obscure state fairs ingesting disagreeable and fattening local food. Caroline Kennedy is normal. Until recently, she wasn't even sure how much she wanted to work at all.

It was, evidently, Jacqueline Kennedy's intention to raise children who were as unaffected as possible by the extraordinary circumstances of their lives, and it seems that she succeeded: Caroline Kennedy's life has in many ways been indistinguishable from that of any other smart and reasonably diligent child raised on Fifth Avenue in the nineteen-sixties. She went to Sacred Heart School in New York in the lower grades, and then to Brearley. She was close to her brother; she resented her stepfather. In tenth grade, she went to boarding school at Concord Academy, where she smoked, like everybody else, and wore clogs, like everybody else. She put on weight and was hounded by her mother about it. (At her fiftieth-birthday party, according to one guest, many of the family toasts were about her obsession with being thin.) She had moments of greatness: according to the biographer C. David Heymann, when the police discovered pot plants that her cousin David was growing in her back yard in Hyannis Port, she took the blame.

After high school, she spent a year in London taking an art course at Sotheby's. She went to nightclubs and had a love affair. She went to Radcliffe. She majored in fine arts. She did the usual college things. The summer after her freshman year, contacts of her mother's helped her obtain an internship at the *News*, and after college she went to work in the educational-film department of the Metropolitan Museum of Art. While there, she met a designer of museum installations named Edwin Schlossberg, and married him when she was twenty-eight.

After a few years at the Met, she decided to go to law school at Columbia. She interned for a summer at her mother's lawyer's firm, but then decided she didn't want to practice. "I think that, like a lot of people who go to law school, she wasn't entirely sure what she wanted to do with her law degree," Ellen Alderman, a friend from law school, says. "We were taking it more as we went along." It seems as though Caroline did not, at the time, have a sense of what she wanted to do with her life or a measure of her own ambition. "I would say it was very much like her mom's," a friend says. "Her mom wanted to get smart things done, and she wanted to have some fun, and I think that's probably what Caroline thought. She thought, I'm going to stay in New York, on the Upper East Side, I'll marry this smart guy, that's good, I'll hang out with my three good friends from school, and we won't do anything crazy. I'm stabilizing things up here—John can move downtown. Jackie was like, Relax, let's have lunch, let's go for a swim, have you read this book?"

At law school, she and Ellen Alderman decided that, since the two-hundredth anniversary of the Bill of Rights was coming up, they would write a book together about it. They traveled around the country, interviewing people who had been involved in cases in which the principles of the Bill of Rights had been tested. The result, *In Our Defense: The Bill of Rights in Action*, was more pedagogical than analytical: "A 1987 newspaper poll showed that 59 percent of Americans could not identify the Bill of Rights," the Authors' Note at the front of the book begins. "It seemed to us that an unfortunate gulf exists between those who know about the law and those who do not." The book sold very well, and a little while later Alderman and Kennedy decided to write a similar book, *The Right to Privacy*, about privacy law.

Meanwhile, she was having children. She had her first baby right after she graduated from law school, and by the time *The Right to Privacy* was published, when she was thirty-seven, she had three children—Rose, Tatiana, and John—and she decided that, rather than write another book or take a job of some kind, she would concentrate on raising them. For the next six or seven years, she served on a few boards (the John F. Kennedy Library Foundation, the American Ballet Theatre, the Citizens Committee for New York City), but basically she was a stay-at-home mother. "I think she understood, as her mother did, that the first responsibility is motherhood and being a good spouse," Paul Kirk, the chairman of the board of the John F. Kennedy Library Foundation, says.

In her early forties, she began publishing a series of anthologies. The first, *The Best-Loved Poems of Jacqueline Kennedy Onassis*, had a photograph on the cover of Caroline at age three or four, looking at a book with her mother, and on the back a painting of her mother reading to her brother and herself. The poems (Frost, Shakespeare) are interspersed with more family photos and short reflections by Kennedy on her parents. ("My mother was a true romantic. She lived her life on a dramatic scale and responded to the poetry of love with a passionate intensity.") *A Family of Poems: My Favorite Poetry for Children* also came with a cover photograph of her at three or four, this time sitting on a chair looking at a book, next to a Teddy bear sitting on a smaller chair. *A Patriot's Handbook* collected songs, poems, stories, and speeches celebrating America, with a photograph of her as an adult on the cover. *A Family Christmas*, a selection of poetry, Christmas carols, and excerpts from fiction and nonfiction, had a photograph on the back of herself and her brother and mother, with their Christmas stockings hanging from the mantelpiece. She also edited *Profiles in Courage for Our Time*, a collection of essays about the winners of the Profile in Courage Award, given by the John F. Kennedy Library Foundation to elected officials who have taken brave stands. The anthologies all sold extremely well— *The Best-Loved Poems of Jacqueline Kennedy Onassis* sold close to half a million copies, and *A Family of Poems* stayed on the *Times* best-seller list for months.

It appears from Kennedy's commentaries that the anthologies, like her legal books, have a didactic purpose, and are intended for people without prior knowledge of the subject. "Sometimes, poems like these can seem old-fashioned," she writes in the love-poetry section of her Jacqueline Kennedy Onassis book. "The language is complex, the flowery style at odds with modern life and the changing roles of men and women. But if you do make the effort, you will find that the emotions these poets express are not foreign or faraway but ones that all of us have felt for those we love." The same book includes, in an appendix, a selection of poetry by her mother. "Although I know my mother would have felt slightly embarrassed to have her own poems included with the ones in this book that she so admired, they have meant a lot to our family, and I wanted to share them," she writes. "She allowed them to be published during her life, and they reveal a bit about her in her own words. Though writing poetry can seem difficult, I hope these poems will also encourage readers to write poetry of their own."

≺⊹ • ⊹≻

During the weeks before Caroline Kennedy withdrew her bid, her friends said that her quest for the Senate seat followed naturally from her work in the New York City public schools. As her kids had neared college age, they said, she had started to think about what she was going to do with the rest of her life, and decided on public service. She cared about education, so she went to work for the schools; she cared about America, so she decided to run for the Senate. But her life and her decision, like most lives and decisions, were more haphazard than that.

In the summer of 2001, she ran into her old college friend Nicole Seligman at a party on Martha's Vineyard and went for a walk on the beach with Seligman's husband, Joel Klein, the chancellor of the New York City schools. They started talking about her life, and she started talking about public service and government. Not long afterward, Klein offered her a job. As the executive director of the Office for Strategic Partnerships, she was charged with raising money for the schools from private companies, and with changing public education's reputation in the city. Caroline Kennedy did some fund-raising herself, but mostly she visited a lot of schools and planned strategy. Many of the teachers at the schools were thrilled to have such a celebrated person come to visit. And, as always, people came to her because they wanted to help her and be associated with her. A public-relations man she knew persuaded AOL, one of his clients, to sponsor a Dave Matthews Band concert in Central Park and donate a million dollars to the schools. Inspired by the concert, Rosie O'Donnell gave another million. Some months later, Kennedy worked alongside the chairperson of

Time, Inc., to organize a giant tag sale in Central Park, selling items that stores would donate.

She quit the job after two years, and although she continued to serve as the vice-chair of the board of the Fund for Public Schools, and spoke to her successor several times a week, for the most part she returned to being a stay-at-home mother. Then Obama appeared on the scene. She didn't pay much attention at first, but her children thought he was terrific, so she started to tune in to his speeches on television. She watched some of the debates. "She had a real yearning to serve in a more meaningful way than she had up to now," Gary Ginsberg, an executive vice-president at the News Corporation and a friend, says. "She started really watching the campaign in the fall of 2007, and I could sense then that she had started to think of it in more practical terms for herself."

It seemed that she knew she was not a natural politician—certainly not a rousing, ecstatic speechmaker. In January 2008, she endorsed Obama in a speech at American University, and although she had given many endorsement speeches before, she was quite awkward, charmingly so. Dressed with almost overstated understatement in a gray dress and a gray cardigan, she compared Obama to her father—"Fortunately, there is one candidate who offers that same sense of hope and inspiration"—with her mouth in a twisted half smile, as though anticipating the applause with a mixture of joy and embarrassment. When she stated that she was endorsing him, she did so as though she were saying, "Yes, I do realize you already knew what I was going to say." As she finished her endorsement, the crowd started chanting "Yes we can! Yes we can!" and she joined in, but in a low voice, and wagging her head from side to side as though she were making fun of it, except that she clearly wasn't—she was making fun of herself for being so self-conscious.

She started to stump for Obama around the country. "She campaigned in places like Orlando and Indiana and Ohio, getting her hands dirty, doing real retail politics, and I think she was surprised by how much she really enjoyed it," Gary Ginsberg says. "I think she just found the whole political process to be much more satisfying and engaging than she would have thought." Still, while she was campaigning for Obama, she was in control of her time. She wasn't required to show up anywhere or do anything in particular: any amount of time she gave to him was a gift for which the campaign was grateful. At one point last year, she was visiting the Obama campaign office in West Palm Beach and was interviewed for a local television station by a small boy about ten years old. They sat on a table, side by side, cases of bottled water stacked behind them against the wall. She was wearing a gray Obama "Hope" T-shirt and a string of pearls; he wore a jacket and tie. Each time he asked a question, he twisted around and aimed his very large microphone right at her mouth, as though carefully feeding a zoo animal. He asked her why she was supporting Barack Obama for president, what were her favorite subjects in school, whether she thought Joe Biden was long-winded (the boy had previously interviewed Biden, he explained, and had been told that that's what he was), and what "long-winded" meant. She had a faint smile on her face as she answered his questions, but she did not otherwise react to his cuteness with any cuteness of her own. Sometimes while he asked his questions, she gazed around the room, as though she were thinking about something else.

She enjoyed campaigning for Obama, but running for office on her own behalf was different. Drawing attention to herself, asking people to look at her, begging for favors—these were things she'd never had to do. Before the Senate opportunity came along, she'd never been inclined to political arguments, never been one to pontificate about an issue. "I thought she understood her place in the culture," one friend says. "If you asked her opinion on something, she would back off. She was comfortingly self-effacing." And what if she lost? What if she didn't get the job? That would be humiliating. Kennedys don't like losers, Caroline Kennedy especially. "In the case of the Profiles in Courage awards, she's made it clear in recent years that she doesn't always want us to recognize people who are political losers," John Shattuck, the C.E.O. of the John F. Kennedy Library Foundation, says. "She wants the award to be given to people who succeed. That was reflected last year in two women she championed who are still in office. And that was quite an interesting philosophical discussion, because I think almost all the cases that her father described"—in the book that inspired the award, *Profiles in Courage*—"were cases of people who paid a huge political price for their actions. She felt that there was more than room for courage in politics among those who are successful."

Then, there were the legacy issues. She would never know whether people were voting for her or just for a Kennedy. But friends thought that, over the years, she'd grown more comfortable with being a Kennedy, with all that it implied—comfortable enough to run for her Uncle Robert's old Senate seat. "For Caroline, maybe this is a thing that, ironically, she feels that she can own because it's so against her nature," a friend says. "For you to be able to take this kind of step and withstand it—even if you don't get the appointment, but that you jumped off that cliff—that's a real psychological accomplishment." Moreover, by endorsing Obama, at a time when it was not at all clear that he would win the primary, and from Hillary Clinton's home state, Caroline Kennedy had won the allegiance of a younger constituency on her own behalf. "This generation salutes her and Ted for what they did for Obama," Al Sharpton said in early January. "I'll give you an example. When she got out of the car in front of Sylvia's, people in the streets were screaming 'Caroline!' 'Caroline!' 'Senator!' I was amazed. Young people. And when we walked in, the people in the restaurant stood up and started clapping. And let me tell you why I thought that was interesting: they didn't react that way to *Obama* when I brought him there. When I brought Obama there, people were shaking his hand, but they weren't standing up and applauding. I was like, Wow, what is this? I talked to them, and people said, 'No, man, she risked a lot for us.' And, see, when you did something for people that nobody does something for, and you didn't have to do it, it hits an emotional thing with us."

And yet, of course, the best argument for appointing Caroline Kennedy to the seat had been that she *was* Caroline Kennedy. That was her chief value to New York. "There are very few people who walk into the Senate and know they'll be heard immediately," Richard Plepler said. "What have two-thirds of the Senate done before they got there? Served in the state legislature? You think that is a better qualification than her intellect, her breadth of experience, her ability to get things done for the state? I don't think so." "Let's say I'm David Paterson and I choose Maloney," Al Sharpton says, referring to Carolyn Maloney, the downstate congresswoman. "Well, why didn't you choose somebody that can get President Obama on the phone? He's gonna have hard questions either way. So it's almost like, what medicine do you wanna take?"

"She's the only person that New York can send to the Senate who is immediately valuable to other senators," Lawrence O'Donnell said. "Because there are really only three people in the Democratic Party who you can say is coming to your fund-raiser and sell tickets from that, and they are Barack and Michelle Obama and Caroline Kennedy. Hillary Clinton had that, too, and that enabled her to have a value to other senators right off the bat that she could then translate into what she could get for New York. . . . Harry Reid, in an unprecedented moment, has said that this is the senator he wants, and that is hugely important for practical purposes—he would have this star player who could be deployed to help get other senators elected. Andrew Cuomo is the only other person whom other people in the Senate have heard of, but, with all due respect, there isn't a senator in the country who would ask Andrew Cuomo to come to their fund-raiser in his first year in the Senate."

⤛ • ⤜

When Caroline Kennedy first announced her intention to seek the Senate seat, some of her friends were surprised that she would volunteer for such a role, given how shy and reserved she seemed, and how obsessed with maintaining her privacy. ("Jackie and Caroline had similar personalities," Andy Warhol told C. David Heymann. "They tended to bury their emotions. They were like icebergs. They revealed only a small portion of themselves—everything else was deeply submerged.") Unlike her brother, who didn't usually seem to mind when photographers took his picture or reporters approached him, Caroline Kennedy has always appeared to dislike the press. (She declined to be interviewed for this article.) Her friends understand that to speak about her in public would mean banishment. When she announced her bid for the Senate, she gave a few of her friends permission to speak with reporters, but several of those friends, after making the most anodyne or laudatory comments, panicked and withdrew them, or demanded anonymity. (This was no more than prudence: according to one biography, when a few of her brother's friends spoke fondly of him to reporters, in the wake of his death, they were told they were no longer welcome at his memorial service.)

She is often sarcastic when she talks to the press, and she can be short to the point of rudeness. She is easily annoyed by what she perceives to be prying or stupid questions. When Wolf Blitzer, of CNN, asked her why Hillary Clinton was not formally vetted by Obama's vice-presidential search committee, of which she was a member, Kennedy interrupted him.

"Boy, you know an awful lot about this, don't you?" she said. "'Cause I'm not telling you anything else, O.K.?"

"But just walk us through that decision," Blitzer asked.

"No, I'm not going to walk you through that decision!" she said indignantly.

"Why not?"

"It's a confidential process!"

Near the end of an interview after Kennedy's speech at the 2008 Democratic Convention, Katie Couric started talking about the Kennedy dynasty and what it has meant to America, laying it on a bit thick. Then she began, "Do you ever feel any pressure, I know you're very shy—" and Kennedy interrupted her (rather loudly, and not shyly at all): "Are you going to ask me if I'm going to run for office, by any chance? Is that where you're going with this question?"

"What do you think?" Couric asked.

Kennedy shook her head in irritated disbelief. "Well, you know, it's incredible, you're just so *creative*."

"Well, no, but I think people do," Couric said, trying again, a little taken aback. "Maybe if you have any renewed interest in going into political office, I mean, you already are in public service, but because of Teddy's illness and because of the era sort of coming to a close, I'm just wondering if you feel any kind of responsibility at all or if you feel completely comfortable with the path you've taken."

"Well, I don't make a lot of long-range plans."

But whereas her mother liked to keep her family out of the public eye altogether, insofar as that was possible, with Caroline Kennedy the issue seems to be not so much privacy as control. She is happy to reprint family photographs in her books and sell off intimate family artifacts, as long as she is in charge of the process. She organized two auctions of Kennedy memorabilia, in which she sold family letters, old toys, and bric-a-brac from the family homes. The two auctions brought in about forty million dollars. ("Only the Kennedys could hold a garage sale at Sotheby's," Alan Jellinek, a London art dealer, commented, about the second auction. "It was just a collection of old junk. . . . She sold everything but her mother's bloomers.")

A few years ago, she permitted the licensing of her mother's jewelry collection to a company that sold cheap replicas of the pieces, the Jacqueline Kennedy Collection, on QVC.

Caroline Kennedy, it seems, is less private in the sense of secretive than private in the peculiar legal sense that the word has taken on, and that she has written about. For the Supreme Court, "privacy" implies control over one's body and its use (the right to marry a person of any race, to use contraception, to abort a first-term fetus); for Caroline Kennedy, control over her body and its use encompasses photographs taken, descriptions written, and habiliments abandoned. "Whether it be the disclosure of intimate details about a person's life or interference with private decisions," she wrote, with Alderman, in *The Right to Privacy*, "there is a growing sense that all of us, well known and unknown, are losing control."

So Caroline Kennedy isn't private in the ordinary sense of the word. "I think there's a little bit of a misperception about that," Alderman says. "I agree that she was never in the public eye just to be there, she wasn't a 'Here I am' being in the public eye, but we went on two book tours together, and we were on television, and she was even, way back then, giving speeches to huge crowds and doing campaign work. I wouldn't describe her as shy. I think she's tasteful and dignified and didn't have a sense of self-promotion for the sake of it. But when there was something she was interested in she was out there." "Addressing a few Democratic Conventions, with twenty thousand people in the hall and twenty million on television—and yet having done that a few times in her life, people still talk about her as this shy, avoid-the-limelight person," Lawrence O'Donnell says.

Caroline Kennedy has a magic about her that is very useful in politics, and politicians in her family and her party have always used it. For most people old enough to remember her as a child in the White House, and to have been affected by her father's assassination, she provokes a mixture of benign emotions—nostalgia, respect, excitement, loyalty, pity, love. "One of the senior administrators in one of our schools broke down in tears to meet Caroline Kennedy," Joel Klein says. "She just couldn't get over it." Everywhere Caroline Kennedy goes, people come up to her and tell her how much some member of her family meant to them. They tell her what they were doing and how they felt when her father was killed. They tell her how elegant her mother was, or that they saw her mother walking in Central

Park. They tell her they once sat next to her brother at a Knicks game. It never stops. She has been pursued by several stalkers. And it's not just strangers—it's friends as well. "No one is ever going to be the one to get off the phone with Caroline," a friend says. "No one's going to say 'I gotta go.' People just don't let her go. The circle around her—they think that if they maintain the friendship with her that they're magic, too."

If Caroline Kennedy wants someone to help her with a project, if she wants advice, or an expert to explain something to her, virtually anyone will make himself available to her right away. A couple of weeks ago, she asked Sister Paulette LoMonaco, who works at Good Shepherd Services, and whom she knew from her time working in education, to organize expert briefings for her on child welfare and youth services. "I called these people on Sunday night of the long weekend or Monday morning, and everybody cleared their calendars for Tuesday," Sister Paulette says. "We're talking about folks who are booked almost every evening. And the e-mails of appreciation were just amazing. Let me read you one: 'Thank you so much for including me in the meeting, it was an incredible honor to be there, she made us all feel so comfortable, she is very much at ease with herself and this was so evident. I was also really impressed with her intelligence and with her ability to absorb so much information so fast.'" When she announced her candidacy for the Senate, a few New York politicians made headlines by resisting her, but many others supported her, even before they'd met. "A few weekends ago, the *New York Observer* called me and asked me about her, and I said I'd never met her but we all feel like we know her because we've watched her grow up, and so the response to her was really quite startling to me," Congresswoman Louise Slaughter, of New York's Twenty-eighth District, around Rochester, Buffalo, and Niagara Falls, who endorsed Kennedy, says. "I said a couple of nice things about her, and she was gracious enough to call me."

While she was in the White House—when she was three, four years old—the public was obsessed with her to the point of madness. Strangers sent her letters. Someone came out with a Caroline Kennedy doll. Press interest in her was insatiable—and while her mother hated the idea of her being in the newspapers, her father tended to encourage it, because it helped him. He would feed cute anecdotes about her to his press secretary. She rode her pony, Macaroni, into the Oval Office; she popped out from behind her father's desk to offer a perky greeting to Harry Truman ("You lived here before us, didn't you?").

Even long after she left the White House, she was badgered by the press. Ron Galella would wait outside her school to shoot pictures of her. "We grew up with her in *Life* magazine, and it was like she was our friend," a friend says. "She was heavy, she was unkempt, she had frizzy hair—for someone my age, everything I was going through she was going through. We read about her birthday parties, we read about her in high school, we read about her wedding." In recent years, she has lived a much more private life, but in one sense in the past decade she has been more than ever the focus of Kennedy reverence: when her brother was alive, when her mother was alive, they created some shade for her, and when they died some of that shade was removed.

It's hardly surprising that, having seen the world stutter and bumble in her presence all her life, she often finds it ridiculous. How could she not? Her mother was known for her witty derision—she referred to Lyndon Johnson and his wife as "Colonel Cornpone and his little pork chop"—and Caroline Kennedy is also funny. She is wry; she can be scornful. She still has a bit of boarding-school blasé about her—the heavy-lidded eyes, the ironic smile, the husky voice. "Caroline tended to see the foibles in people, whereas John looked for more positive traits," George Plimpton once said. "Caroline could cut people down with a few trenchant words; John built them up. She had a dark sense of humor, a rapier wit; his was effervescent. She trusted nobody, he trusted everyone."

Over the years, she has achieved a certain amount of distance from the phenomenon of Caroline Kennedy—she doesn't take herself so seriously that she is above using Kennedy worship to her advantage. At her fiftieth-birthday party, George Bell, the husband of her boarding-school roommate, Carrie Minot, read aloud as a toast the flattering e-mails she had sent to a Harvard professor (and then gleefully forwarded to Bell) asking him to re-arrange his schedule so she could accompany him on a trip. (He did.)

There's a brief scene in which she appears in *Taking on the Kennedys*, a documentary about Kevin Vigilante's race against Patrick Kennedy, son of Teddy Kennedy, when Patrick first ran for Congress, in 1994. She has just flown in on a private plane to stump for him. The press gathers at the airport to meet her, and a television reporter from a local station, WLNE, jostles to the front of the pack and holds his microphone out. He beams at her, and she, in a fuchsia suit and immobile 1994 hair, smiles brilliantly back at him. "How does it feel still being in the public eye, I mean, the name Kennedy, *Caroline Kennedy,*" he babbles, with a giddy little shrug of his shoulders, as though he can't quite believe he is standing there talking to her. "How does it make you feel?" She looks at him, still smiling. "How does it make me feel being Caroline Kennedy?" she asks, and laughs at him, her mockery spiced with a tiny hint of flirtation. He tries to rescue his question by re-phrasing, but appears to realize that he has had his moment and flubbed it.

Now Caroline Kennedy has had her moment and flubbed it. Paterson has appointed Kirsten Gillibrand, a second-term congresswoman from Hudson, near Albany. "Paterson has no comprehension of upstate New York, absolutely none, and has chosen someone better at representing cows than people," Lawrence O'Donnell says. "What you have is the daughter of a lobbyist, instead of the daughter of a former president or the son of a for-mer governor. This is the hack world producing the hack result that the hacks are happy with."

To Caroline Kennedy's friends, her putting herself forward for the Sen-ate, whatever the result, was a step of great courage and significance. "This is a person who has the blessing of using her remarkable position to ad-vance larger issues," Richard Plepler says, "and, because she has never taken advantage of that, that is something that speaks to the integrity and, not to be too corny, but, the nobility of what she's doing now." "To put yourself through that seems like a lot for her, but I take my hat off to her, because changing your life up and trying things at—you know, she's not twenty-five—takes a certain amount of guts," a friend says. "She's not stupid, she knew that the life she knew would come to an end whether she got the ap-pointment or not, and that's a tough thing for anyone, giving away the life you've had."

But in the end, it seems, she could not give away the life she had. De-spite all the work that her friends and supporters put into her bid, despite all the behind-the-scenes campaigning, despite all the fuss and the cover-age and the lunches and the phone calls and the public-relations consultants, she decided that she would prefer not to. Her friends could support her and spin for her and be excited for her, but they couldn't make her *want* it. There would be three more days of bad press, and then everyone would forget about it and leave her alone. She would go back to being Caroline Kennedy, and that would be fine.

16

THE MAN WHO ATE THE GOP

MICHAEL WOLFF
Vanity Fair   May 2009

In last year's election the Democrats, riding Barack Obama's coattails, picked up 21 seats in the House of Representatives, leaving them with a 257–178 advantage over their Republican counterparts. They also added either 7 or 8 seats in the Senate, depending on the final outcome of the Norm Coleman-Al Franken contest in Minnesota, which is still being adjudicated by that state's Supreme Court (as this was written, Franken was clinging to a slight lead).

The leftward shift produced the usual overblown talk about the GOP being washed up as a political party. Before anyone writes their eulogy, however, it's worth noting that the House Democrats actually emerged slightly stronger from the 1992 election when Bill Clinton was voted into the White House (258–176), and did better still in 1976 behind Jimmy Carter (292–143). If you really want to talk about a Republican collapse, consider 1932, the year Franklin Roosevelt was first elected president. The Democrats gained 97 House seats in that election, roaring from a 2-seat deficit to a 313–117 majority. The Dems' high-water mark came four years later in the 1936 election, which left them with a staggering 334–88 advantage. Now that was a Republican Party in peril! Oh, and by the way: In the very next election the GOP picked up 81 seats.

Which is to say, the Republicans will be back—in all likelihood, sooner rather than later. Still, they're in need of some serious repositioning. And with George W. Bush back in Texas, Dick Cheney working the airwaves defending the Bush administration's interrogation policies, and no new A-list political stars on the horizon, the Grand Old Party has something of a leadership vacuum. In this essay, Vanity Fair's *media columnist Michael Wolff reports on how conservative radio host Rush Limbaugh is filling this void—and adding to his already bulging coffers in the process.*

Rush Limbaugh, it seemed to me, had to be in huge trouble. Beyond his history of drug problems—in liberal circles there remains a constant is-he-isn't-he speculation about the status of his prescription-painkiller addiction—beyond even the fact that the mighty conservative tide which he'd ridden to such success had certainly peaked, there were the terrible problems in his core business. Radio advertising rates were falling—even before the recession—Internet competition was rising, and Rush's much-vaunted audience of 14 million was down from its high of 20 to 25 million during the Clinton years to closer to cable-TV size. The view at MSNBC was that, on a minute-by-minute basis, Limbaugh's audience was now no bigger than that of its liberal stars, Keith Olbermann and Rachel Maddow.

So, when, in the beginning of February, Limbaugh said he hoped that the new president would fail in his efforts to deal with economic calamity, this seemed much more like a desperate bid to stay in the game than it did a stroke of master showmanship. By any logical assessment of behavior, it *still* seems as if the man may be imploding. And yet, within a month of his issuing his provocative or nihilistic view about an Obama-led recovery, the argument had become not whether he was hopelessly marginalized but whether he was the most significant figure in the Republican Party.

In a jaunty and rapid-fire manner, he'd dealt with Republican congressman Phil Gingrey, who had mildly suggested—to a reporter's question about Limbaugh's derogatory comments about the Republican leadership—that there were able gentlemen running the party. After a torrential news cycle, Gingrey offered Rush an abject apology, which had the added sweetener (a little carrot and stick) of getting him an appearance—to reiterate his apology—on Rush's show. Then Limbaugh laid into Republicans who had expressed reservations about Louisiana governor Bobby Jindal's response—lame by every estimation—to the president's speech on February 24 before a joint session of Congress. No matter how lame, Jindal still hewed to the orthodox conservative small-government views; hence, according to Rush, Jindal was "brilliant. He's the real deal." And if anybody said otherwise, well, they'd have to deal with Rush. Then, the day after Limbaugh addressed the annual meeting of the Conservative Political Action Conference (CPAC), Republican National Committee chairman Michael Steele gamely tried on CNN to face down D. L. Hughley's assertion that Rush was the effective party leader. "Rush Limbaugh is an entertainer. Rush Limbaugh, his whole thing is entertainment," Steele sputtered, only to find himself apologizing shortly thereafter when Rush had mauled him on the air. (The Democratic Congressional Campaign Committee put up a Web site—I'm Sorry, Rush—offering an automated form through which congressional Republicans could apologize to Limbaugh. Indeed, as I was writing this piece, a half-dozen Republican officials and operatives first committed to talk with me about Limbaugh and his effects on the party, and then, in a process of hand-wringing and revising their views, each decided, on better thought, not to risk even the smallest chance of waking up on the wrong side of Rush.)

The CPAC speech was the Limbaugh topper. The meeting, an annual and usually uncommented-upon gathering of right-wing enthusiasts (Ana Marie Cox, the Washington gossip and political reporter, roaming the halls in her new job as a radio reporter for Air America, described it to me as "Woodstock for wing nuts"), was treated nearly as a third-party political convention because Rush was the main event. The entire three days of the conference, with Mike Huckabee, Ann Coulter, and Newt Gingrich, was a buildup to Rush. Fox News, carrying the speech live, promoted it for several days before.

The 58-year-old, post-pill-popping, post-cochlear-implant (to correct his deafness), post-fat-and-sloppy Rush appeared on the stage to a pounding welcome, looking like nothing more than . . . Johnny Cash. In black suit and black shirt, two buttons open, hair slicked back, he pronounced this—considering Fox's live coverage—to be his "first ever address to the nation."

He'd become, second only to the fortunes of the new president, the biggest political story going, one loved equally by right and left. By the right because he so infuriated the left, and by the left because he so discomfited Republican moderates. He was the perfect political lightning rod, polarizing but entertaining too.

⊰ • ⊱

The most elemental fact about the Limbaugh career might be that, outside of seriously corrupt dictatorships, nobody has made as much money from politics as Rush Limbaugh. Since this Top 40 D.J. and local talker in Sacramento went national, in 1988, as a right-wing voice, he has made hundreds of millions of dollars in salary, bonuses, participation in advertising revenue, and the sale of his show to the Sam Zell–controlled Jacor radio production company (Zell, a real-estate entrepreneur, now controls the *Chicago Tribune*), which was then sold to Clear Channel. His new contract, signed last summer, is worth a reported $400 million over eight years. There are, too, his newsletter, his paid Internet site with its voluminous traffic, his blockbuster best-sellers, his speaking fees, his half-dozen cars, including a Maybach 57S, his Gulfstream G550, and his Palm Beach estate with five houses.

Rush's business plan seriously impacts on the future of the Republican Party.

Indeed, the extraordinary thing Rush has done, something arguably never before accomplished in the history of the co-dependent relationship of media and politics, is manage to keep his media day job while assuming something rather close to direct political power. Every other entertainer who has discovered a political mission—from Ronald Reagan to Sonny Bono to Al Franken—has had to quit show business and run for office. Not Rush.

Rather, one hand ably washes the other.

For instance, the single most important issue in Rush's radio career is now among the hot-button issues in conservative politics: the Fairness Doctrine, a formalized fair-and-balanced rule for covering controversial issues on the nation's airwaves, which the Reagan FCC killed in 1987. The most liberal wing of the Democratic Party, which puts substantial blame on talk radio for a generation of conservative dominance in Washington, wants to revive the doctrine, which would pretty handily destroy conservative talk. According to the official CPAC polling of its members, restoring the Fairness Doctrine is the third-most-significant Democratic Congress policy initiative opposed by the right wing, ranking behind only expanding government and public health care.

There is, with Rush's orchestration, a rabidness to the cause. Opposing the Fairness Doctrine is up there with opposing abortion.

In the hours after Phil Gingrey found himself in the stew for criticizing Rush, much of the intense and angry reaction—Gingrey's office came under instant siege—was focused on the misperception that Gingrey was in favor of the Fairness Doctrine. "Rush has turned opposing Fairness into a core principle," says a Gingrey spokesperson. "That's why we had to apologize."

-<+- • -+>-

Lee Vanden-Handel retired just a few months ago, at 82, from the Clear Channel–owned Premiere Radio Networks. Vanden-Handel, along with Ed McLaughlin, the former head of the ABC radio network who discovered Rush in Sacramento in 1987, helped build the EIB radio network around him, taking advantage of a singular change in the radio business: music had moved to the better, FM band, leaving AM radio without much of an audience. The oompah-pah of Limbaugh's no-breath-taking voice, which McLaughlin flew out to Sacramento to hear for himself, had something like the lulling effect of music.

Curiously, in a wide-ranging discussion about his more than 20 years of working with Limbaugh, Vanden-Handel never once brought up politics. Vanden-Handel's inside view of Limbaugh involves almost entirely a nuts-and-bolts discussion about the peculiar craft and salesmanship involved in the radio business. "Rush," he says, echoing RNC chairman Steele, "is an entertainer. A consummate professional. He knows his audience. He stays with it, and it has stayed with him. That's not politics. That's . . . well . . . good business."

-<+- • -+>-

Similarly, Jon Sinton, founding president of Air America, the network specifically constituted to be the liberal antidote to Limbaugh and the other conservative talkers, doesn't much, in his analysis of the Rush effect, consider ideology, beyond that Rush connected with the country's dedicated population of Reagan-lovers, one of the most faithful demographics in politics and media.

Limbaugh's absolute dominance of this niche produced, according to Sinton, a paradigm-shifting development in radio. "Radio had always been a barter game. You give us your show and we'll give you back some ad spots for you to sell. Rush became so important to AM radio that he could demand both a cash payment and ad time," says Sinton with some professional awe.

The Rush voice and timbre had another effect which changed both radio and politics: format hegemony. "In the way that you could not play Led Zeppelin on a country station," says Sinton, "you could not mix liberal talk with conservative talk, and since the conservatives, as the first talk movers, had come to dominate radio, there was virtually no room in major markets for anything other than a conservative format."

Which would be key to setting the agenda for the next 20 years.

⤙ • ⤚

It's that hegemony that the left has helplessly objected to for so many years (and hence is hoping to deal with by pressing the Democratic Congress to pass new fairness rules) that is now causing problems for the Republicans. "I think, in hindsight, we abdicated a certain responsibility in terms of communication," says a source close to a senior House Republican. "Aspects of the Republican constituency were more efficiently dealt with through the power of talk radio. We let the talkers represent us."

The power of conservative radio is a phenomenon as much of direct marketing as of politics. Radio advertising is about the call to action: Show up at this sale and say that you heard about it here and get an extra 5 percent off. Go to this restaurant for brunch and get a free Bloody Mary (and then enter a contest and win a trip to Las Vegas). Put your money into this bank and, if you do it today, get a toaster. Rush, along with his advertisers' calls to action, adapts this form to his pet political causes. Indeed, this became a curious demonstration of Rush's commercial appeal. "If he could get people to write letters to their congressman, which they did by the bushel," says Vanden-Handel, "then reasonably he might also get people to buy pre-owned cars."

Indeed, for 20 years, three hours a day, nothing in radio has so moved the audience to action as Rush: The Republican base both buys the pre-owned cars he suggests ought to be bought and champions the causes he's hot on. Nothing in politics, or the news cycle, is as direct and powerful as this. In seconds, he can move an awesome tide, unleashing e-mail, telephone calls, and scary Web-site rage. Minutes after RNC chairman Steele tried to suggest to CNN that he, rather than Rush, was the bona fide leader of the party, Rush, reached for comment, merely said he'd respond on the air—which must have sent a chill down Steele's spine.

When moderate Republicans talk about the Rush effect, there's a plaintiveness with which I sympathize. Shortly after the war in Iraq began, when I was reporting from CentCom headquarters in Qatar, I asked an intemperate question of one of the military briefers in the daily televised news conference and, dissed by Rush for my lack of patriotism, got the full effect: more than 20,000 e-mails in 48 hours, shutting down my mail server.

And he isn't just a man alone in a booth. Around himself he's constituted his own political-action committee, or leadership group, of other talkers.

"It's Rush who's talking to Sean Hannity and Mark Levin. And they're talking to others," explains a Republican pundit, discussing with me media relationships among conservatives. "It's incredibly networked. The message, the position is spread." Limbaugh, too, is in regular contact with Roger Ailes, the head of Fox News, which ran the live broadcast of the Limbaugh CPAC address.

Arguably no message apparatus like it exists in the nation, except, perhaps, at the White House (or in Oprah—whose position with American women is curiously analogous to Rush's position with American conservatives). It is concentrated and extraordinary power.

-<- . ->-

Except that this power ought to be ending. It ought to all be on the wane. It is not just the Obama victory and the magnitude of his approval ratings. It is not just that the gravity of the economic crisis, with historic unemployment rates, means it's a lot harder to get people excited about Reagan-and-Rush-esque hands-off government.

It is, rather, a crueler demographic point. The dirty little secret of conservative talk radio is that the average age of listeners is 67 and rising, according to Sinton—the Fox News audience, likewise, is in its mid-60s: "What sort of continuing power do you have as your audience strokes out?"

You can begin to make plausibly large statements about the end of—or at least a crisis in—conservative media. "There are fewer advertisers, fewer listeners, shrinking networks, shallower penetration," says Sinton. "A lowering tide lowers all ships."

What's more, it's the Internet that is the fast-growing and arguably more powerful political medium—and it is the province of the young and liberal. The only sensible market view of conservative talk is that it will contract and be reduced, in the coming years, to a much more rarefied format.

And yet, by the end of Rush Limbaugh's fractious month of calculated outrage, his audience was back up to 20 million.

⤛ • ⤜

That's showmanship. "Or," said a moderate Republican of my acquaintance, "nuttiness. The man has no behavioral regulators."

Certainly he can pick a fight like nobody's business. It is a contrarian talent and temperament. The ordinary sacred cows which Don Imus, for instance, might get run off the air for messing with are, in Rush's hands, statements of challenge. He can go after Michael J. Fox, ridiculing his Parkinson's symptoms, or he can publicly hope for the President to fail, or announce Teddy Kennedy's imminent demise, because these assaults are cast not just as slurs but as threats. "If you disagree with him, you have to confront him, and then it's you against Rush. In that match, you simply can't win," says Sinton.

There is, too, his specific political position. In the battle between what David Brooks characterizes as the reformers in the party and the orthodox Ronald Reagan loyalists, the Rush position is clear. A kinder, gentler Republican consensus would be much worse for the Rush brand and business model than even an F.D.R.-type era of Democratic dominance.

Rush is so much more lively, scary, jaw-dropping, and fabulous when he's on the attack. Add to this that he might actually be crazy—the big fear of the moderates—that it isn't showmanship but a train wreck that we're all watching, one in which he takes everyone with him. "How far will he go? You don't know what might come out of his mouth. What if he truly goes to war against the leadership? He could, you know, if he wanted to just split the party. Walk out with the hard-core conservatives. He could and he knows it," said my moderate-Republican interlocutor.

At least he can until the demographic reality catches up with him. "It's a last hurrah," says Sinton, "because it isn't and has never been first and foremost about politics. It's always been about radio. And that endgame is written."

17

SPECTER'S EPILOGUE

TERENCE SAMUEL

The American Prospect Online   May 1, 2009

In late April 2009, Arlen Specter, a Republican senator for the past twenty-nine years, announced he was switching parties and becoming a Democrat. On the face of it, this was great news for the Dems because it would potentially give them sixty seats in the Senate (assuming Al Franken is eventually ruled the victor over Norm Coleman by the Minnesota Supreme Court)—enough to override any Republican attempt to filibuster unwanted legislation. But as his erstwhile GOP colleagues know all too well, Specter is famously prickly about voting the party line. In making his switch, he readily admitted that he'd done so because he didn't think he could win the upcoming Republican primary in his home state of Pennsylvania. As if to underscore his ambivalence about his new affiliation, a day after announcing his defection, Specter promptly voted against President Obama's budget.

If Specter's change of party is a mixed blessing for the Democrats, however, it was a body blow to the Republicans. As Terence Samuel notes in this online piece for The American Prospect, *it's one more sign that the GOP's Big Tent is getting smaller by the day.*

The dramatic party-switch by Pennsylvania bulldog Senator Arlen Specter can be read as a final denouement in the slow, steady collapse of the Republican Party. Though the decline was triggered by the disastrous presidency of George W. Bush, it was the decision by congressional Republicans to so fully and uncritically embrace the Bush agenda and the president's arrogance that cost the GOP so dearly.

In retrospect, it is interesting to note how early the signs of the implosion began to appear: The seeds of the GOP's current demise were sown in the triumphal moments following Bush's victory in 2000. Had they heeded the warning signs, Republicans could have saved themselves a lot of trouble—and maybe even a few congressional seats. Specter's reasons for leaving are the same as Republican-turned-Independent Sen. Jim Jeffords' were eight years ago. Perhaps more importantly, they were the same reasons that drove so many Americans into the arms of the Democrats over the last four years of the Bush administration.

On May 23, 2001, while Bush still basked in the glow of his new presidency, then-Senate Majority Leader Trent Lott held a reception honoring Gerald Ford. The bitterness of the election had begun to dissipate, but not in the Senate, where the divisions were playing out in a 50–50 chamber split. Lott was the majority leader by virtue of the fact that Vice President Dick Cheney, as president of the Senate, had the tie-breaking vote.

At Lott's reception, the drinks were served in crystal. The embossed coasters that sat under each glass read: "Majority Leader"; I remember thinking, "Yes, but for how long?"

There were already rumors that Jeffords, upset by the size of the Bush tax cuts and by huge cuts in environmental and education spending, would leave the GOP. He would become an independent and caucus with the Democrats, giving them the majority. The very next day, he did exactly that.

"I became a Republican not because I was born into the party, but because of the kind of fundamental principles that these and many Republicans stood for: moderation; tolerance; fiscal responsibility. Their party—our party—was the party of Lincoln," Jeffords said by way of explanation.

And Jeffords made clear that he was leaving because of Bush: "In the past, without the presidency, the various wings of the Republican Party in Congress have had some freedom to argue and influence and ultimately to shape the party's agenda. The election of President Bush changed that dramatically."

There was no room to argue with or influence the White House; the pressure to toe the line was already too much for Jeffords. He predicted that the political situation was only going to get worse. "I can see more and more instances where I'll disagree with the president on very fundamental issues—the issues of choice, the direction of the judiciary, tax and spending decisions, missile defense, energy and the environment, and a host of other issues, large and small."

In so many ways, Jeffords was talking for those swing voters who had been the decisive bloc in the recent national elections. But for the ideological purists who controlled the Republican Party, it was a time of opportunity. For six years they were in charge but frustrated. Though Republicans had controlled Congress since 1994, many of their best efforts were quashed by Bill Clinton's veto pen.

It may have been that frustration more than anything else that led them to be so unquestioningly loyal to a president who had not even won the popular vote.

With the Bush win, they seized their moment, and quickly fell in line. Lott told me back then that he would wake up pinching himself with joy that Bush was in the White House. After the Supreme Court made Bush the winner, Tom DeLay, the house majority leader at the time, similarly stated, "The things we have been dreaming about, we can now do."

Suddenly all of that pent up ideological frustration meant there was no place for a moderate like Jeffords. Dissent became inconvenient at the very least—and traitorous at worst.

But Bush's stridency on issues like Iraq, tax cuts, climate change, stem cell research, and Social Security—along with congressional Republicans' willingness to support him—quickly became a political turnoff for a lot of Americans. They saw a world in tatters and a government taking an ideological stand in response. The Terri Schiavo fiasco, Hurricane Katrina, and the worsening economy did not help their cause; there was a sense that ideologues were driving the bus and they were going to take it over the cliff.

Despite their declining popularity, Democrats could not quite get their act together. Republicans kept control of the House in 2002 and, in 2004, retook the Senate and held onto the White House. Smugness metastasized into full-blown arrogance. "I earned capital in the campaign, political capital," Bush said the morning after his reelection in 2004, "and now I intend to spend it."

Bush's first goal after his reelection was to try to partially privatize Social Security, which infuriated people who were already seeing the sign of a worsening economy and who were now much more skeptical of the administration because the war in Iraq was not going well. Then came Katrina, which turned the widespread unease with the president's swagger into disdain for his incompetence. Republicans had lost both houses of Congress in the 2006 elections, and the president could only lament his misspent capital the morning after: "Look, this is a close election. If you look at it race by race, it was close. The cumulative effect, however, was not too close. It was a thumping."

Two of those elections carried special significance for Arlen Specter. The first election called that night was in Pennsylvania, where the incumbent Republican, Rick Santorum, lost his Senate seat by 18 points. Clearly, there was no ambivalence about that rejection. More telling was the Republican loss in Rhode Island. Lincoln Chaffee was Arlen Specter without the law-yerly pomposities: He was a moderate who opposed Bush and his party on many important issues. His approval rating in his state was in the mid-sixties, but he lost 53 percent to 47 percent to Democrat Sheldon White-house, because voters decided that they wanted to punish Bush and the Republicans.

Specter could not miss the meaning: Republicans are dying and moder-ate Republicans are headed for extinction. There was no other option but to switch.

OVER THERE

PAKISTANI NUCLEAR TOTEM POLE

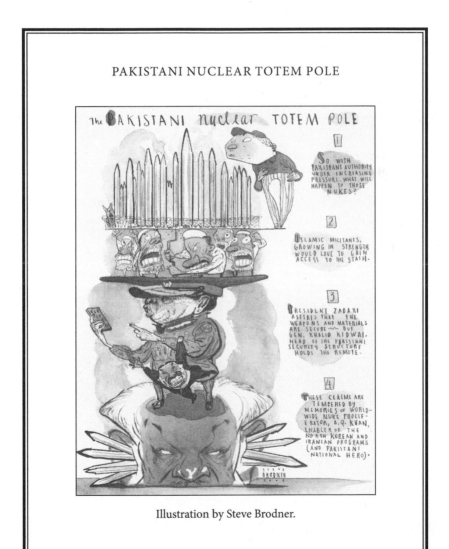

Illustration by Steve Brodner.

18

OBAMA'S FOREIGN POLICY AT 100

ILAN GOLDENBERG

The American Prospect Online   April 28, 2009

Whereas the new Obama administration has moved swiftly on the domestic front, its international effort, spearheaded by Hillary Clinton's State Department, is still a work in progress. The president's decision to retain George Bush's defense secretary, Robert Gates, was a signal that he intends to move cautiously in Iraq and Afghanistan—the two countries where the United States has significant numbers of combat troops. As for Afghanistan's troubled nuclear neighbor, Pakistan, the world can only hope that it manages to contain and ultimately overcome the resurgent Taliban. America's options are also limited in North Korea and Iran, two nations seemingly determined to develop nuclear weapons. (Most recently, following North Korea's series of missile tests, Secretary Gates warned that any attempt by that country to export its nuclear technology could result in a military response.) At the same time, Obama and his team clearly place more value on diplomacy than their predecessors did—a stance that has largely been welcomed by the international community. In this American Prospect *column, written at the 100-day point of Obama's presidency, Ilan Goldenberg—who was named a special adviser to the Pentagon on the Middle East just weeks after this article was published— sketches the contours of the new administration's emerging foreign policy.*

For the first 100 days of Barack Obama's presidency, coverage of his foreign policy has focused primarily on his dramatic diplomatic gestures and the overwhelmingly positive response he has received from foreign publics and leaders. It feels good to see an American leader being treated as a hero instead of a pariah. On a more substantive level, restoring our prestige has real benefits—cooperation is easier when having a close relationship with the President of the United States is a political boon and not a liability (just ask Gordon Brown and Tony Blair). But diplomacy is only a means to an end. What is much more significant are some of the early changes the president has made in how he prioritizes U.S. interests and the strategies used to achieve them. Below, the *Prospect* considers four of the major changes to U.S. foreign policy made by President Obama in his first 100 days.

Putting terrorism in its proper place. The president has restructured our priorities so that terrorism is treated as one of a number of significant challenges but no longer dominates all other policy objectives. This does not mean abandoning counterterrorism as a priority. Obama made that clear when he explained the goal of his new Afghanistan-Pakistan strategy: "To disrupt, dismantle and defeat al Qaeda in Pakistan and Afghanistan, and to prevent their return to either country in the future." But it is a rebuke of the Bush-era concept of a "war on terror," which viewed all extremist groups and state sponsors of terrorism as a cohesive threat—a policy that resulted in our invasion of Iraq, a country that had nothing to do with 9/11 or al Qaeda.

It has also meant a reframing of our relationship with the Muslim world. As the president explained during a speech to the Turkish Parliament, "America's relationship with the Muslim community, the Muslim world, cannot, and will not, just be based upon opposition to terrorism."

This approach has carried over to the president's decision to close Guantánamo Bay and put an end to torture. These practices are morally reprehensible, of questionable efficacy, and act as a recruiting tool for terrorists. As Obama explained, "America's moral example must be the bedrock and the beacon of our global leadership."

Prioritizing the elimination of nuclear weapons. During the Bush era, there was bipartisan agreement that the use of nuclear weapons by terrorists was at the top of the list of national security concerns. During the 2004 presidential debates, Senator John Kerry and President George W. Bush agreed on this point. The problem with the Bush approach was that it focused exclusively on the perpetrators of such an attack while ignoring the weapons themselves.

Obama has overturned this policy and embraced the global arms control regime that played such a crucial role in limiting the spread of nuclear weapons during the Cold War. During a seminal speech in Prague on April 5, he committed to the goal of a nuclear-free world.

After years of deteriorating relations with Russia, Obama and Russian President Dmitry Medvedev agreed to restart negotiations and come to an agreement by the end of this year on a new Strategic Arms Reduction Treaty (START), which would dramatically reduce U.S. and Russian nuclear stockpiles. Considering that the two nations possess a combined 95 percent of the world's nuclear weapons, this was a critical step both in reducing nuclear weapons and also making clear that the world's foremost nuclear powers are committed to a nuclear-free world.

The president has also signaled his commitment to the Comprehensive Test Ban Treaty (CTBT) by making Vice President Joe Biden the point man on achieving Senate ratification. This crucial agreement to ban testing failed ratification in 1999, thus undermining America's position to credibly lead international non-proliferation initiatives.

Rebalancing the national security budget. For years the allocation of spending in the national security budget has been characterized by badly misplaced priorities. It overemphasized military spending while ignoring the other tools of diplomacy and development. It included billions in funds for ineffective and unnecessary Cold War weapons systems, while falling short on basic needs like armor and troop strength for the wars we are fighting today. The result has been a national security infrastructure unprepared to deal with the problems of the 21st century.

The Obama administration's budget adds 10 percent to the combined State Department and foreign assistance budget. Moreover, by hiring the highly respected Jack Lew as deputy secretary of State for Management—a position that went unfilled in the Bush administration—the administration has sent a clear signal that the State Department will be a real player when it comes to fighting for resources.

The Defense budget also represents a dramatic strategic shift away from big expensive toys to the programs and personnel that are needed for current and future conflicts. This has involved cutting: the F22 Raptor, which was designed to fight the next generation of Soviet fighters; the DDG1000 surface destroyer—a program so expensive and unwieldy even the Navy decided it did not want it; and the Future Combat Systems, which included the Army's plans for replacement vehicles but did not take into account the experiences and needs from Iraq and Afghanistan. In place, Gates committed to expanding the size of the ground forces and investing in weapons systems designed for irregular operations such as the wars in Iraq and Afghanistan.

Connecting the dots on regional strategies. The Bush administration too often subscribed to simplistic theories that looked for regional silver bullets. The most egregious example was the claim that the invasion of Iraq would spread democracy and lead to a permanent Middle East peace. Obama has taken a different approach, choosing to simultaneously address multiple regional problems and recognizing that important linkages exist.

In the Middle East, the president moved on a number of fronts at once. He set a firm deadline for withdrawal from Iraq—a decision that sent a clear signal to the region that the U.S. was not there to create a permanent military presence. He has pursued aggressive public outreach towards Iran in an attempt to overcome years of bad blood and pave the way towards diplomatic negotiations. But he has also worked to gain greater support from Russia—the country most capable of exerting real pressure on Iran—on the nuclear question. He has engaged Syria sending two senior officials to Damascus after years of diplomatic isolation. And, from day one he has put negotiating an Arab-Israeli peace at the top of his agenda.

In Latin America, the president has recognized that our anachronistic Cuba policy serves as a barrier between the United States and the entire region. He has begun the critical process of improving relations by removing barriers preventing Cuban Americans from traveling to the island or sending remittances and by also striking a new tone, which received a positive response from Raul Castro. He followed this up by attending the Summit of the Americas where he received a warm welcome, in stark contrast to Bush's isolation four years ago.

The administration has also prioritized the fight with the drug cartels in Mexico and released new initiatives meant to stop the flow of money and weapons south and strengthen Mexico's internal security and capability to deal with the cartels. Perhaps the greatest signal of how seriously Obama is taking this problem is the fact that the president as well as three cabinet members (Hillary Clinton, Eric Holder, and Janet Napolitano) have all visited within the first 100 days.

Overall, it is too early to ascribe to the president a fully formed foreign policy philosophy. But 100 days into his administration, it is clear that these changes have already gone a long way towards redefining American foreign policy and they will likely continue to be central elements of the president's policies for years to come.

19

OBAMA'S WAR

MICHAEL HASTINGS

GQ magazine   May 2009

While Iraq finally appears to be achieving some level of stability—providing a measure of vindication for the outgoing Bush administration—the U.S. combat effort in Afghanistan seems to be losing ground: To date, more than 600 American GIs and an equivalent number of allied troops have died since Operation Enduring Freedom was launched there in 2001, and the monthly casualty rates in Afghanistan now routinely surpass those in Iraq. During the past year, the Taliban have become increasingly aggressive on both sides of the Afghanistan-Pakistan border, while Hamid Karzai's unpopular and reputedly corrupt government holds little sway outside of Kabul.

Barack Obama underscored Afghanistan's importance with his announcement in February that he would deploy another 17,000 troops to that country—bringing the total U.S. military presence to 55,000—and with his recent appointment of Lt. General Stanley McChrystal, a special-ops expert who played a major role in the success of the "surge" in Iraq, to replace General David McKiernan as head of U.S. and NATO troops there. Still, maintaining order in a mountainous nation the size of Texas is a daunting task. And as this report from the front lines by GQ *magazine's Michael Hastings makes clear, the soldiers on the ground are anything but optimistic.*

On a Sunday afternoon the past fall, 22-year-old Private First Class Brian Thomas pulled guard duty, which sucks, as he'll have you know. Two- or three- or four-hour shifts, staring at the same mountains and the same piles of rock. Maybe you sneak a cigarette, maybe take your helmet off, maybe lean forward and close your eyes for a few minutes, trying to remain conscious enough to wonder if that white Toyota Corolla snaking its way along the road in the distance is just another beat-up Corolla or if it's on the BOLO (be on the lookout) list, and if that dirty-bearded goat-herding motherfreaker sitting like a gargoyle up there on the ridge is working with the driver and scoping you out and getting ready to run a car bomb up your ass. Probably not today, but who knows? You have to try and stay alert, have to pick up the binoculars every fifteen minutes or so, because one day they just might.

It's Private Thomas's turn on ECP, or entry-control point, which is military-speak for the entrance to the outpost, known as District Center Terezayi. Located in Khost Province in eastern Afghanistan, Terezayi is eight miles from the Pakistan border, which is an absolute nowhere land—beautiful, in its way, but nowhere, with muddy wadis and rubble-strewn valleys and distant mountain peaks and strange mud huts that bring to mind terms like *prebiblical* and *Stone Age*. It's also the new front in America's continuing "war on terror," and the soldiers who are currently stationed here—and at outposts like this all along the border—are the beta-testers for how that war will be fought.

Not that Thomas is concerned with any of that right now. At the moment, in addition to thinking about the goat herder and the Corolla, he's watching three of his fellow American soldiers hunt a pack of dogs in the valley in front of him. "The great dog massacre of 2008," he says. A few months earlier, the twenty-five soldiers stationed here (they are responsible for patrolling 350 square miles, including a stretch of fifty miles along the border where Taliban and other militants pass freely) received orders from their battalion headquarters to kill the dogs around the base. They could be rabid, they posed a threat to the locals and the troops, and also they kept attacking cows and were just constantly barking their asses off. The catch was, the unit had adopted some of the wild dogs as pets, and they had to go, too. "We loved those fucking dogs," Thomas says. After the purge, a new brood eventually appeared, and a new puppy was adopted, nicknamed Convoy Dog, and he was out there running around right now.

From where he stands, in addition to the valley that doubles as a firing range when it's not the site of a dog hunt, Thomas has a view of a hill to the right, on which the Afghan police force has an observation post, and a hill to the left, beyond which a road leads toward him and the ECP. He can see the first checkpoint, about one hundred yards up the road, manned by Afghan Security Guards, a supplement force that has been trained by private contractors and hired by the U.S. military to help out here with security because the Afghan police are so bad at it.

As in Iraq, one of the guiding principles is that we can recruit and train security forces to take part in stabilizing their own country, which will eventually allow the number of U.S. troops to be drawn down. But the training has gone poorly. There are all sorts of practical problems, the main one being that Afghan police get killed at a ridiculously high rate. (Over the course of two years, they've lost an average of fifty-six men a month.) The other, more insidious issue is one of trust. In September an Afghan police officer turned on the Americans he was with and killed a U.S. soldier; in another incident in a nearby village, the Afghan police were suspected of burning down their own district center and pretending it was a Taliban attack. Plus, they're corrupt, and they get paid almost nothing, and they have other issues—like, for instance, younger police officers at the district center are kept at separate observation posts from older police officers, because of the younger officers' fear that they'll be raped.

Thomas gets on his radio and reports back to the sergeant of the guard at headquarters that the men are out there shooting dogs.

"Say again?"

"Roger, they're shooting dogs. Over."

"Roger. Copy."

Thomas is on his second deployment. "When I get back, I'm getting my ass out of the army," he says. He's from Big Springs, Texas, and he plans on using the new GI Bill to go to the University of Texas to study music, after he saves a little money working on an oil rig. He watches through his binoculars as two soldiers take aim with their M-4's. Six shots ring out.

"They just killed Convoy Dog," Thomas says. He shakes his head. "I automatically do not like that guy. That dog is domesticated, you know what I mean? That really irritates the crap out of me." Another shot. "I'm depressed."

Thomas was in the ECP when the base was attacked by rockets a month ago. Because of the echoing effect of the mountains, the loud explosions "scrambled my brains," he says. They never got the attackers, even though the next morning they found a local Afghan civilian loitering out near where the rockets were fired. They swabbed the guy for explosives, and he came up positive, but they still weren't allowed to detain him. The Americans operate under strict rules when it comes to engaging Afghans, and getting found near the scene of an attack and then testing positive for explosives isn't considered enough evidence for detention. "It was frustrating," Thomas says. "'Hey, go ahead and hit us again! We're not going to do anything!' They know they aren't going to get in trouble. They probe us all the time. A guy standing on the pile of rocks right there scanned my entire AO [area of operation]. I saw him standing up there, probing us like a champ. I picked up my binos, and he saw us and left. You know they're getting ready to hit us again. It's just a matter of time."

⤛ ● ⤜

Throughout the presidential campaign, Barack Obama talked about how we "took our eyes off the ball" in Afghanistan and promised that after he was elected, he would focus on moving tens of thousands of troops into the country to fight the terrorists where they live. By some measures, that makes sense, since at least some of the guys responsible for the September 11 attacks are still operating near here. But if protecting ourselves from terrorists is the primary goal of American foreign policy, then is placing that many soldiers on the ground in Afghanistan the best and most efficient way to do so? "If our strategic aim is to beat the shit out of al Qaeda, we don't need an existential American combat presence to do that," a senior U.S. military official who spoke with me on condition of anonymity said. "If it's in our strategic interest to maintain stability in Afghanistan and along the Pakistan border, I think that having an existential ground-combat presence actually makes that interest suspect."

It's hard to make that case, though, because despite the rhetoric about changing course, so much of what we're doing now feels inevitable, a natural progression of the decisions that have determined our foreign policy for the past eight years. In the immediate aftermath of the World Trade Center attacks, we acted on the belief that fighting terrorism meant invading Afghanistan—and subsequently Iraq. Overnight, invasion became occupation. And once we were involved in those occupations, we quickly learned that the people we were fighting were generally not the kind who would be plotting against America but were instead militaristic groups involved in their own power struggles (in Iraq, Shiite militias and Sunni insurgents; in Afghanistan, the Taliban and local warlords and mujahideen). Rather than reexamining the original assumptions, though, the U.S. military got swept up in developing a counterinsurgency strategy (which eventually we conducted with moderate success in Iraq). And thus counter*terrorism* and counter*insurgency* became hopelessly confused. As one military-intelligence official put it to me: "It's not about bin Laden anymore. It's about fixing the mess."

This winter I spoke with Michael Scheuer, a twenty-two-year veteran of the CIA who ran the agency's bin Laden–hunting unit in the late '90s and is the author of *Marching Toward Hell: America and Islam After Iraq.* "In Afghanistan, I don't think we have a clue of what we're after," Scheuer said. When I asked him what he would do if he were in charge of American policy, he explained that he'd inflict as much damage as possible on al Qaeda now—through targeted air strikes and assassinations and Special Forces operations—and "get out in six months." To actually "win" the war in any traditional sense—to crush al Qaeda and the Taliban—Scheuer says we'd need "a force of 300,000 to 400,000, one that would go into Pakistan." Since we're not going to do that, he says, "why bother? We stayed way too long at the fair. We can't redeem it."

But redeeming it by now fighting the "good war," as it's being called, is exactly what we're trying to do. One of the officers in charge of redeeming things, at least in the 350 square miles around DC Terezayi, is Captain Terry Hilt, a 32-year-old father of two from North Carolina. He's the kind of sturdy and thoughtful, permanently even-keeled commander who embodies the best military traditions. This is the third year of the past five that Hilt has been overseas, but he seems free of bitterness and is still positive when he talks about his job. He has a regular habit of keeping his thumb pressed against his wedding ring, which he's done since the invasion of Iraq in 2003, when he pulled off his gloves and his gold band flew off into the sand. By a stroke of luck, one of his soldiers found it in the dirt, and since then Hilt's been paranoid about losing it again.

As Hilt explains it, the primary job of the men at DC Terezayi is to frequently go out on "show of force" missions to let the enemy know that the

Americans are around. The other goal is to "separate the enemy from the civilian population." In Iraq, that eventually meant paying the bad guys not to shoot at us and setting up smaller outposts that were more integrated with the population. But here, with fewer troops and an even more complex tribal system (it's very hard to know whom we need to pay off), the agenda is more piecemeal—modest patrolling while keeping an eye on the various reconstruction projects that are part of winning over Afghan hearts and minds. Though "reconstruction" is misleading. Really, it's straight-up construction: building roads (which cost up to $500,000 per kilometer) or schools that never existed to begin with.

It's an accepted fact among Hilt and his men that the area they are responsible for is so large it's nearly impossible for them to have any lasting impact. So they do what they can, going out each day as long as the wrecker is around to pull the MRAPs (the million-dollar armored vehicles that can withstand a roadside bomb) out of the mud if they get stuck, teaching the Afghan police how not to be fuckups, trying to resolve the occasional complex tribal dispute, and running into the enemy and engaging in battle with increasing frequency.

⤙ • ⤚

Six days after the dog massacre, the sun is out again and the soldiers at DC Terezayi are preparing their trucks for a two-day stay at the border, eight miles away, where the plan is to check in on the Afghan Border Police. They're fueling up and loading supplies onto their trucks when suddenly there's a huge blast at the ECP and a funnel of smoke shoots to the sky. The private on guard screams over the radio, "Oh God, we've been hit by a suicide bomber," and everyone starts to move, throwing their body armor and helmets on and sprinting toward the ECP. There's gunfire from an AK-47, though it's impossible to see who it's directed at. The Afghan Security Guards come stumbling through the gate, carrying one of the guards, a teenager, who looks like he's dying. They have an older Afghan man, too, a police officer, whose blood is running down his face. Specialist Daniel Allen, the unit's medic, tells them to put the two men down, and he starts working on them, taking off their clothes, trying to find where all the blood is coming from. The kid has about forty or fifty small holes in him, made by the ball bearings that exploded out of the suicide vest. Doc Allen takes off the kid's pants to make sure he hasn't been hit in the groin, and the kid's lying there naked and bleeding on a slab of concrete outside the motor pool, a white bandage pressed over his penis. One of his friends is kneeling by him and holding his hand.

Outside the gate, Sergeant Joseph Biggs is making sure no one else is hit. Biggs is a 24-year-old from Florida. He has over a dozen tattoos, including one on his right biceps that says WAR and one on his left that says KILL, as well as another on his right forearm that spells out the Arabic word for "infidel." He points to a live grenade on the ground, near one of the severed legs of the bomber. "He was about to throw that," he says.

For forty-five minutes, they keep the kid alive, waiting for a Black Hawk helicopter to come in and take the two men away. After they leave, several of the men meet in the Tactical Operations Center, where Hilt is trying to piece together what happened. The suicide bomber came up through the valley between the two hills, he says. A group of five or six boys ran up and surrounded him as he approached the gate. The children are 8 or 9 years old and are regulars at the base. They come over most days after school, and the Americans give them chores to do, like filling sandbags or gathering up golf balls that have been hit into the valley. Most of the guys here like having them around.

The security cameras near the ECP captured the attack, and now four soldiers are gathered around, watching the footage as the bomber gets close to the gate (the kids, at this point, have run away, taking a seat on the Hesco barriers that have been set up as backstops out on the firing range). He stops outside the barbed-wire fence, and the young guard stands up and calls to him to stand where he is and wait to be searched. The guard moves across the screen from right to left, toward the bomber, and then suddenly stops and backs up, cocking his AK-47 and lifting it up to fire, and that's when the suicide vest explodes. Smoke fills the screen and the guard disappears, then reappears, staggering backward and screaming before falling to the ground.

"We're going to need to clean that whole yard," Hilt says. "Once everyone is inside, I'll talk to everyone real quick. We're going to try to HIIDE him [identify using a retinal or fingerprint scan], if we can find the head. Hey, Sergeant Biggs."

"Hoo-ah," Biggs says.

"You said the head was out there?"

"No, just the scalp, just the hair."

"The flesh out there," another soldier adds, "it's everywhere."

"I guess we don't bring them kids back no more," Biggs says. "I always said with the kids around, there's going to be some shit like that. The kids are the ones who brought him over here, the little terrorist bastards."

The rest of the soldiers gather in the living room (or, as it's known among the men, the MWR—short for "moral-welfare and recreation area"), where at night they watch DVDs and play the video game Rock Band.

"Everyone knows what just happened," Hilt says to the group. "A suicide bomber at the front gate blew himself up. A couple things are going to happen. The kids that typically hang around were walking with the guy prior to detonating. They won't be coming back here. The mission [to the border] is going to be off. Hey, what typically happens after one bomber?"

"Another one," the soldiers answer in chorus.

"There are body parts all over the place, all through the district center," Hilt says. "Doc, we got plenty of rubber gloves? We're going to get some and do a police crawl across the DC. If you find fingers, any of that stuff, don't touch it. Call for one of the HIIDE guys. We might be able to get it to hit on the HIIDE system."

Hilt pauses and then adds, "Pictures. Do not be taking pictures of friggin' body parts. You'll get in a lot of trouble if you try to take pictures of body parts home. We got really lucky. Stay vigilant. Here's the good news: The sandbags worked, the gate worked. Because of that, we're not putting anybody in the ground."

The soldiers pull on rubber gloves and go outside and begin walking slowly over the gravel, looking for pieces of the bomber. One soldier scrapes up a chunk of flesh with a shovel. "Mmm, pancakes," he says. "Why the fuck couldn't they have used a car bomb? I don't mind cleaning up after car bombs. Everything's burned up."

They dump the body parts in a clear plastic garbage bag. The bomber's legs are still there near the gate, intact from the knee down. His legs are hairy. He was wearing white high-tops with yellow stripes. The scalp is on the ground next to a Hesco barrier, a blood-wet mop of black hair.

Staff Sergeant Daniel Smith spots a blackened finger hanging off the concertina wire, and Staff Sergeant Aaron Smelley, who's in charge of identification, takes it and places it on the portable HIIDE machine and presses hard to get a scan. After a few tries, he gets a reading, but the fingerprint doesn't match any known terrorist in the database.

The Afghan police bury the leftover body parts a few hundred meters away from the base in a small cemetery. They place a pile of rocks on top to mark the grave, then lay the bomber's yellow-striped high-tops next to the rocks. Later that afternoon, two Afghan men from one of the nearby villages come to look at the grave site. As they start to walk away, one of them turns back and picks up the high-tops and takes them for himself.

That night the dogs are back, barking and fighting over the bits of flesh that flew so far from the base they were missed during the cleanup.

≺≺ • ≻≻

Two days later, the mission to the border is back on and the MRAPs crawl out to an outpost called Border Security Point 7, BSP 7, an eight-mile trip that takes around two hours because there's no paved road. It's to the hills and caves along the border that al Qaeda and the Taliban retreated during the 2001 invasion and where, to this day, Taliban leader Mullah Omar is said to be hiding, as well as Jalaluddin Haqqani, a former mujahideen fighter for the U.S. against the Soviets, who now runs a network of Afghan fighters closely allied with al Qaeda.

Controlling the border with the supposed help of the Pakistani military is a major part of the newly intensified American strategy. Eighteen new border facilities have recently been completed, with 147 more under construction or in planning stages, costing upward of $845 million. Along with bringing an additional 17,000 American troops into the country, the goal is for private military contractors Xe (formerly Blackwater) and DynCorp to train thousands of Afghan Border Police to help the Americans patrol the area.

When I met with Major General Robert Cone, he was the U.S. commander in charge of training all the Afghan security services, including police, army, and border patrol. "What I've learned about Afghanistan," Cone told me, "is that if something is broken, somebody wants it that way. There

are a lot of people who would benefit from not having border police"—
drug traffickers, Taliban insurgents, al Qaeda terrorists.

On the Pakistan side, for nearly three decades, there have been factions
within the army and the ISI (Pakistan's intelligence service) who are ideologically anti-Western and sympathetic to Islamic fanaticism (primarily because it represents a base of fighters to counter the historic threat from
India) and who have done as little as possible to rein in extremists in the
Federally Administered Tribal Areas. Pakistan is nominally an American
ally—we've given the military $8.7 billion in aid since 2002—but the coun-
try is beset with its own rivalries and factions, and there often seem to be
as many enemies as friends. U.S. military and intelligence officials say there
are camps of Taliban fighters out in the open, a few kilometers into Pakistan,
and that the Pakistani military does very little to restrict them. Militants
frequently attack the NATO supply convoys that run from Karachi up
through the Khyber Pass; in a series of incidents last December, NATO lost
400 vehicles and containers.

From the top of BSP 7, the Pakistani military checkpoint is clearly vis-
ible. The sun is setting behind us, we're about 4,000 feet up, and between
the mountains, about two miles away, is a dark brown building that marks
the official presence of Pakistan. I'm standing with Hilt and his Afghan-
border-patrol counterpart, Captain Sadeq, who won't tell me his last name
because his family doesn't know that his real job is commanding a company of Afghan Border Police on a mountaintop along the Pakistan border
and not, as he tells them when he leaves for months on end, teaching in a
school in Kabul.

Every few weeks, Sadeq explains, Pakistani and Afghan Taliban, along
with soldiers in the Pakistani military, come over the mountain and take
up positions and start shooting at them. "My informant [in Pakistan] calls
me and tells when the Taliban are coming," he says, "so we know when they
are going to attack. The Taliban have a meeting in the day, and when they
have this meeting, I get a phone call."

Sadeq also says that suicide bombers are often ferried in along a path in
plain view of the Pakistani border guards. "Pakistan doesn't want Afghanistan to have peace," he says. "Pakistan wants to keep Afghanistan unstable
and destroyed."

BSP 7 consists of just one small building where the border guards sleep, surrounded by a perimeter of sandbags and Hesco barriers with a steep drop-off all around that is littered with claymore mines. Earlier in the day, when we arrived, Hilt wasn't pleased with what he saw. The place was strewn with garbage from one end of the outpost to the other, and there was also, as Sergeant Smith noted, "man-shit everywhere."

The fighting position on the north side of the outpost, nearest to the Pakistani military checkpoint, was also wrecked. Plywood boards and sandbags had collapsed, and the Russian machine gun that had been set up wasn't working. Hilt asks Sadeq why the most important fighting position was knocked down.

"A storm blew it down two weeks ago," Sadeq answers.

"Why didn't you fix it?"

"We were waiting for you."

Sadeq is pretty sure that the outpost isn't going to be attacked tonight. He didn't get a phone call. But the Americans prepare for one anyway, filling up more sandbags and rebuilding the collapsed bunkers.

The sun sets and it starts to get colder; the night sky is filled with stars. The Americans settle into their fighting positions on the edge of the mountain. In a guard tower on the north side of the hilltop, some of the Afghan border guards start smoking hash. The smell wafts down to where I'm sitting with a few American soldiers, and we can also hear the electronic pings of an old handheld video game they're playing. More confident now that the Americans are around, the border guards start yelling and taunting the Taliban, shouting into the darkness.

One of the guards thinks it would be funny to shine his flashlight down on us. "What the fuck are you doing?" one of the Americans yells up, and then says, "We need to get a translator over here to talk to these guys."

A little later, one of the border guards appears in front of us and says to Biggs, "Hash is *gooooood,*" then makes a crazy face and runs away into the night.

In defense of the border guards, BSP 7 is the perfect place to get high. There's no light pollution out here, just dozens of shooting stars in the crisp high-altitude air. The border guards spend two or three months at a time on this mountaintop with the constant threat of being shot or mortared, so why not get high? If you know your history, you could stare out and reflect on how Alexander the Great passed through here, how Rudyard Kipling's tales were inspired by the adventurer who, disguised as a Mohammedan, stumbled through this very terrain, how thirty-odd years ago some poor Soviet bastards were probably wishing for a toke on this same mountain bluff after the CIA armed the mujahideen with Stinger missiles to blast their comrades out of the sky.

It's a history in which the various occupiers who have tried to control this part of the world haven't fared so well. And it's a place where the disparate and often warring factions have never united around much except their shared desire to get rid of foreigners—most recently the Soviets, who at one point had over 100,000 soldiers in Afghanistan.

General David McKiernan, the American commander of the NATO coalition in Afghanistan, rejects the comparison to the Soviet experience here. "We're not here to occupy the place," he told me during an interview in Kabul last fall. "It's apples and oranges. . . . We are winning in Afghanistan, but it's much slower and much more uneven than anybody would like." He continued, "I don't have a specific time [for when we'll leave]. We have a program to grow the Afghan army and police that will at least extend over the next three or four years. The additional forces would be provided in that same period of time. If you come back in three or four years and ask me, 'Have we got to the tipping point?' I don't know if we'll be. But we'll have committed the resources to get to it. I think a lot depends on what happens across the border in Pakistan." He paused for a moment and then added, "There's no way this place is going to be the next Switzerland."

⤙ • ⤚

At 10 P.M., Hilt gives the order for all the fighting positions to fire off flares. The flares are green and yellow and red and go up in all directions, arcing this way and that, lighting up the surrounding moonscape. Two land on the dry vegetation 300 yards from us, and a number of bushes catch fire and go up fast, bonfires burning on the mountain side.

"That's fucking awesome," a soldier I'm sitting with says.

The flares let the Taliban know that the Americans are there, to lure them from their hideouts and into a fight. The Americans have a lot of impressive weapons lined up and ready to go: the Mark 19, which can fire grenades more than a mile, the M-240 Bravo machine gun, and a shoulder-fired an-titank missile, as well as the heavy artillery they can call in to be dropped on top of the Taliban and blow the place up. Most of the guys here are itch-ing to see the enemy tonight. "You finally feel like you're doing your job," Private First Class Julio Hurtado tells me as we slouch down behind sand-bags. "You get to go after them." He's here, Hurtado says, "for the adrena-line dump. Winning or losing the war, it doesn't matter to me."

Around eleven, Hilt comes over to the position where I'll be spending the night with two soldiers, Private First Class Cody Byrd and Specialist Jacques "Linny" Linnemeier. He sits on a green metal army cot that Byrd and Linny found and moved up to their position. "I think we're going to be here for a long time," he says, looking out into Pakistan. "This will be like the new DMZ."

He means that the American military presence along this border is going to become more or less permanent, as it is on the thirty-eighth parallel in Korea. It's the kind of "long war" that General Petraeus and his supporters continue to talk about. But many others, both inside and outside the mili-tary, think what that really means is a sort of half-assed colonialism. Re-tired colonel Douglas Macgregor is a widely respected military thinker who was integrally involved in planning the air strikes over Kosovo and who also advised the Defense Department on the second Iraq war. Macgregor is skeptical of, as he puts it, "the merits of wasting more blood and treasure in the Islamic world." In an e-mail he sent me this winter, he wrote: "I receive a great deal of feedback from officers who've served in Iraq and Afghani-stan. With very few exceptions, they tend to regard operations in these places as colonial expeditions against weak peoples mired in failed cultures and societies. In contrast to the British, who until 1914 extracted billions in profits from these ventures, most officers think we've simply poured our wealth into the sand."

What Macgregor argues for, rather than a prolonged counterinsurgency, is "a strategy in which American military action is short, sharp, decisive, and rare. Such a strategy involves knowing when to fight and when to re-fuse battle." Our counterterrorism should look more like America's in-volvement in El Salvador in the 1980s, he says, in which we treated El Salvador as a sovereign state and did not flood it with American troops. (Counterinsurgency proponents like Petraeus look to less promising historic examples for guidance, like French commander David Galula's fight in Algiers in the 1950s or the British campaign against Communist insurgents in Malaysia in 1960.) "The answer has always been low footprint, high impact," he wrote. "The notion that we are going to field vast forces of riflemen with little or no protection, firepower, or mobility who will be Renaissance men—fluent in multiple languages and familiar with the complexities of non-European cultures—is simply nonsense. The idea these will be welcome anywhere in the non-Western world is foolish."

At midnight, Hilt gets up and heads back down to the command post. The night drags on. At 2 A.M., it's face-freezing cold. At four, even colder. Eventually, the sun starts to rise, and we pack up and get ready to go back to Terezayi. Byrd and Linny take down the Mark 19. The other soldiers are heading back to the MRAPs.

Around 8:30 A.M., a pickup truck full of Afghan Border Police drives past, heading to a checkpoint at the bottom of the hill. I'm throwing my gear into the MRAP when I hear an explosion, maybe a mortar or an RPG, quickly followed by three or four more. The truck carrying the border police has been attacked, and the Americans scramble to set up their guns again. An Afghan border guard, the one who last night had said how good hash was, stands barefoot behind a Soviet Dishka left over from two wars ago, firing wildly into the hillside. "Taliban! Shoot!" he yells, glaring at me. "Taliban! Shoot!"

It's unclear if anyone has seen the enemy yet or if they're just laying down suppressing fire. Hilt orders up air support, two Kiowa helicopters. I run to a fighting position occupied by Sergeant Biggs, Doc Allen, and another soldier, and stay there as the helicopters come in and make four passes over the ravine, launching Hellfire missiles and strafing with machine-gun fire. Each time the helicopters launch a missile, Biggs fires a single shot down into the ravine. "Hell, I might as well get mine in," he says.

The fight lasts about forty-five minutes. Afterward the soldiers go on a foot patrol into the ravine, looking for bodies. There aren't any. There are rocks and heavy vegetation and a few caves. I get the sense that we could have walked right past them. There are so many hiding places. The soldiers scan the ridges for a few more minutes and then give up and head back to the MRAPs for the slow crawl back to Terezayi. Hilt shakes his head and scans the landscape around us, a tiny portion of the 350 square miles he and his men are responsible for. "They're already back in Pakistan," he says.

20

RIGHT AT THE EDGE

DEXTER FILKINS

The New York Times Magazine   September 7, 2008

It's telling that this article, reported from inside Pakistan by New York Times *correspondent Dexter Filkins, and the preceding piece, written from the perspective of American troops in Afghanistan, both conclude with the same image: Islamic insurgents drifting back across the border into Pakistan after conducting an operation in the country next door. For years, this stretch of rugged territory on the eastern side of the Af-Pak border has been a safe haven for the Taliban and al Qaeda. Officially off-limits to U.S. ground troops, the area has also been largely left alone by Pakistan's forces—a policy that's come back to haunt them in recent months, as the Taliban have stepped up their military efforts in Pakistan itself. Pakistan's new counteroffensive to reclaim Taliban-held territory in the picturesque Swat valley seems to meeting with some success. However, as Filkins notes, it's still unclear exactly whose side the Pakistani government—now headed by Benazir Bhutto's widower, Asif Ali Zardari—is on.*

I. THE BORDER INCIDENT

Late in the afternoon of June 10, during a firefight with Taliban militants along the Afghan-Pakistani border, American soldiers called in airstrikes to beat back the attack. The firefight was taking place right on the border itself, known in military jargon as the "zero line." Afghanistan was on one side, and the remote Pakistani region known as the Federally Administered Tribal Areas, or FATA, was on the other. The stretch of border was guarded by three Pakistani military posts.

The American bombers did the job, and then some. By the time the fighting ended, the Taliban militants had slipped away, the American unit was safe and 11 Pakistani border guards lay dead. The airstrikes on the Pakistani positions sparked a diplomatic row between the two allies: Pakistan called the incident "unprovoked and cowardly"; American officials regretted what they called a tragic mistake. But even after a joint inquiry by the United States, Pakistan and Afghanistan, it remained unclear why American soldiers had reached the point of calling in airstrikes on soldiers from Pakistan, a critical ally in the war in Afghanistan and the campaign against terrorism.

The mystery, at least part of it, was solved in July by four residents of Suran Dara, a Pakistani village a few hundred yards from the site of the fight. According to two of these villagers, whom I interviewed together with a local reporter, the Americans started calling in airstrikes on the Pakistanis after the latter started shooting at the Americans.

"When the Americans started bombing the Taliban, the Frontier Corps started shooting at the Americans," we were told by one of Suran Dara's villagers, who, like the others, spoke on condition of anonymity for fear of being persecuted or killed by the Pakistani government or the Taliban. "They were trying to help the Taliban. And then the American planes bombed the Pakistani post."

For years, the villagers said, Suran Dara served as a safe haven for jihadist fighters—whether from Afghanistan or Pakistan or other countries—giving them aid and shelter and a place to stash their weapons. With the firefight under way, one of Suran Dara's villagers dashed across the border into Afghanistan carrying a field radio with a long antenna (the villager called it "a Motorola") to deliver to the Taliban fighters. He never made it. The man with the Motorola was hit by an American bomb. After the fight, wounded Taliban members were carried into Suran Dara for treatment. "Everyone supports the Taliban on both sides of the border," one of the villagers we spoke with said.

Later, an American analyst briefed by officials in Washington confirmed the villagers' account. "There have been dozens of incidents where there have been exchanges of fire," he said.

That American and Pakistani soldiers are fighting one another along what was meant to be a border between allies highlights the extraordinarily chaotic situation unfolding inside the Pakistani tribal areas, where hundreds, perhaps thousands, of Taliban, along with al Qaeda and other foreign fighters, enjoy freedom from American attacks.

But the incident also raises one of the more fundamental questions of the long war against Islamic militancy, and one that looms larger as the American position inside Afghanistan deteriorates: Whose side is Pakistan really on?

≺≺ • ≻≻

Pakistan's wild, largely ungoverned tribal areas have become an untouchable base for Islamic militants to attack Americans and Afghans across the border. Inside the tribal areas, Taliban warlords have taken near-total control, pushing aside the Pakistani government and imposing their draconian form of Islam. And for more than a year now, they have been sending suicide bombers against government and military targets in Pakistan, killing hundreds of people. American and Pakistani investigators say they believe it was Baitullah Mehsud, the strongest of FATA's Taliban leaders, who dispatched assassins last December to kill Benazir Bhutto, the former prime minister. With much of the North-West Frontier Province, which borders the tribal areas, also now under their control, the Taliban are increasingly in a position to threaten the integrity of the Pakistani state.

Then there is al Qaeda. According to American officials and counterterrorism experts, the organization has rebuilt itself and is using its sanctuaries inside the tribal areas to plan attacks against the United States and Europe. Since 2004, six major terrorist plots against Europe or the United States—including the successful suicide attacks in London that killed 52 people in July 2005—have been traced back to Pakistan's tribal areas, according to Bruce Hoffman, a professor of security studies at Georgetown University. Hoffman says he fears that al Qaeda could be preparing a major attack before the American presidential election. "I'm convinced they are planning something," he told me.

At the center of all this stands the question of whether Pakistan really wants to control the Talibs and their Qaeda allies ensconced in the tribal areas—and whether it really can.

This was not supposed to be a major worry. After the attacks of September 11, President Pervez Musharraf threw his lot in with the United States. Pakistan has helped track down al Qaeda suspects, launched a series of attacks against militants inside the tribal areas—a new offensive got under way just weeks ago—and given many assurances of devotion to the antiterrorist cause. For such efforts, Musharraf and the Pakistani government have been paid handsomely, receiving more than $10 billion in American money since 2001.

But as the incident on the Afghan border suggests, little in Pakistan is what it appears. For years, the survival of Pakistan's military and civilian leaders has depended on a double game: assuring the United States that they were vigorously repressing Islamic militants—and in some cases actually doing so—while simultaneously tolerating and assisting the same militants. From the anti-Soviet fighters of the 1980s and the Taliban of the 1990s to the homegrown militants of today, Pakistan's leaders have been both public enemies and private friends.

When the game works, it reaps great rewards: billions in aid to boost the Pakistani economy and military and Islamist proxies to extend the government's reach into Afghanistan and India.

Pakistan's double game has rested on two premises: that the country's leaders could keep the militants under control and that they could keep the United States sufficiently placated to keep the money and weapons flowing. But what happens when the game spins out of control? What happens when the militants you have been encouraging grow too strong and set their sights on Pakistan itself? What happens when the bluff no longer works?

II. BEING A WARLORD

Late in June, to great fanfare, the Pakistani military began what it described as a decisive offensive to rout the Taliban from Khyber agency, one of seven tribal areas that make up the FATA. "Forces Move In on Militants," declared a headline in *Dawn*, one of Pakistan's most influential newspapers. Reporters were kept away, but footage on Pakistani television showed troops advancing behind trucks and troop carriers. The Americans were pleased. "We think that's a positive development and certainly hope and expect that this government will continue," Tom Casey, the deputy spokesman at the State Department, said.

The situation was serious indeed: Peshawar, the capital of North-West Frontier Province and just east of Khyber agency, was almost entirely surrounded by Taliban militias, which had begun making forays into the city.

The encirclement of Peshawar was the culmination of the Taliban's advance: first they conquered the tribal areas, then much of the North-West Frontier Province, and now they were aiming for the province's capital itself. The Talibs were cutting their well-known medieval path: shutting girls' schools, banishing women from the streets, blowing up CD kiosks and beating barbers for shaving beards.

A few days into the military operation, the photographer Lynsey Addario and I, dressed in traditional clothes and with a posse of gunmen protecting us, rode into Khyber agency ourselves. "Entry by Foreigners Prohibited Beyond This Point," the sign said on the way in. As we drove past the dun-colored buildings and corrugated-tin shops, every trace of government authority vanished. No policemen, no checkpoints, no guards. Nothing to keep us from our appointment with the Taliban.

It was a Friday afternoon, and our guides suggested we pull off the main road until prayers were over; local Taliban enforcers, they said, would not take kindly to anyone skipping prayers. For a couple of hours we waited inside the home of an uncle of one of our guides, listening to the muezzin call the locals to battle.

"What is the need of the day?" a man implored in Pashto over a loudspeaker. "Holy war—holy war is the need of the day!"

After a couple of hours, we resumed our journey, traveling down a mostly empty road. And that is when it struck me: there was no evidence, anywhere, of the military operation that had made the news. There were no Pakistani soldiers, no trucks, no tanks. Nothing.

After a couple of miles, we turned off the road and headed down a sandy path toward a high-walled compound guarded by young men with guns. I had come to my destination: Takya, the home village of Haji Namdar, a Taliban commander who had taken control of a large swath of Khyber agency.

Pulling into Namdar's compound, I felt transported back in time to the Kabul of the 1990s, when the Taliban were at their zenith. A group of men and boys—jittery, clutching rifles and rocket-propelled grenades—sat in the bed of a Toyota Hi-Lux, the same model of truck the Taliban used to ride to victory in Afghanistan. A flag nearly identical to that of the Afghan movement—a pair of swords crossed against a white background—fluttered in the heavy air. Even the name of Namdar's group, the Vice and Virtue brigade, came straight from the Taliban playbook: in the 1990s, bands of young men under the same name terrorized Afghanistan, flogging men for shaving their beards, caning women for walking alone and thrashing children for flying kites.

The young fighters were chattering excitedly about a missile that had recently destroyed one of their ammunition dumps. An American missile, the kids said. "It was a plane without a pilot," one of the boys explained through an interpreter. His eyes darted back and forth among his fellows. "We saw a flash. And then the building exploded."

His description matched that of a Predator, an airborne drone that America uses to hunt militants in the tribal areas. Publicly, at least, the Predator is the only American presence the Pakistani government has so far allowed inside its borders.

We walked into the compound's main building. In a corner, Namdar sat on the floor, wearing a traditional *salwar kameez*, but also a vest that looked as if it had been plucked from a three-piece suit. He stood to shake my hand, and he gave a small bow. To break the ice, I handed him a map of Pakistan and asked him to show me where we were. Namdar peered at the chart for several seconds, his eyes registering nothing. He handed it to one of his deputies. He resumed his stare.

Trying again, I asked about the Pakistani military operation—the one that was supposed to be unfolding right now, chasing the Taliban from Khyber.

Why, I asked Namdar, aren't the Pakistani forces coming after you?

"The government cannot do anything to us, because we are fighting the holy war," he said. "We are fighting the foreigners—it is our obligation. They are killing innocent people." Namdar's aides, one of whom spoke fluent English, looked at him and shook their heads to make him speak more cautiously. Namdar carried on.

"When the Americans kill innocent people, we must take revenge," he said.

Tell me about that, I asked Namdar, and his aides again shook their heads. Finally Namdar changed his line. "Well, we can't stop anyone from going across" into Afghanistan, he said. "I'm not saying we send them ourselves." And with that, Namdar raised his hand, declining to offer any more details.

By many accounts—on the streets, among Western analysts, even according to his own deputies—Namdar was regularly training and dispatching young men to fight and blow themselves up in Afghanistan. An aide,

Munsif Khan, told me that his group had sent "hundreds of people" to fight the Americans. At one point, he described for me how the Vice and Virtue brigade had recently set a minimum-age requirement for suicide bombers. "We are opposed to children carrying out suicide bombings," Khan said. "We get so many young people coming to us—15, 16 years old—wanting to go on martyrdom operations. This is not the age to be a suicide bomber. Any man who wants to be a suicide bomber should be at least 20 or 25."

Khan himself, a former magazine reporter in Peshawar, had been gravely wounded in a car-bomb attack last year. His feet were mangled, and he could walk only with crutches. A bloody struggle for power rages among the many Taliban warlords of the FATA; Khan said his assailants had likely been dispatched by Baitullah Mehsud, the powerful warlord in South Waziristan, because Namdar had refused to submit to Mehsud's authority.

Another of Namdar's aides had spoken enthusiastically of his commander's prowess in battle. "He is a great fighter!" the aide told me. "He goes to Afghanistan every month to fight the Americans."

So here was Namdar—Taliban chieftain, enforcer of Islamic law, usurper of the Pakistani government and trainer and facilitator of suicide bombers in Afghanistan—sitting at home, not three miles from Peshawar, untouched by the Pakistani military operation that was supposedly unfolding around us.

What's going on? I asked the warlord. Why aren't they coming for you?

"I cannot lie to you," Namdar said, smiling at last. "The army comes in, and they fire at empty buildings. It is a drama—it is just to entertain."

Entertain whom? I asked.

"America," he said.

III. PLAYING THE GAME

The idea that Pakistan's military and intelligence agencies could simultaneously be aiding the Taliban and like-minded militants while taking money from the United States is not as far-fetched as it may seem.

The relationship dates to the 1980s, when, following the Soviet invasion of Afghanistan, Pakistan became the conduit for billions of dollars of American and Saudi money for the Afghan rebels. Pakistan's leader, the fundamentalist General Zia ul-Haq, funneled the bulk of the cash to the most religiously extreme guerrilla leaders. After the Soviet Union withdrew in 1989, Pakistani military and intelligence services kept on supporting Islamist militants, notably in the Muslim-majority Indian state of Kashmir, where they threw their support behind a local uprising. Through time, with the Pakistanis closely involved, the Kashmiri movement was taken over by Islamist extremists and foreign fighters who moved easily between Pakistan and Kashmir.

Then, in 1994, Pakistani leaders made their most fateful move. Alarmed by the civil war that engulfed Afghanistan following the Soviet retreat, Prime Minister Benazir Bhutto and her government intervened on behalf of a small group of former anti-Soviet fighters known for their religious fanaticism. They called themselves "the students": the Taliban.

With Pakistan providing support and the United States looking the other way, the Taliban took control of Kabul in 1996. "We created the Taliban," Nasrullah Babar, the interior minister under Benazir Bhutto, told me in an interview at his home in Peshawar in 1999. "Mrs. Bhutto had a vision: that through a peaceful Afghanistan, Pakistan could extend its influence into the resource-rich territories of Central Asia." That never happened—the Taliban, even with Pakistani support, never completed the conquest of Afghanistan. But the training camps they ran, sometimes with the help of Pakistani intelligence officers, were beacons to Islamic militants from around the world.

By all accounts, Pakistan's spymasters were never terribly discriminating about who showed up in their training camps. In 1998, when President Bill Clinton ordered missile strikes against camps in Afghanistan following al Qaeda's bombings of American embassies in East Africa, several trainers from Pakistan's Inter-Services Intelligence, or ISI, were killed. Osama bin Laden was supposed to be there when the missiles struck but apparently had already left.

After 9/11, President George W. Bush and other senior American officials declared in the strongest terms that Pakistani leaders had to end their support for the Taliban and other Islamic militants. Pakistan's military dictator, Pervez Musharraf, promised to do so.

Yet the game did not end; it merely changed. In the years after 9/11, Musharraf often made great shows of going after militants inside Pakistan, while at the same time supporting and protecting them.

In 2002, for instance, Musharraf ordered the arrest of some 2,000 suspected militants, many of whom had trained in Pakistani-sponsored camps. And then, quietly, he released nearly all of them. Another revealing moment came in 2005, when Fazlur Rehman, the leader of Jamiat Ulema-e-Islam, one of the most radical Islamist parties, denounced Musharraf for denying the existence of jihadi groups. Everyone knows, Rehman said in a speech before Pakistan's National Assembly, that the government supports the holy warriors. "We will have to openly tell the world whether we want to support jihadis or crack down on them," Rehman declared. "We cannot afford to be hypocritical any more."

In 2006, a senior ISI official, speaking on the condition of anonymity, told a *New York Times* reporter that he regarded Serajuddin Haqqani as one of the ISI's intelligence assets. "We are not apologetic about this," the ISI official said. For a presumed ally of the United States, that was a stunning admission: Haqqani, an Afghan, is currently one of the Taliban's most senior commanders battling the Americans in eastern Afghanistan. His father, Jalaluddin, is a longtime associate of bin Laden's. The Haqqanis are believed to be overseeing operations from a hiding place in the Pakistani tribal agency of North Waziristan.

But such evidence, however intriguing, fails to answer the critical questions: Exactly who in the Pakistani government is helping the militants and why?

⤙⤙ ⦁ ⤚⤚

The most common theory offered to explain Pakistan's continued contact with Islamic militants is the country's obsession with India. Pakistan has fought three major wars with India, from which it split violently upon independence from Britain in 1947. To the east, the Pakistani military and intelligence services have long tolerated and sometimes directed militants moving into Indian Kashmir. To the west, Afghanistan has long been seen as a potentially critical arena of competition with India. After the U.S.-led invasion in the fall of 2001, for example, India lost no time in setting up consulates throughout Afghanistan and beginning an extensive aid program. According to Pakistani and Western officials, Pakistan's officer corps remains obsessed by the prospect of Indian domination of Afghanistan should the Americans leave. The Taliban are seen as a counterweight to Indian influence. "We are saving the Taliban for a rainy day," one former Pakistani official put it to me.

Another explanation is growing popular hatred of the United States. Pakistan's leaders—whether Musharraf or the army chief, General Ashfaq Pervez Kayani, or the country's leading civilian politicians—are finding it more and more difficult to mobilize their own army and intelligence services to act against the Taliban and other militants inside the country. And while the Pakistan Army used to be a predominantly secular institution, increasingly it is being led by Islamist-minded officers.

The pro-Islamist and anti-American sentiments pervading the armed forces might help explain why a group of ill-trained, underpaid Pakistani Frontier Corps soldiers would open fire on American troops fighting the Taliban. Those same sentiments buttress the notion, offered by some American and Pakistani officials, that rogue officers inside the army and ISI are supporting the militants against the wishes of their superiors.

Finally, there is the problem of the Pakistan Army's competence. For all the myths that officers like Musharraf have spread about the institution, the simple fact is that it isn't very good. The Pakistan Army has lost every war it has ever fought. And it isn't trained to battle an insurgency. Each of the half-dozen offensives the army has launched into the tribal areas since 2004 has left it bloodied and humbled.

For all these reasons, when it comes to the militants in their midst, it's easier for Pakistan to do as little as possible.

"There is a growing Islamist feeling in the military, and it's inseparable from anti-Americanism," I was told by a Western military officer with several years' experience in the region. "The vast majority of Pakistani officers feel they are fighting our war. There is a lot of sympathy for the Taliban. The result is that the Pakistanis do as little as they possibly can to combat the militants."

These are reasonable explanations, offered by reasonable people. But are such explanations enough? The more Pakistanis I talked to, the more I came to believe that the most reasonable explanations were not necessarily the most plausible ones.

⤙ • ⤚

One sweltering afternoon in July, I ventured into the elegant home of a former Pakistani official who recently retired after several years of serving in senior government posts. We sat in his book-lined study. A servant brought us tea and biscuits.

Was it the obsession with India that led the Pakistani military to support the Taliban? I asked him.

"Yes," he said.

Or is it the anti-Americanism and pro-Islamic feelings in the army?

"Yes," he said, that too.

And then the retired Pakistani official offered another explanation—one that he said could never be discussed in public. The reason the Pakistani security services support the Taliban, he said, is for money: after the 9/11 attacks, the Pakistani military concluded that keeping the Taliban alive was the surest way to win billions of dollars in aid that Pakistan needed to survive. The military's complicated relationship with the Taliban is part of what the official called the Pakistani military's "strategic games." Like other Pakistanis, this former senior official spoke on the condition of anonymity because of the sensitivity of what he was telling me.

"Pakistan is dependent on the American money that these games with the Taliban generate," the official told me. "The Pakistani economy would collapse without it. This is how the game works."

As an example, he cited the Pakistan Army's first invasion of the tribal areas—of South Waziristan in 2004. Called Operation Shakai, the offensive was ostensibly aimed at ridding the area of Taliban militants. From an American perspective, the operation was a total failure. The army invaded, fought and then made a deal with one of the militant commanders, Nek Mohammed. The agreement was capped by a dramatic meeting between Mohammed and Safdar Hussein, one of the most senior officers in the Pakistan Army.

"The corps commander was flown in on a helicopter," the former official said. "They had this big ceremony, and they embraced. They called each other *mujahids.*"

"*Mujahid*" is the Arabic word for "holy warrior." The ceremony, in fact, was captured on videotape, and the tape has been widely distributed.

"The army agreed to compensate the locals for collateral damage," the official said. "Where do you think that money went? It went to the Taliban. Who do you think paid the bill? The Americans. This is the way the game works. The Taliban is attacked, but it is never destroyed.

"It's a game," the official said, wrapping up our conversation. "The U.S. is being taken for a ride."

IV. A NEW GOVERNMENT, A NEW TACK

In February, nationwide elections lifted to power Pakistan's first full-fledged civilian government in nine years. The elections followed the tumultuous events of Benazir Bhutto's return from exile and her assassination.

If there was any reason to hope that the government's games with the Taliban would end, this was it: Pakistan's new leaders declared they had a popular mandate to steer the country in a new direction. That meant, implicitly, reining in the military and the spy agencies. At the same time, the country's new civilian leaders, led by Prime Minister Yousaf Raza Gilani, made it clear that they would not be taking orders from officials in the Bush administration, whom they resented for having supported Musharraf for so long. (Musharraf, facing impeachment, finally resigned from the presidency last month.) Instead of launching military operations into the tribal areas, Pakistan's new leaders promised to embark on negotiations to neutralize the militants.

The leader of this new civilian effort in the tribal areas is Owais Ahmed Ghani, governor of the North-West Frontier Province. Since February, Ghani is said to have embarked on a series of negotiations in tribal areas.

I went to see Ghani earlier this summer at the governor's mansion in Peshawar, inside a lovely compound built by the British at the height of their imperial power. Ghani seemed as if he might have stepped from the Raj himself: he gave off an air of faint amusement, a British affectation common in the upper tiers of Pakistani society. On his wall hung a British-made Enfield rifle, preserved from colonial days. Outside, peacocks strolled across the manicured lawn.

"You know the joke about the Pathans," Ghani began, using the old British name for the Pashtuns, the ethnic group that dominates the tribal areas and the Taliban. "A Pathan's heart hammers harder when he has a gun than a woman!"

Suddenly turning serious, Ghani spelled out a state-of-the-art counterinsurgency campaign to defeat the militants in control of the FATA. He emphasized that the purely military approach to the tribal areas had failed—not merely because the army has been unable to succeed militarily but also because it no longer could count on popular support. "No government can afford to make war on its own people for very long," Ghani said.

The new approach, Ghani said, would entail negotiations and economic development. Under the plan, the government would pour billions into the region over the next five years to build schools, roads and health clinics. (The United States has agreed to pitch in $750 million.) The political negotiations, Ghani said, would be conducted by civilian members of the government and the region's tribal leaders, not, as in the past, by military officers and Taliban militants. Ghani called this new strategy "Jang and Jirga"—the Pashto words for "war" and "tribal council." Carrot and stick.

"The idea is to drive a wedge between the militants and the people," Ghani said. "There will be no negotiations with the militants themselves."

Ghani's previous post had been as governor of Baluchistan Province, to the south, where he had weakened an ethnically based insurgency that had churned on for decades. He said he was confident he could do the same here. "Don't underestimate the Pakistani desire to confront the militants," he insisted. "Ninety percent of the country is behind us."

It was sundown when Ghani and I finished talking. As I strolled across the grounds of the governor's compound, a group of soldiers had just begun lowering the Pakistani flag. Another man blew into a bugle, playing "A Hundred Pipers," a Scottish air.

◄◄ • ►►

For Ghani and Pakistan's civilian government, the crucial players in achieving peace are traditional tribal leaders whose power is independent of the Taliban or other militants. This method of governing the tribal areas—indirect rule through local chiefs—dates back to the British imperial period. The British put tribal leaders—known as *maliks*—on the payroll to stand in for the central government, which imposed no taxes or customs duties and, in turn, did very little. At the same time, imperial administrators reserved for themselves extraordinary powers of arrest and punishment that extended to collective reprisals against entire tribes. The purpose of the malik system was to keep the tribal areas quiet and at least nominally under the thumb of the imperial government. This preserved a feudal political structure, and feudal levels of economic development, into the 20th century.

The British system, with a little tinkering, has survived to this day: the FATA stands apart from the rest of Pakistan, with little or no government presence and little or no development. Not one person in five can read or write. Pakistani political parties are banned. Universal suffrage wasn't allowed until 1997. Until recently, tribesmen could claim no protection by Pakistan's Constitution or its courts. Inside the FATA, the locals do not even change the time on their clocks, as other Pakistanis do, when daylight savings begins. "English time," it is called.

A few days after my talk with Ghani, I met an elder of one of the two main tribes of South Waziristan. He refused to give his name and insisted that I refer to him as Jan. South Waziristan is believed to contain the largest number of militant Arabs and other foreign fighters, possibly even bin Laden and his deputy, Ayman al-Zawahiri. To be more specific about Jan— to use his name, to identify the tribe he leads, to name the town where he lives—would almost certainly, he said, result in his death at the hands of the militants and Taliban fighters who control South Waziristan.

"There are many Arab fighters living in South Waziristan," Jan told me. "Sometimes you see them in the town; you hear them speaking Arabic.

"But the important Arabs are not in the city," he continued. "They are in the mountains."

Important Arabs? I asked.

"They ride horses, Arabian horses; we don't have horses like this in Waziristan," Jan said. "The people from the town take food to the Arabs' horses in the mountains. They have seen the horses. They have seen the Arabs. These horses eat better than the common people in the town."

How do you know?

"I am a leader of my tribe. People come to me—everyone comes to me. They tell me everything."

What about Osama? I asked. Is he in South Waziristan?

"Osama?" Jan said. "I don't know. But they"—the Arabs in the mountains—"are important."

The labor it took to persuade Jan to speak to me is a measure of what has become of the area over which his family still officially presides. Since it was not possible for me to go to South Waziristan—"Baitullah Mehsud would cut off your head," the Taliban leader, Namdar, told me—I had to persuade Jan to come to Peshawar. For several days, military checkpoints and roadblocks made it impossible for Jan to travel. Finally, after two weeks, Jan left his home at midnight in a taxi so no one would notice either him or his car.

Jan had reason to worry. Seven members of his family—his father, two brothers, two uncles and two cousins—have been murdered by militants who inhabit the area. Jan said he believed his father was killed by Uzbek and Tajik gunmen who fled to South Waziristan after the American invasion of Afghanistan in 2001. His father had opposed them. Jan's cousins, he said, were killed by men working for Baitullah Mehsud. Jan's father was a malik, and thousands of Waziri tribesmen came to his funeral: "the largest funeral in the history of Waziristan," Jan said.

The rise of the Taliban and al Qaeda has come at the expense of the maliks, who have been systematically murdered and marginalized in a campaign to destroy the old order. In South Waziristan, where Mehsud presides, the Taliban and al Qaeda have killed more than 150 maliks since 2005, all but destroying the tribal system. And there are continual reminders of what happens to the survivors who do not understand this—who, for example, attempt to talk with Pakistan's civilian government and assert their authority. In June, Mehsud's men gunned down 28 tribal leaders who had formed a "peace committee" in South Waziristan. Their bodies were dumped on the side of a road. "This shows what happens when the tribal elders try to challenge Baitullah Mehsud," Jan said.

Like Taliban militias in other parts of Pakistan, Mehsud's men have been strong-arming families into turning over their young sons to join. "They have taken my own son to be a suicide bomber," Jan said. "He is gone." The Talibs, he said, now control the disbursement of all government money that comes into the area.

The Taliban have not achieved this by violence alone. They have capitalized on the resentment many Pakistanis feel toward the hereditary maliks and the government they represent. Taliban leaders and their foot soldiers come mostly from the lower classes. Mehsud, the Taliban chieftain, was an unemployed man who spent his time lifting weights before he picked up a gun. Manghal Bagh, the warlord in Khyber agency whom the

Pakistan military went after in June, swept public buses. "They are illiterate people, and now they have power," Jan said.

◄─ • ─►

Everywhere I traveled during my stay in the tribal areas and in Peshawar, I met impoverished Pakistanis who told me Robin Hood–like stories about how the Taliban had challenged the wealthy and powerful people on behalf of the little guys. Hamidullah, for instance, was an illiterate wheat farmer living in Khyber agency when, in 2002, a wealthy landowner seized his home and six acres of fields. Hamidullah and his family were forced to eke out a living from a nearby shanty. Neither the local malik nor the government agent, Hamidullah told me, would intervene on his behalf. Then came Namdar, the Taliban commander. He hauled the rich man before a Vice and Virtue council and ordered him to give back Hamidullah's home and farm.

Now Hamidullah is one of Namdar's loyal militiamen.

"There are so many guys like me," he said, cradling a Kalashnikov.

The social revolution that has swept the tribal areas does not bode well for the plans, laid out by Governor Ghani, to oust the Taliban by boosting the tribal elders. Nor does it hold out much promise for the Americans, who have expressed hope that they could do in the FATA what they were able to do with the Sunni tribes in Iraq. There, local tribesmen rose up against, and have substantially weakened, al Qaeda of Mesopotamia.

Indeed, in some cases the distinction between tribe and Taliban has vanished altogether. Baitullah Mehsud, for instance, comes from the Mehsud tribe, one of the two largest clans of South Waziristan. ("The Taliban is the Mehsud tribe," Jan said. "They are one and the same now.")

Mehsud is the most powerful of dozens of Taliban chieftains who control the tribal areas. Some of them answer to Mehsud; some do not. The others are no less brutal: in July, for instance, in Bajaur tribal agency, the Taliban leader Faqir Mohammed staged a public execution of two men "convicted" of spying for the United States. One was shot; the other beheaded. A photograph of the men's last moments was displayed on the front page of *The News*, a Pakistani newspaper.

The chieftains' rivalries are intense, too. Six weeks after I met Namdar, he was gunned down by one of his bodyguards, in the very house where I met him. It isn't entirely clear who ordered the killing of Namdar, but many of his followers suspect it was Mehsud.

V. THE GAME CHANGES

While most of the Taliban chieftains do share a basic ideology, they appear to be divided into two distinct groups: those who send fighters into Afghanistan to fight the Americans and those who do not. And that is an important distinction for the Pakistanis, as well as for the Americans.

After the rout of the Taliban government in Afghanistan in the fall of 2001, many militants fled across the border, and the Taliban inside Pakistan grew. At first, they largely confined their activities to the tribal areas themselves, from where they could send fighters into Afghanistan. That started to change last year. Militants began moving out of the FATA and into the rest of Pakistan, taking control of the towns and villages in the neighboring North-West Frontier Province. Militants began attacking Pakistani police and soldiers. Inside the FATA, Mehsud was forming Tehrik-e-Taliban Pakistan, an umbrella party of some 40 Taliban groups that claimed as its goal the domination of Pakistan. Suddenly, the Taliban was not merely a group of militants who were useful in extending Pakistan's influence into Afghanistan. They were a threat to Pakistan itself.

The turning point came in July last year, when the government laid siege to a mosque in Islamabad called Lal Masjid, where dozens of militants had taken shelter. The presence of the militants inside Islamabad itself, Pakistan's stately, secular-minded capital, was shock enough to the country's ruling class. Then, after eight days, on orders from Musharraf, security forces stormed the mosque, sparking a battle that left 87 dead. The massacre at Lal Masjid became a rallying cry for Islamic militants across the country. Mehsud and other Islamists declared war on the government and launched a campaign of suicide bombings; there were 60 in 2007 alone. In an act of astonishing humiliation, Mehsud's men captured 300 Pakistan Army soldiers that came into South Waziristan; Mehsud eventually let them go. And then, in December, a suicide bomber, possibly dispatched by Mehsud, killed Bhutto.

The bloody siege of Lal Masjid, Western and Pakistani officials say, finally convinced senior Pakistani military and ISI leaders that the Taliban fighters they had been nurturing for so many years had grown too strong. "Now, the militants are autonomous," one retired Pakistani official told me. "No one can control them anymore."

⤛ • ⤜

In January of this year, Pakistan opened an offensive into South Waziristan that was far fiercer than any that had come before. It inflicted hundreds of casualties on Mehsud's forces and caused at least 15,000 families to flee. Then, after just three weeks, the operation ended. As they had before, Pakistani commanders and Mehsud struck a deal. But this time, remarkably, the deal seemed to stick. The army dismantled its checkpoints and pulled back its troops, and the suicide bombings all but stopped.

What happened? A draft of the peace agreement struck between the army and Mehsud may help explain. The agreement itself, which has not been officially released, provides a look into the Pakistani government's new strategy toward the militants. According to the agreement, members of the Mehsud tribe agreed to refrain from attacking the Pakistani state and from setting up a parallel government. They agreed to accept the rule of law.

But sending fighters into Afghanistan? About that, the agreement says nothing at all.

And that appears to be the essence of the new Pakistani game. As long as the militants refrain from attacking the state, they are free to do what they want inside the tribal areas—and across the border in Afghanistan. While peace has largely prevailed between the government and the militants inside Pakistan since earlier this year, the infiltration of Taliban fighters from the tribal areas into Afghanistan has risen sharply. Even the current Pakistani offensive, according to Major General Jeffrey J. Schloesser, the top American commander in eastern Afghanistan, has failed to slow the influx.

In short, the chaos has been redirected.

This must have been why Namdar told me with such confidence that "fighting the jihad" insulated him from the Pakistani government. The real purpose of the government's Khyber operation became clear: to tame Manghal Bagh, the warlord who does not send men into Afghanistan and who was encroaching on Peshawar. Indeed, after more than a week of enduring the brunt of the army's assault, Bagh agreed to respect the Pakistani state. Namdar had been left alone by government troops all the while.

If channeling the Taliban into Afghanistan and against NATO and the Americans is indeed the new Pakistani game, then one more thing is also clear: the leaders of the Pakistan Army and the ISI must still be confident they can manage the militants. And it is certainly the military and ISI officers who are doing the managing—not the country's elected leaders. When I asked Jan, the tribal elder, about the negotiations that Ghani had described for me—talks between the country's new civilian leaders and FATA's tribal elders—Jan laughed. "The only negotiations are between the army and the Taliban, between the army and Baitullah Mehsud," he said. "There are no government officials taking part in any negotiations. There are no tribal elders taking part. I'm a tribal elder. I think I would know."

Western officials agreed that the influence of Pakistan's new civilian leaders over strategy in the tribal areas was close to nil. "Until the civilians get their act together, the military will play the dominant role," a Western analyst in Pakistan, speaking on the condition of anonymity, told me. The parliamentary coalition cobbled together earlier this year is already falling apart.

"It's a very close relationship," Jan said, describing the meetings between the Pakistan Army and the Taliban. "The army and the Taliban are friends. Whenever a Taliban fighter is killed, army officers go to his funeral. They bring money to the family."

Indeed, American officials said in July that the ISI helped Jalaluddin Haqqani's fighters bomb the Indian Embassy in Kabul. The attack killed 54, including an Indian defense attaché. American officials said the evidence of the ISI's involvement was overwhelming. "It was sort of this 'aha' moment," one of them said.

VI. THE PATH OF JIHAD

After I met Namdar, the Taliban commander, he ordered some of his young fighters to take me to the Afghan border. The mountains that ran along the border shimmered in the monsoon rains, and a new stream was running down from the peaks. It was this range, called the White Mountains, through which Osama bin Laden escaped from Tora Bora in December 2001. The Afghan frontier, the fighters told me, was a day's walk over the hills.

It was along a similar route, two years ago, that an 18-year-old Pakistani named Mudasar trekked into Afghanistan to blow himself up. His family, who live in the town of Shakhas in Khyber agency, told me they learned of his fate in a telephone call. "Your son has carried out a suicide operation inside of Afghanistan," a man said without identifying himself. There was no corpse to send home to Pakistan, so Mudasar's family and the rest of the villagers of Shakhas gathered for a *ghaibana*, a funeral without a body.

"It is very respectable to die this way," Abu Omar, Mudasar's brother, told me one day at a cafe in Peshawar. Mudasar and Abu Omar were both part of the tide of young Pakistani men that has been surging across the Afghan border to fight the Americans. Abu Omar described his brother as intensely religious, without hobbies—unlike Abu Omar himself, whose passion was playing fullback on the soccer field. "Mudasar would lie awake at night crying for the martyred people in Afghanistan," Abu Omar said.

What finally drove Mudasar to want to kill Americans was a single spectacular event. In January 2006, the Americans maneuvered a Predator drone across the border into Pakistan and fired a missile at a building they thought contained Ayman al-Zawahiri, al Qaeda's deputy leader. The missile reportedly missed Zawahiri by a couple of hours, but it killed his son-in-law and several other senior al Qaeda members. A number of civilians died as well, including women and children. Television footage from the scene, showing corpses lying amid the rubble, sparked protests across Pakistan.

"My brother saw that and resolved to become a martyr," Abu Omar told me.

Confiding in only his mother and brother, Mudasar enrolled in a local camp for suicide bombers. Abu Omar declined to tell me who ran the camp or where it was, saying such things were military secrets. "There are many such camps," he said and shrugged.

It was during our second meeting, in Peshawar's main shopping area, that Abu Omar agreed to talk about his own mission across the border. We sat in a shabby second-floor office in the Saddar bazaar. Last October, following the death of his brother, Abu Omar enrolled in one of the Taliban training camps inside Khyber agency operated by Mehsud's organization. The camp, Abu Omar said, was split into three sections: one for bomb making, one for reconnaissance and ambushes and one for firing large weapons. Abu Omar's section was given a heavy machine gun.

"Big enough to shoot down helicopters," he said.

Abu Omar spoke listlessly but in great detail. The militant camp sat within a few miles of the Afghan border, he said, and only a few miles from a Pakistan military base. Most of the volunteers were Pakistani, he said, although foreigners trained, too, including a Muslim convert from Great Britain.

"He had blond hair, but a very long beard," Abu Omar said, breaking into his only smile of the afternoon. "A good Muslim."

When the time finally came, Abu Omar said, he and about 20 of his comrades moved at night to a safe house near the Afghan frontier, in Mohmand tribal agency. They were just across the border from Kunar, one of the most violent of Afghanistan's provinces. There, he said, he and his comrades waited for two days until the way was clear. Then, when the signal came, they moved across. None of the men, Abu Omar said, were particularly worried about what would happen if they were spotted by Pakistani troops. "They are Muslims," he told me. "They support what we are doing."

Fighting in Afghanistan, Abu Omar said, was a hit-and-miss, sometimes tedious affair: once across the border, he and the other fighters sat inside another safe house for two days, waiting for word to launch their attack. Finally, Abu Omar's commander told them that there were too many American and Afghan soldiers about and that they would have to return to Pakistan.

The second time, the mission worked. Crossing into Kunar once more, Abu Omar and the other fighters attacked a line of Afghan army check posts just inside the border. Omar put his heavy machine gun to good use, he said, and four of the posts were overrun. "We killed seven Afghan soldiers," he claimed. "Unfortunately, there were no Americans."

Their attack successful, Abu Omar and his comrades trekked back across the Pakistani border. The sun was just rising. The fighters saw a Pakistani checkpoint and headed straight for it.

"They gave us some water," he said of the Pakistani border guards. "And then we continued on our way."

VII. THE ROSE GARDEN

From the Rose Garden of the White House, you could just make out the profile of the Pakistani prime minister, Yousaf Raza Gilani, sitting across from President Bush inside the Oval Office. It was Gilani's first official visit and, by all accounts, not a typical one. That same day, July 28, as Gilani's plane neared the United States, a Predator drone had fired a missile into a compound in South Waziristan, killing Abu Khabab al-Masri, an al Qaeda poison and bombing expert. The hit was a significant one, and al Qaeda posted a eulogy to al-Masri on the Internet a couple of days later. Gilani, according to the American analyst who was briefed by officials, knew nothing of the incident when he arrived in Washington. "They just did it," the analyst said. The Americans pressed Gilani, telling him that his military and security services were out of his control and that they posed a threat to Pakistan and to American forces in Afghanistan.

At the Rose Garden, though, appearances were kept up in grand style. Bush and Gilani strode from the Oval Office side by side. Gilani laughed as the two leaders stopped to face the assembled reporters. Over to the side, to the right of the reporters, the senior members of Bush's foreign-policy team had gathered, including Secretary of State Condoleezza Rice and her deputy, John Negroponte.

"Pakistan is a strong ally and a vibrant democracy," Bush said. "We talked about the common threat we face: extremists who are very dangerous people. We talked about the need for us to make sure that the Afghan border is secure as best as possible: Pakistan has made a very strong commitment to that."

"Thank you," Gilani said, hesitating, looking at Bush. "Now?"

"Please, yes, absolutely," the president said.

Gilani played his part. "We are committed to fight against those extremists and terrorists who are destroying and making the world not safe," Gilani said. "There are few militants—they are hand-picked people, militants, who are disturbing this peace," he concluded. "And I assured Mr. President we'll work together for democracy and for the prosperity and peace of the world."

And then the two men walked together back into the White House, with Rice and Negroponte trailing after them.

21

BELIEVE ME, IT'S TORTURE

CHRISTOPHER HITCHENS
Vanity Fair   August 2008

One of the biggest obstacles in the ongoing debate over the "enhanced interrogation" techniques employed by the CIA in the years following the September 11 terrorist attacks is that the issue remains oddly abstract to everyone other than those who were actually interrogated. Who else could possibly know, for example, what it's like to be chained in standing position for days on end, or repeatedly deprived of oxygen? In this gripping article, Christopher Hitchens goes where no other journalist has dared to tread, voluntarily submitting himself to the simulated drowning process known as waterboarding—and then writing eloquently about the experience. It's a must-read for anyone who thinks they've formed an opinion on the subject.

Here is the most chilling way I can find of stating the matter. Until recently, "waterboarding" was something that Americans did to other Americans. It was inflicted, and endured, by those members of the Special Forces who underwent the advanced form of training known as SERE (Survival, Evasion, Resistance, Escape). In these harsh exercises, brave men and women were introduced to the sorts of barbarism that they might expect to meet at the hands of a lawless foe who disregarded the Geneva Conventions. But it was something that Americans were being trained to *resist,* not to *inflict.*

Exploring this narrow but deep distinction, on a gorgeous day last May I found myself deep in the hill country of western North Carolina, prepar-

ing to be surprised by a team of extremely hardened veterans who had confronted their country's enemies in highly arduous terrain all over the world.
They knew about everything from unarmed combat to enhanced interrogation and, in exchange for anonymity, were going to show me as nearly as
possible what real waterboarding might be like.

It goes without saying that I knew I could stop the process at any time,
and that when it was all over I would be released into happy daylight rather
than returned to a darkened cell. But it's been well said that cowards die
many times before their deaths, and it was difficult for me to completely
forget the clause in the contract of indemnification that I had signed. This
document (written by one who knew) stated revealingly:

> "Water boarding" is a potentially dangerous activity in which the
> participant can receive serious and permanent (physical, emotional
> and psychological) injuries and even death, including injuries and
> death due to the respiratory and neurological systems of the body.

As the agreement went on to say, there would be safeguards provided
"during the 'water boarding' process, however, these measures may fail and
even if they work properly they may not prevent Hitchens from experiencing serious injury or death."

≺⊹ ⚬ ⊹≻

On the night before the encounter I got to sleep with what I thought was
creditable ease, but woke early and knew at once that I wasn't going back to
any sort of doze or snooze. The first specialist I had approached with the
scheme had asked my age on the telephone and when told what it was (I am
59) had laughed out loud and told me to forget it. Waterboarding is for
Green Berets in training, or wiry young jihadists whose teeth can bite
through the gristle of an old goat. It's not for wheezing, paunchy scribblers.
For my current "handlers" I had had to produce a doctor's certificate assuring them that I did not have asthma, but I wondered whether I should
tell them about the 15,000 cigarettes I had inhaled every year for the last
several decades. I was feeling apprehensive, in other words, and beginning
to wish I hadn't given myself so long to think about it.

I have to be opaque about exactly where I was later that day, but there came a moment when, sitting on a porch outside a remote house at the end of a winding country road, I was very gently yet firmly grabbed from behind, pulled to my feet, pinioned by my wrists (which were then cuffed to a belt), and cut off from the sunlight by having a black hood pulled over my face. I was then turned around a few times, I presume to assist in disorienting me, and led over some crunchy gravel into a darkened room. Well, mainly darkened: there were some oddly spaced bright lights that came as pinpoints through my hood. And some weird music assaulted my ears. (I'm no judge of these things, but I wouldn't have expected former Special Forces types to be so fond of New Age techno-disco.) The outside world seemed very suddenly very distant indeed.

Arms already lost to me, I wasn't able to flail as I was pushed onto a sloping board and positioned with my head lower than my heart. (That's the main point: the angle can be slight or steep.) Then my legs were lashed together so that the board and I were one single and trussed unit. Not to bore you with my phobias, but if I don't have at least two pillows I wake up with acid reflux and mild sleep apnea, so even a merely supine position makes me uneasy. And, to tell you something I had been keeping from myself as well as from my new experimental friends, I do have a fear of drowning that comes from a bad childhood moment on the Isle of Wight, when I got out of my depth. As a boy reading the climactic torture scene of *1984*, where what is in Room 101 is the worst thing in the world, I realize that somewhere in my version of that hideous chamber comes the moment when the wave washes over me. Not that that makes me special: I don't know anyone who *likes* the idea of drowning. As mammals we may have originated in the ocean, but water has many ways of reminding us that when we are in it we are out of our element. In brief, when it comes to breathing, give me good old air every time.

⤜ • ⤛

You may have read by now the official lie about this treatment, which is that it "simulates" the feeling of drowning. This is not the case. You feel that you are drowning because you *are* drowning—or, rather, being drowned, albeit slowly and under controlled conditions and at the mercy (or otherwise) of those who are applying the pressure. The "board" is the instrument, *not* the method. You are not being boarded. You are being watered. This was very rapidly brought home to me when, on top of the hood, which still admitted a few flashes of random and worrying strobe light to my vision, three layers of enveloping towel were added. In this pregnant darkness, head downward, I waited for a while until I abruptly felt a slow cascade of water going up my nose. Determined to resist if only for the honor of my navy ancestors who had so often been in peril on the sea, I held my breath for a while and then had to exhale and—as you might expect—inhale in turn. The inhalation brought the damp cloths tight against my nostrils, as if a huge, wet paw had been suddenly and annihilatingly clamped over my face. Unable to determine whether I was breathing in or out, and flooded more with sheer panic than with mere water, I triggered the pre-arranged signal and felt the unbelievable relief of being pulled upright and having the soaking and stifling layers pulled off me. I find I don't want to tell you how little time I lasted.

This is because I had read that Khalid Sheikh Mohammed, invariably referred to as the "mastermind" of the atrocities of September 11, 2001, had impressed his interrogators by holding out for upwards of two minutes before cracking. (By the way, this story is not confirmed. My North Carolina friends jeered at it. "Hell," said one, "from what I heard they only washed his damn face before he babbled.") But, hell, I thought in my turn, no Hitchens is going to do worse than *that*. Well, O.K., I admit I didn't outdo him. And so then I said, with slightly more bravado than was justified, that I'd like to try it one more time. There was a paramedic present who checked my racing pulse and warned me about adrenaline rush. An interval was ordered, and then I felt the mask come down again. Steeling myself to remember what it had been like last time, and to learn from the previous panic attack, I fought down the first, and some of the second, wave of nausea and terror but soon found that I was an abject prisoner of my gag reflex. The interrogators would hardly have had time to ask me any questions, and I knew that I would quite readily have agreed to supply any answer. I still feel ashamed when I think about it. Also, in case it's of interest, I have since woken up trying to push the bedcovers off my face, and if I do anything that makes me short of breath I find myself clawing at the air with a horrible sensation of smothering and claustrophobia. No doubt this will pass. As if detecting my misery and shame, one of my interrogators comfortingly said, "Any time is a long time when you're breathing water." I could have hugged him for saying so, and just then I was hit with a ghastly sense of the sadomasochistic dimension that underlies the relationship between the torturer and the tortured. I apply the Abraham Lincoln test for moral casuistry: "If slavery is not wrong, nothing is wrong." Well, then, if waterboarding does not constitute torture, then there is no such thing as torture.

I am somewhat proud of my ability to "keep my head," as the saying goes, and to maintain presence of mind under trying circumstances. I was completely convinced that, when the water pressure had become intolerable, I had firmly uttered the pre-determined code word that would cause it to cease. But my interrogator told me that, rather to his surprise, I had not spoken a word. I had activated the "dead man's handle" that signaled the onset of unconsciousness. So now I have to wonder about the role of false memory and delusion. What I do recall clearly, though, is a hard finger feeling for my solar plexus as the water was being poured. What was that for? "That's to find out if you are trying to cheat, and timing your breathing to the doses. If you try that, we can outsmart you. We have all kinds of enhancements." I was briefly embarrassed that I hadn't earned or warranted these refinements, but it hit me yet again that this is certainly the *language* of torture.

Maybe I am being premature in phrasing it thus. Among the veterans there are at least two views on all this, which means in practice that there are two opinions on whether or not "waterboarding" constitutes torture. I have had some extremely serious conversations on the topic, with two groups of highly decent and serious men, and I think that both cases have to be stated at their strongest.

⤛ • ⤜

The team who agreed to give me a hard time in the woods of North Carolina belong to a highly honorable group. This group regards itself as out on the front line in defense of a society that is too spoiled and too ungrateful to appreciate those solid, underpaid volunteers who guard us while we sleep. These heroes stay on the ramparts at all hours and in all weather, and if they make a mistake they may be arraigned in order to scratch some domestic political itch. Faced with appalling enemies who make horror videos of torture and beheadings, they feel that they are the ones who confront denunciation in our press, and possible prosecution. As they have just tried to demonstrate to me, a man who has been waterboarded may well emerge from the experience a bit shaky, but he is in a mood to surrender the relevant information and is unmarked and undamaged and indeed ready for another bout in quite a short time. When contrasted to actual torture, waterboarding is more like foreplay. No thumbscrew, no pincers, no electrodes, no rack. Can one say this of those who have been captured by the tormentors and murderers of (say) Daniel Pearl? On this analysis, any call to indict the United States for torture is therefore a lame and diseased attempt to arrive at a moral equivalence between those who defend civilization and those who exploit its freedoms to hollow it out, and ultimately to bring it down. I myself do not trust anybody who does not clearly understand this viewpoint.

Against it, however, I call as my main witness Mr. Malcolm Nance. Mr. Nance is not what you call a bleeding heart. In fact, speaking of the coronary area, he has said that, in battlefield conditions, he "would personally cut bin Laden's heart out with a plastic M.R.E. spoon." He was to the fore on September 11, 2001, dealing with the burning nightmare in the debris of the Pentagon. He has been involved with the SERE program since 1997. He speaks Arabic and has been on al Qaeda's tail since the early 1990s. His most recent book, *The Terrorists of Iraq*, is a highly potent analysis both of the jihadist threat in Mesopotamia and of the ways in which we have made its life easier. I passed one of the most dramatic evenings of my life listening to his cold but enraged denunciation of the adoption of waterboarding by the United States. The argument goes like this:

1. Waterboarding is a deliberate torture technique and has been prosecuted as such by our judicial arm when perpetrated by others.

2. If we allow it and justify it, we cannot complain if it is employed in the future by other regimes on captive U.S. citizens. It is a method of putting American prisoners in harm's way.

3. It may be a means of extracting information, but it is also a means of extracting junk information. (Mr. Nance told me that he had heard of someone's being compelled to confess that he was a hermaphrodite. I later had

an awful twinge while wondering if I myself could have been "dunked" this far.) To put it briefly, even the C.I.A. sources for the *Washington Post* story on waterboarding conceded that the information they got out of Khalid Sheikh Mohammed was "not all of it reliable." Just put a pencil line under that last phrase, or commit it to memory.

4. It opens a door that cannot be closed. Once you have posed the notorious "ticking bomb" question, and once you assume that you are in the right, what will you *not* do? Waterboarding not getting results fast enough? The terrorist's clock still ticking? Well, then, bring on the thumbscrews and the pincers and the electrodes and the rack.

⤞ • ⤝

Masked by these arguments, there lurks another very penetrating point. Nance doubts very much that Khalid Sheikh Mohammed lasted that long under the water treatment (and I am pathetically pleased to hear it). It's also quite thinkable, *if* he did, that he was trying to attain martyrdom at our hands. But even if he endured so long, and since the United States has in any case bragged that *in fact* he did, one of our worst enemies has now become one of the founders of something that will someday disturb your sleep as well as mine. To quote Nance:

> Torture advocates hide behind the argument that an open discussion about specific American interrogation techniques will aid the enemy. Yet, convicted al Qaeda members and innocent captives who were released to their host nations have already debriefed the world through hundreds of interviews, movies and documentaries on exactly what methods they were subjected to and how they endured. Our own missteps have created a cadre of highly experienced lecturers for al Qaeda's own virtual SERE school for terrorists.

Which returns us to my starting point, about the distinction between training *for* something and training to resist it. One used to be told—and surely with truth—that the lethal fanatics of al Qaeda were schooled to lie, and instructed to claim that they had been tortured and maltreated whether they had been tortured and maltreated or not. Did we notice what a frontier we had crossed when we admitted and even proclaimed that their stories might in fact be true? I had only a very slight encounter on that frontier, but I still wish that my experience were the only way in which the words "waterboard" and "American" could be mentioned in the same (gasping and sobbing) breath.

22

U.S. TORTURE: VOICES FROM THE BLACK SITES

MARK DANNER

The New York Review of Books   April 9, 2009

One of the first things Barack Obama did as president was to declassify a number of documents outlining the detention and interrogation policies of the Bush administration—an act that some conservatives, most notably former Vice President Dick Cheney, have angrily denounced as endangering national security. In this New York Review of Books *article, Mark Danner takes an in-depth look at the recently-released Red Cross report on the techniques used by the CIA in the early part of this decade on suspected terrorists. It's a compelling—and harrowing—account. But Danner also makes an important political argument in this piece and in his follow-up essay in the April 30, 2009, issue of* NYRB: *namely, that the only way to resolve the issue of American-sanctioned torture for future generations is to have a detailed inquiry into exactly what was accomplished by these extralegal methods. "Only a credible investigation into what was done and what information was gained," he writes, "can begin to alter the political calculus around torture by replacing the public's attachment to the ticking bomb with an understanding of what torture is and what is gained, and lost, when the United States reverts to it."*

**ICRC Report on the Treatment of Fourteen
"High Value Detainees" in CIA Custody**
by the International Committee
of the Red Cross
43 pp., February 2007

> *We need to get to the bottom of what happened—and why—so we make
> sure it never happens again.*[1]
>
> —Senator Patrick Leahy, Chairman, Senate Judiciary Committee

1.

We think time and elections will cleanse our fallen world but they will not.
Since November, George W. Bush and his administration have seemed to be
rushing away from us at accelerating speed, a dark comet hurtling toward
the ends of the universe. The phrase "War on Terror"—the signal slogan of
that administration, so cherished by the man who took pride in proclaim-
ing that he was "a wartime president"—has acquired in its pronouncement
a permanent pair of quotation marks, suggesting something questionable,
something mildly embarrassing: something past. And yet the decisions
that that president made, especially the monumental decisions taken after
the attacks of September 11, 2001—decisions about rendition, surveillance,
interrogation—lie strewn about us still, unclaimed and unburied, like
corpses freshly dead.

How should we begin to talk about this? Perhaps with a story. Stories
come to us newborn, announcing their intent: Once upon a time.... In the
beginning.... From such signs we learn how to listen to what will come.
Consider:

> I woke up, naked, strapped to a bed, in a very white room. The room
> measured approximately 4m x 4m [13 feet by 13 feet]. The room
> had three solid walls, with the fourth wall consisting of metal bars
> separating it from a larger room. I am not sure how long I remained
> in the bed....

A man, unnamed, naked, strapped to a bed, and for the rest, the elemental facts of space and of time, nothing but whiteness.

The storyteller is very much a man of our time. Early on in the "War on Terror," in the spring of 2002, he entered the dark realm of "the disappeared"—and only four and a half years later, when he and thirteen other "high-value detainees" arrived at Guantánamo and told their stories in interviews with representatives of the International Committee of the Red Cross (reported in the confidential document listed above) did he emerge partly into the light. Indeed, he is a famous man, though his fame has followed a certain path, peculiar to our modern age: jihadist, outlaw, terrorist, "disappeared." An international celebrity whose name, one of them anyway, is instantly recognizable. How many people have their lives described by the President of the United States in a nationally televised speech?

> Within months of September the 11th, 2001, we captured a man known as Abu Zubaydah. We believe that Zubaydah was a senior terrorist leader and a trusted associate of Osama bin Laden. . . . Zubaydah was severely wounded during the firefight that brought him into custody—and he survived only because of the medical care arranged by the CIA. [2]

A dramatic story: big news. Wounded in a firefight in Faisalabad, Pakistan, shot in the stomach, groin, and thigh after jumping from a roof in a desperate attempt to escape. Massive bleeding. Rushed to a military hospital in Lahore. A trauma surgeon at Johns Hopkins awakened by a late-night telephone call from the director of central intelligence and flown in great secrecy to the other side of the world. The wounded man barely escapes death, slowly stabilizes, is shipped secretly to a military base in Thailand. Thence to another base in Afghanistan. Or was it Afghanistan?

⋘⋆ • ⋆⋙

We don't know, not definitively. For from the moment of his dramatic capture, on March 28, 2002, the man known as Abu Zubaydah slipped from one clandestine world, that of al Qaeda officials gone to ground in the days after September 11, into another, a "hidden global internment network" intended for secret detention and interrogation and set up by the Central Intelligence Agency under authority granted directly by President George W. Bush in a "memorandum of understanding" signed on September 17, 2001.

This secret system included prisons on military bases around the world, from Thailand and Afghanistan to Morocco, Poland, and Romania—"at various times," reportedly, "sites in eight countries"—into which, at one time or another, more than one hundred prisoners . . . disappeared.[3] The secret internment network of "black sites" had its own air force and its own distinctive "transfer procedures," which were, according to the writers of the International Committee of the Red Cross (ICRC) report, "fairly standardised in most cases":

> The detainee would be photographed, both clothed and naked prior to and again after transfer. A body cavity check (rectal examination) would be carried out and some detainees alleged that a suppository (the type and the effect of such suppositories was unknown by the detainees), was also administered at that moment.
>
> The detainee would be made to wear a diaper and dressed in a tracksuit. Earphones would be placed over his ears, through which music would sometimes be played. He would be blindfolded with at least a cloth tied around the head and black goggles. In addition, some detainees alleged that cotton wool was also taped over their eyes prior to the blindfold and goggles being applied. . . .
>
> The detainee would be shackled by [the] hands and feet and transported to the airport by road and loaded onto a plane. He would usually be transported in a reclined sitting position with his hands shackled in front. The journey times . . . ranged from one hour to over twenty-four to thirty hours. The detainee was not allowed to go to the toilet and if necessary was obliged to urinate and defecate into the diaper.

One works the imagination trying to picture what it was like in this otherworldly place: blackness in place of vision. Silence—or "sometimes" loud music—in place of sounds of life. Shackles, together sometimes with gloves, in place of the chance to reach, touch, feel. One senses metal on wrist and ankle, cotton against eyes, cloth across face, shit and piss against skin. On "some occasions detainees were transported lying flat on the floor of the plane . . . with their hands cuffed behind their backs," causing them "severe pain and discomfort," as they were moved from one unknown location to another.

For his part, Abu Zubaydah—thirty-one years old, born Zein al-Abedeen Mohammad Hassan, in Riyadh, Saudi Arabia, though coming of Palestinian stock, from the Gaza Strip—

> alleged that during one transfer operation the blindfold was tied very tightly resulting in wounds to his nose and ears. He does not know how long the transfer took but, prior to the transfer, he reported being told by his detaining authorities that he would be going on a journey that would last twenty-four to thirty hours.

A long trip then: perhaps to Guantánamo? Or Morocco? Then back, apparently, to Thailand. Or was it Afghanistan? He thinks the latter but can't be sure. . . .

2.

All classified, compartmentalized, deeply, deeply secret. And yet what is "secret" exactly? In our recent politics, "secret" has become an oddly complex word. From whom was "the secret bombing of Cambodia" secret? Not from the Cambodians, surely. From whom was the existence of these "secret overseas facilities" secret? Not from the terrorists, surely. From Americans, presumably. On the other hand, as early as 2002, anyone interested could read on the front page of one of the country's leading newspapers:

U.S. Decries Abuse but Defends Interrogations: "Stress and Duress" Tactics Used on Terrorism Suspects Held in Secret Overseas Facilities

> Deep inside the forbidden zone at the U.S.-occupied Bagram air base in Afghanistan, around the corner from the detention center and beyond the segregated clandestine military units, sits a cluster

of metal shipping containers protected by a triple layer of concertina wire. The containers hold the most valuable prizes in the war on terrorism—captured al Qaeda operatives and Taliban commanders....

"If you don't violate someone's human rights some of the time, you probably aren't doing your job," said one official who has supervised the capture and transfer of accused terrorists. "I don't think we want to be promoting a view of zero tolerance on this. That was the whole problem for a long time with the CIA...."

This lengthy article, by Dana Priest and Barton Gellman, appeared in *The Washington Post* on December 26, 2002, only months after the capture of Abu Zubaydah. A similarly lengthy report followed a few months later on the front page of *The New York Times* ("Interrogations: Questioning Terror Suspects in a Dark and Surreal World"). The blithe, aggressive tone of the officials quoted—"We don't kick the [expletive] out of them. We send them to other countries so they can kick the [expletive] out of them"—bespeaks a very different political temper, one in which a prominent writer in a national newsmagazine could headline his weekly column "Time to Think About Torture," noting in his subtitle that in this "new world ... survival might well require old techniques that seemed out of the question."[4]

So there are secrets and secrets. And when, on a bright sunny day two years ago, just before the fifth anniversary of the September 11 attacks, the President of the United States strode into the East Room of the White House and informed the high officials, dignitaries, and specially invited September 11 survivor families gathered in rows before him that the United States government had created a dark and secret universe to hold and interrogate captured terrorists—or, in the president's words, "an environment where they can be held secretly [and] questioned by experts"—he was not telling a secret but instead converting a known and well-reported fact into an officially confirmed truth:

In addition to the terrorists held at Guantánamo, a small number of suspected terrorist leaders and operatives captured during the war have been held and questioned outside the United States, in a separate program operated by the Central Intelligence Agency.... Many specifics of this program, including where these detainees have been held and the details of their confinement, cannot be divulged. . . .

We knew that Abu Zubaydah had more information that could save innocent lives, but he stopped talking. . . . And so the CIA used an alternative set of procedures. These procedures were designed to be safe, to comply with our laws, our Constitution, and our treaty obligations. The Department of Justice reviewed the authorized methods extensively and determined them to be lawful. I cannot describe the specific methods used—I think you understand why. . . .

I was watching the live broadcast that day and I remember the uncanny feeling that came over me as, having heard the president explain the virtues of this "alternative set of procedures," I watched him stare straight into the camera and with fierce concentration and exaggerated emphasis intone once more: "The United States does not torture. It's against our laws, and it's against our values. I have not authorized it—and I will not authorize it." He had convinced himself, I thought, of the truth of what he said.

This speech, though not much noticed at the time, will stand, I believe, as George W. Bush's most important: perhaps the only "historic" speech he ever gave. In telling his version of Abu Zubaydah's story, and versions of the stories of Khaled Shaik Mohammed and others, the president took hold of many things that were already known but not acknowledged and, by means of the alchemical power of the leader's voice, transformed them into acknowledged facts. He also, in his fervent defense of his government's "alternative set of procedures" and his equally fervent denials that they constituted "torture," set out before the country and the world the dark moral epic of the Bush administration, in the coils of whose contradictions we find ourselves entangled still. Later that month, Congress, facing the midterm elections, duly passed the president's Military Commissions Act of 2006, which, among other things, sought to shelter from prosecution those who had applied the "alternative set of procedures" and had done so, said the president, "in a thorough and professional way."

-<- • ->-

At the same time, perhaps unwittingly, President Bush made it possible that day for those on whom the "alternative set of procedures" were performed eventually to speak. Even as the president set out before the country his version of what had happened to Abu Zubaydah and the others and argued for its necessity, he announced that he would bring him and thirteen of his fellow "high-value detainees" out of the dark world of the disappeared and into the light. Or, rather, into the twilight: the fourteen would be transferred to Guantánamo, the main acknowledged offshore prison, where—"as soon as Congress acts to authorize the military commissions I have proposed"— they "can face justice." In the meantime, though, the fourteen would be "held in a high-security facility at Guantánamo" and the International Committee of the Red Cross would be "advised of their detention, and will have the opportunity to meet with them."

A few weeks later, from October 6 to 11 and then from December 4 to 14, 2006, officials of the International Committee of the Red Cross—among whose official and legally recognized duties is to monitor compliance with the Geneva Conventions and to supervise treatment of prisoners of war— traveled to Guantánamo and began interviewing "each of these persons in private" in order to produce a report that would "provide a description of the treatment and material conditions of detention of the fourteen during the period they were held in the CIA detention program," periods ranging "from 16 months to almost four and a half years."

As the ICRC interviewers informed the detainees, their report was not intended to be released to the public but, "to the extent that each detainee agreed for it to be transmitted to the authorities," to be given in strictest secrecy to officials of the government agency that had been in charge of holding them—in this case the Central Intelligence Agency, to whose acting general counsel, John Rizzo, the report was sent on February 14, 2007. Indeed, though almost all of the information in the report has names attached, and though annexes contain extended narratives drawn from interviews with three of the detainees, whose names are used, we do find a number of times in the document variations of this formula: "One of the detainees who did not wish his name to be transmitted to the authorities alleged ..."— suggesting that at least one and perhaps more than one of the fourteen, who are, after all, still "held in a high-security facility at Guantánamo," worried about repercussions that might come from what he had said.

In virtually all such cases, the allegations made are echoed by other, named detainees; indeed, since the detainees were kept "in continuous solitary confinement and incommunicado detention" throughout their time in "the black sites," and were kept strictly separated as well when they reached Guantánamo, the striking similarity in their stories, even down to small details, would seem to make fabrication extremely unlikely, if not impossible. "The ICRC wishes to underscore," as the writers tell us in the introduction, "that the consistency of the detailed allegations provided separately by each of the fourteen adds particular weight to the information provided below."

⤙ • ⤚

The result is a document—labeled "confidential" and clearly intended only for the eyes of those senior American officials to whom the CIA's Mr. Rizzo would show it—that tells a certain kind of story, a narrative of what happened at "the black sites" and a detailed description, by those on whom they were practiced, of what the President of the United States described to Americans as an "alternative set of procedures." It is a document for its time, literally "impossible to put down," from its opening page—

Contents
Introduction
1. Main Elements of the CIA Detention Program
1.1 Arrest and Transfer
1.2 Continuous Solitary Confinement and Incommunicado Detention
1.3 Other Methods of Ill-treatment
    1.3.1 Suffocation by water
    1.3.2 Prolonged Stress Standing
    1.3.3 Beatings by use of a collar
    1.3.4 Beating and kicking
    1.3.5 Confinement in a box
    1.3.6 Prolonged nudity
    1.3.7 Sleep deprivation and use of loud music
    1.3.8 Exposure to cold temperature/cold water
    1.3.9 Prolonged use of handcuffs and shackles
    1.3.10 Threats

1.3.11 Forced shaving

1.3.12 Deprivation/restricted provision of solid food

1.4 Further elements of the detention regime....

—to its stark and unmistakable conclusion:

> The allegations of ill-treatment of the detainees indicate that, in many cases, the ill-treatment to which they were subjected while held in the CIA program, either singly or in combination, constituted torture. In addition, many other elements of the ill-treatment, either singly or in combination, constituted cruel, inhuman or degrading treatment.

Such unflinching clarity, from the body legally charged with overseeing compliance with the Geneva Conventions—in which the terms "torture" and "cruel, inhuman, and degrading treatment" are accorded a strictly defined legal meaning—couldn't be more significant, or indeed more welcome after years in which the President of the United States relied on the power of his office either to redefine or to obfuscate what are relatively simple words. "This debate is occurring," as President Bush told reporters in the Rose Garden the week after he delivered his East Room speech,

> because of the Supreme Court's ruling that said that we must conduct ourselves under the Common Article III of the Geneva Convention. And that Common Article III says that, you know, there will be no outrages upon human dignity. It's like—it's very vague. What does that mean, "outrages upon human dignity"?[5]

In allowing Abu Zubaydah and the other thirteen "high-value detainees" to tell their own stories, this report manages to answer, with great power and authority, the president's question.

3.

We return to a man, Abu Zubaydah, a Palestinian who, in his thirty-one years, has lived a life shaped by conflicts on the edge of the American consciousness: the Gaza Strip, where his parents were born; Riyadh, Saudi Arabia, where he apparently first saw the light of day; Soviet-occupied Afghanistan, where he took part in the jihad against the Russians, perhaps with the help, directly or indirectly, of American dollars; then, post-Soviet Afghanistan, where he ran al Qaeda logistics and recruitment, directing aspiring jihadists to the various training camps, placing them in cells after they'd been trained. The man has been captured now: traced to a safe house in Faisalabad, gravely wounded by three shots from an AK-47. He is rushed to the Faisalabad hospital, then to the military hospital at Lahore. When he opens his eyes he finds at his bedside an American, John Kiriakou of the CIA:

> I asked him in Arabic what his name was. And he shook his head. And I asked him again in Arabic. And then he answered me in English. And he said that he would not speak to me in God's language. And then I said, "That's okay. We know who you are."
>
> And then he asked me to smother him with a pillow. And I said, "No, no. We have plans for you."[6]

Kiriakou and the "small group of CIA and FBI people who just kept 24/7 eyes on him" knew that in Abu Zubaydah they had "the biggest fish that we had caught. We knew he was full of information . . . and we wanted to get it." According to Kiriakou, on a table in the house where they found him, "Abu Zubaydah and two other men were building a bomb. The soldering [iron] was still hot. And they had plans for a school on the table. . . . " The plans, Kiriakou told ABC News correspondent Brian Ross, were for the British school in Lahore. Their prisoner, they knew, was "very current. On top of the current threat information."

With the help of the American trauma surgeon, Abu Zubaydah's captors nursed him back to health. He was moved at least twice, first, reportedly, to Thailand; then, he believes, to Afghanistan, probably Bagram. In a safe house in Thailand the interrogation began:

> I woke up, naked, strapped to a bed, in a very white room. The room measured approximately [13 feet by 13 feet]. The room had three solid walls, with the fourth wall consisting of metal bars separating it from a larger room. I am not sure how long I remained in the bed. After some time, I think it was several days, but can't remember ex-

actly, I was transferred to a chair where I was kept, shackled by [the] hands and feet for what I think was the next 2 to 3 weeks. During this time I developed blisters on the underside of my legs due to the constant sitting. I was only allowed to get up from the chair to go [to] the toilet, which consisted of a bucket. Water for cleaning myself was provided in a plastic bottle.

I was given no solid food during the first two or three weeks, while sitting on the chair. I was only given Ensure [a nutrient supplement] and water to drink. At first the Ensure made me vomit, but this became less with time.

The cell and room were air-conditioned and were very cold. Very loud, shouting type music was constantly playing. It kept repeating about every fifteen minutes twenty-four hours a day. Sometimes the music stopped and was replaced by a loud hissing or crackling noise.

The guards were American, but wore masks to conceal their faces. My interrogators did not wear masks.

During this first two to three week period I was questioned for about one to two hours each day. American interrogators would come to the room and speak to me through the bars of the cell. During the questioning the music was switched off, but was then put back on again afterwards. I could not sleep at all for the first two to three weeks. If I started to fall asleep one of the guards would come and spray water in my face.

A naked man chained in a small, very cold, very white room is for several days strapped to a bed, then for several weeks shackled to a chair, bathed unceasingly in white light, bombarded constantly with loud sound, deprived of food; and whenever, despite cold, light, noise, hunger, the hours and days force his eyelids down, cold water is sprayed in his face to force them up.

≺≺ • ≻≻

One can translate these procedures into terms of art: "Change of Scenery Down." "Removal of Clothing." "Use of Stress Positions." "Dietary Manipulation." "Environmental Manipulation." "Sleep Adjustment." "Isolation."

"Sleep Deprivation." "Use of Noise to Induce Stress." All these terms and many others can be found, for example, in documents associated with the debate about interrogation and "counter-resistance" carried on by Pentagon and Justice Department officials beginning in 2002. Here, however, we find a different standard: the Working Group says, for example, that "Sleep Deprivation" is "not to exceed 4 days in succession," that "Dietary Manipulation" should include "no intended deprivation of food or water," that "removal of clothing," while "creating a feeling of helplessness and dependence," must be "monitored to ensure the environmental conditions are such that this technique does not injure the detainee."[7] Here we are in a different place.

But what place? Abu Zubaydah was not only the "biggest fish that we had caught" but the first big fish. According to Kiriakou, Zubaydah, as he recovered, had "wanted to talk about current events. He told us a couple of times that he had nothing personal against the United States. . . . He said that 9/11 was necessary. That although he didn't think that there would be such a massive loss of life, his view was that 9/11 was supposed to be a wake-up call to the United States."

In those initial weeks of healing, before the white room and the chair and the light, Zubaydah seems to have talked freely with his captors, and during this time, according to news reports, FBI agents began to question him using "standard interview techniques," ensuring that he was bathed and his bandages changed, urging improved medical care, and trying to "convince him they knew details of his activities." (They showed him, for example, a "box of blank audiotapes which they said contained recordings of his phone conversations, but were actually empty.") According to this account, Abu Zubaydah, in the initial days before the white room, "began to provide intelligence insights into al Qaeda."[8]

Or did he? "How Good Is Abu Zubaydah's Information?" asked a *Newsweek* "Web exclusive" on April 27, 2002, less than a month after his capture. The extreme secrecy and isolation in which Abu Zubaydah was being held, at a location unknown to him and to all but a tiny handful of government officials, did not prevent his "information" being leaked from that unknown place directly into the American press—in the cause, apparently, of a bureaucratic struggle between the FBI and the CIA. Even Americans who were not following closely the battling leaks from Zubaydah's interrogation would have found their lives affected, whether they knew it or not, by what was happening in that faraway white room; for about the same time the Bush administration saw fit to issue two "domestic terrorism warnings," derived from Abu Zubaydah's "tips"—about "possible attacks on banks or financial institutions in the Northeastern United States" and possible "attacks on U.S. supermarkets and shopping malls." As *Newsweek* learned from a "senior U.S. official," presumably from the FBI—whose "standard interview techniques" had produced that information and the "domestic terrorism warnings" based on it—the prisoner was "providing detailed information for the 'fight against terrorism.'" At the same time, however, "U.S. intelligence sources"—presumably CIA—"wonder whether he's trying to mislead investigators or frighten the American public."[9]

For his part, John Kiriakou, the CIA man, told ABC News that in those early weeks Zubaydah was "willing to talk about philosophy, [but] he was unwilling to give us any actionable intelligence." The CIA officers had the "sweeping classified directive signed by Mr. Bush," giving them authority to "capture, detain and interrogate terrorism suspects," and Zubaydah was "a test case for an evolving new role, ... in which the agency was to act as jailer and interrogator of terrorism suspects." Eventually a team from the CIA's Counterterrorism Center was "sent in from Langley" and the FBI interrogators were withdrawn.

> We had these trained interrogators who were sent to his location to use the enhanced techniques as necessary to get him to open up, and to report some threat information. . . . These enhanced techniques included everything from what was called an attention shake, where you grab the person by their lapels and shake them, all the way up to the other end, which is waterboarding.

-<- • ->-

They began, apparently, by shackling him to the chair, and applying light, noise, and water to keep him awake. After two or three weeks of this Abu Zubaydah, still naked and shackled, was allowed to lie on the bare floor and to "sleep a little." He was also given solid food—rice—for the first time.

Eventually a doctor, a woman, came and examined him, and "asked why I was still naked." The next day he was "provided with orange clothes to wear." The following day, however, "guards came into my cell. They told me to stand up and raise my arms above my head. They then cut the clothes off of me so that I was again naked and put me back on the chair for several days. I tried to sleep on the chair, but was again kept awake by the guards spraying water in my face."

What follows is a confusing period, in which harsh treatment alternated with more lenient. Zubaydah was mostly naked and cold, "sometimes with the air conditioning adjusted so that, one official said, Mr. Zubaydah seemed to turn blue."[10] Sometimes clothing would be brought, then removed the next day. "When my interrogators had the impression that I was cooperating and providing the information they required, the clothes were given back to me. When they felt I was being less cooperative the clothes were again removed and I was again put back on the chair." At one point he was supplied with a mattress, at another he was "allowed some tissue paper to use when going to toilet on the bucket." A month passed with no questioning. "My cell was still very cold and the loud music no longer played but there was a constant loud hissing or crackling noise, which played twenty-four hours a day. I tried to block out the noise by putting tissue in my ears." Then, "about two and half or three months after I arrived in this place, the interrogation began again, but with more intensity than before."

It is difficult to know whether these alterations in attitude and procedure were intended, meant to keep the detainee off-guard, or resulted from disputes about strategy among the interrogators, who were relying on a hastily assembled "alternative set of procedures" that had been improvised from various sources, including scientists and psychiatrists within the intelligence community, experts from other, "friendly" governments, and consultants who had worked with the U.S. military and now "reverse-engineered" the resistance training taught to American elite forces to help them withstand interrogation after capture. The forerunners of some of the theories being applied in these interrogations, involving sensory deprivation, disorientation, guilt and shame, so-called "learned helplessness," and the need to induce "the debility-dependence-dread state," can be found in CIA documents dating back nearly a half-century, such as this from a notorious "counterintelligence interrogation" manual of the early 1960s:

> The circumstances of detention are arranged to enhance within the
> subject his feelings of being cut off from the known and the reas-
> suring, and of being plunged into the strange. . . . Control of the
> source's environment permits the interrogator to determine his diet,
> sleep pattern and other fundamentals. Manipulating these into ir-
> regularities, so that the subject becomes disorientated, is very likely
> to create feelings of fear and helplessness.[11]

A later version of the same manual emphasizes the importance of guilt:
"If the 'questioner' can intensify these guilt feelings, it will increase the subject's anxiety and his urge to cooperate as a means of escape." Isolation and
sensory deprivation will "induce regression" and the "loss of those defenses
most recently acquired by civilized man," while the imposition of "stress
positions" that in effect force the subject "to harm himself" will produce a
guilt leading to an irresistible desire to cooperate with his interrogators.

4.

Two and a half months after Abu Zubaydah woke up strapped to a bed in the
white room, the interrogation resumed "with more intensity than before":

> Two black wooden boxes were brought into the room outside my
> cell. One was tall, slightly higher than me and narrow. Measuring
> perhaps in area [3 1/2 by 2 1/2 feet by 6 1/2 feet high]. The other
> was shorter, perhaps only [3 1/2 feet] in height. I was taken out of my
> cell and one of the interrogators wrapped a towel around my neck,
> they then used it to swing me around and smash me repeatedly
> against the hard walls of the room. I was also repeatedly slapped in
> the face. . . .
>
> I was then put into the tall black box for what I think was about
> one and a half to two hours. The box was totally black on the inside
> as well as the outside. . . . They put a cloth or cover over the outside
> of the box to cut out the light and restrict my air supply. It was diffi-
> cult to breathe. When I was let out of the box I saw that one of the
> walls of the room had been covered with plywood sheeting. From
> now on it was against this wall that I was then smashed with the

towel around my neck. I think that the plywood was put there to provide some absorption of the impact of my body. The interrogators
realized that smashing me against the hard wall would probably
quickly result in physical injury.

One is reminded here that Abu Zubaydah was not alone with his interrogators, that everyone in that white room—guards, interrogators, doctor—
was in fact linked directly, and almost constantly, to senior intelligence
officials on the other side of the world. "It wasn't up to individual interrogators to decide, 'Well, I'm gonna slap him. Or I'm going to shake him.
Or I'm gonna make him stay up for 48 hours,'" said John Kiriakou.

> Each one of these steps . . . had to have the approval of the Deputy
> Director for Operations. So before you laid a hand on him, you had
> to send in the cable saying, "He's uncooperative. Request permission
> to do X." And that permission would come. . . . The cable traffic back
> and forth was extremely specific. And the bottom line was these
> were very unusual authorities that the agency got after 9/11. No one
> wanted to mess them up. No one wanted to get in trouble by going
> overboard. . . . No one wanted to be the guy who accidentally did
> lasting damage to a prisoner.

Smashing against hard walls before Zubaydah enters the tall black coffin-
like box; sudden appearance of plywood sheeting affixed to the wall for him
to be smashed against when he emerges. Perhaps the deputy director of operations, pondering the matter in his Langley, Virginia, office, suggested the
plywood?

Or perhaps it was someone higher up? Shortly after Abu Zubaydah was
captured, according to ABC News, CIA officers "briefed high-level officials
in the National Security Council's Principals Committee," including Vice
President Dick Cheney, National Security Adviser Condoleezza Rice, and
Attorney General John Ashcroft, who "then signed off on the [interroga-
tion] plan." At the time, the spring and summer of 2002, the administration
was devising what some referred to as a "golden shield" from the Justice
Department—the legal rationale that was embodied in the infamous "torture memorandum," written by John Yoo and signed by Jay Bybee in August

2002, which claimed that for an "alternative procedure" to be considered torture, and thus illegal, it would have to cause pain of the sort "that would be associated with serious physical injury so severe that death, organ failure, or permanent damage resulting in a loss of significant body function will likely result." The "golden shield" presumably would protect CIA officers from prosecution. Still, Director of Central Intelligence George Tenet regularly brought directly to the attention of the highest officials of the government specific procedures to be used on specific detainees—"whether they would be slapped, pushed, deprived of sleep or subject to simulated drowning"—in order to seek reassurance that they were legal. According to the ABC report, the briefings of principals were so detailed and frequent that "some of the interrogation sessions were almost choreographed." At one such meeting, John Ashcroft, then attorney general, reportedly demanded of his colleagues, "Why are we talking about this in the White House? History will not judge this kindly."[12]

⤙ • ⤚

We do not know if the plywood appeared in Zubaydah's white room thanks to orders from his interrogators, from their bosses at Langley, or perhaps from their superiors in the White House. We don't know the precise parts played by those responsible for "choreographing" the "alternative set of procedures." We do know from several reports that at a White House meeting in July 2002 top administration lawyers gave the CIA "the green light" to move to the "more aggressive techniques" that were applied to him, separately and in combination, during the following days:

> After the beating I was then placed in the small box. They placed a cloth or cover over the box to cut out all light and restrict my air supply. As it was not high enough even to sit upright, I had to crouch down. It was very difficult because of my wounds. The stress on my legs held in this position meant my wounds both in the leg and stomach became very painful. I think this occurred about 3 months after my last operation. It was always cold in the room, but when the cover was placed over the box it made it hot and sweaty inside. The wound on my leg began to open and started to bleed. I don't

know how long I remained in the small box, I think I may have slept or maybe fainted.

I was then dragged from the small box, unable to walk properly and put on what looked like a hospital bed, and strapped down very tightly with belts. A black cloth was then placed over my face and the interrogators used a mineral water bottle to pour water on the cloth so that I could not breathe. After a few minutes the cloth was removed and the bed was rotated into an upright position. The pressure of the straps on my wounds was very painful. I vomited. The bed was then again lowered to horizontal position and the same torture carried out again with the black cloth over my face and water poured on from a bottle. On this occasion my head was in a more backward, downwards position and the water was poured on for a longer time. I struggled against the straps, trying to breathe, but it was hopeless. I thought I was going to die. I lost control of my urine. Since then I still lose control of my urine when under stress.

I was then placed again in the tall box. While I was inside the box loud music was played again and somebody kept banging repeatedly on the box from the outside. I tried to sit down on the floor, but because of the small space the bucket with urine tipped over and spilt over me. . . . I was then taken out and again a towel was wrapped around my neck and I was smashed into the wall with the plywood covering and repeatedly slapped in the face by the same two interrogators as before.

I was then made to sit on the floor with a black hood over my head until the next session of torture began. The room was always kept very cold.

This went on for approximately one week. During this time the whole procedure was repeated five times. On each occasion, apart from one, I was suffocated once or twice and was put in the vertical position on the bed in between. On one occasion the suffocation was repeated three times. I vomited each time I was put in the vertical position between the suffocation.

During that week I was not given any solid food. I was only given Ensure to drink. My head and beard were shaved every day.

I collapsed and lost consciousness on several occasions. Eventually the torture was stopped by the intervention of the doctor.

I was told during this period that I was one of the first to receive these interrogation techniques, so no rules applied. It felt like they were experimenting and trying out techniques to be used later on other people.

5.

All evidence from the ICRC report suggests that Abu Zubaydah's informant was telling him the truth: he was the first, and, as such, a guinea pig. Some techniques are discarded. The coffin-like black boxes, for example, barely large enough to contain a man, one six feet tall and the other scarcely more than three feet, which seem to recall the sensory-deprivation tanks used in early CIA-sponsored experiments, do not reappear. Neither does the "long-time sitting"—the weeks shackled to a chair—that Abu Zubaydah endured in his first few months.

Nudity, on the other hand, is a constant in the ICRC report, as are permanent shackling, the "cold cell," and the unceasing loud music or noise. Sometimes there is twenty-four-hour light, sometimes constant darkness. Beatings, also, and smashing against the walls seem to be favored procedures; often, the interrogators wear gloves.

In later interrogations new techniques emerge, of which "long-time standing" and the use of cold water are notable. Walid Bin Attash, a Yemeni national involved with planning the attacks on the U.S. embassies in Africa in 1998 and on the USS *Cole* in 2000, was captured in Karachi on April 29, 2003:

> On arrival at the place of detention in Afghanistan I was stripped naked. I remained naked for the next two weeks. I was put in a cell measuring approximately [3 1/2 by 6 1/2 feet]. I was kept in a standing position, feet flat on the floor, but with my arms above my head and fixed with handcuffs and a chain to a metal bar running across the width of the cell. The cell was dark with no light, artificial or natural.
>
> During the first two weeks I did not receive any food. I was only given Ensure and water to drink. A guard would come and hold the

bottle for me while I drank.... The toilet consisted of a bucket in the cell.... I was not allowed to clean myself after using the bucket. Loud music was playing twenty-four hours each day throughout the three weeks I was there.

This "forced standing," with arms shackled above the head, a favorite Soviet technique (*stoika*) that seems to have become standard procedure after Abu Zubaydah, proved especially painful for Bin Attash, who had lost a leg fighting in Afghanistan:

> After some time being held in this position my stump began to hurt so I removed my artificial leg to relieve the pain. Of course my good leg then began to ache and soon started to give way so that I was left hanging with all my weight on my wrists. I shouted for help but at first nobody came. Finally, after about one hour a guard came and my artificial leg was given back to me and I was again placed in the standing position with my hands above my head. After that the interrogators sometimes deliberately removed my artificial leg in order to add extra stress to the position....

By his account, Bin Attash was kept in this position for two weeks—"apart [from] two or three times when I was allowed to lie down." Though "the methods used were specifically designed not to leave marks," the cuffs eventually "cut into my wrists and made wounds. When this happened the doctor would be called." At a second location, where Bin Attash was again stripped naked and placed "in a standing position with my arms above my head and fixed with handcuffs and a chain to a metal ring in the ceiling," a doctor examined his lower leg every day—"using a tape measure for signs of swelling."

> I do not remember for exactly how many days I was kept standing, but I think it was about ten days.... During the standing I was made to wear a diaper. However, on some occasions the diaper was not replaced and so I had to urinate and defecate over myself. I was washed down with cold water everyday.

Cold water was used on Bin Attash in combination with beatings and the use of a plastic collar, which seems to have been a refinement of the towel that had been looped around Abu Zubaydah's neck:

> Every day for the first two weeks I was subjected to slaps to my face and punches to my body during interrogation. This was done by one interrogator wearing gloves....
>
> Also on a daily basis during the first two weeks a collar was looped around my neck and then used to slam me against the walls of the interrogation room. It was also placed around my neck when being taken out of my cell for interrogation and was used to lead me along the corridor. It was also used to slam me against the walls of the corridor during such movements.
>
> Also on a daily basis during the first two weeks I was made to lie on a plastic sheet placed on the floor which would then be lifted at the edges. Cold water was then poured onto my body with buckets.... I would be kept wrapped inside the sheet with the cold water for several minutes. I would then be taken for interrogation....

Bin Attash notes that in the "second place of detention"—where he was put in the diaper—"they were rather more sophisticated than in Afghanistan because they had a hose-pipe with which to pour the water over me."

6.

A clear method emerges from these accounts, based on forced nudity, isolation, bombardment with noise and light, deprivation of sleep and food, and repeated beatings and "smashings"—though from this basic model one can see the method evolve, from forced sitting to forced standing, for example, and acquire new elements, like immersion in cold water.

Khaled Shaik Mohammed, the key planner of the September 11 attacks who was captured in Rawalpindi on March 1, 2003—nine of the fourteen "high-value detainees" were apprehended in Pakistan—and, after a two-day detention in Pakistan during which he alleges that a "CIA agent ... punched him several times in the stomach, chest and face [and] ... threw him on the floor and trod on his face," was sent to Afghanistan using the standard "transfer procedures." ("My eyes were covered with a cloth tied around my head and with a cloth bag pulled over it. A suppository was inserted into my rectum. I was not told what the suppository was for.") In Afghanistan, he was stripped and placed in a small cell, where he "was kept in a standing position with my hands cuffed and chained to a bar above my head. My feet were flat on the floor." After about an hour,

> I was taken to another room where I was made to stand on tiptoes for about two hours during questioning. Approximately thirteen persons were in the room. These included the head interrogator (a man) and two female interrogators, plus about ten muscle guys wearing masks. I think they were all Americans. From time to time one of the muscle guys would punch me in the chest and stomach.

These "full-dress" interrogations—where the detainee stands naked, on tiptoe, amid a crowd of thirteen people, including "ten muscle guys wearing masks"—were periodically interrupted by the detainee's removal to a separate room for additional procedures:

> Here cold water from buckets was thrown onto me for about forty minutes. Not constantly as it took time to refill the buckets. After which I would be taken back to the interrogation room.
>
> On one occasion during the interrogation I was offered water to drink, when I refused I was again taken to another room where I was made to lie [on] the floor with three persons holding me down. A tube was inserted into my anus and water poured inside. Afterwards I wanted to go to the toilet as I had a feeling as if I had diarrhoea. No toilet access was provided until four hours later when I was given a bucket to use.
>
> Whenever I was returned to my cell I was always kept in the standing position with my hands cuffed and chained to a bar above my head.

❮❮ • ❯❯

After three days in what he believes was Afghanistan, Mohammed was again dressed in a tracksuit, blindfold, hood, and headphones, and shackled and placed aboard a plane "sitting, leaning back, with my hands and ankles shackled in a high chair." He quickly fell asleep—"the first proper sleep in over five days"—and remains unsure of how long the journey took. On arrival, however, he realized he had come a long way:

> I could see at one point there was snow on the ground. Everybody was wearing black, with masks and army boots, like Planet-X people. I think the country was Poland. I think this because on one occasion a water bottle was brought to me without the label removed. It had [an] e-mail address ending in ".pl."

He was stripped and put in a small cell "with cameras where I was later informed by an interrogator that I was monitored 24 hours a day by a doctor, psychologist and interrogator." He believes the cell was underground because one had to descend steps to reach it. Its walls were of wood and it measured about ten by thirteen feet.

It was in this place, according to Mohammed, that "the most intense interrogation occurred, led by three experienced CIA interrogators, all over 65 years old and all strong and well trained." They informed him that they had received the "green light from Washington" to give him "*a hard time.*" "They never used the word 'torture' and never referred to 'physical pressure,' only to '*a hard time.*' I was never threatened with death, in fact I was told that they would not allow me to die, but that I would be brought to the '*verge of death and back again.*'"

> I was kept for one month in the cell in a standing position with my hands cuffed and shackled above my head and my feet cuffed and shackled to a point in the floor. Of course during this month I fell asleep on some occasions while still being held in this position. This resulted in all my weight being applied to the handcuffs around my wrist resulting in open and bleeding wounds. [Scars consistent with this allegation were visible on both wrists as well as on both ankles.] Both my feet became very swollen after one month of almost continual standing.[13]

For interrogation, Mohammed was taken to a different room. The sessions last for as long as eight hours and as short as four.

> The number of people present varied greatly from one day to another. Other interrogators, including women, were also sometimes present.... A doctor was usually also present. If I was perceived not to be cooperating I would be put against a wall and punched and slapped in the body, head and face. A thick flexible plastic collar would also be placed around my neck so that it could then be held at the two ends by a guard who would use it to slam me repeatedly against the wall. The beatings were combined with the use of cold water, which was poured over me using a hose-pipe. The beatings and use of cold water occurred on a daily basis during the first month.

⤛ • ⤜

Like Abu Zubaydah; like Abdelrahim Hussein Abdul Nashiri, a Saudi who was captured in Dubai in October 2002, Mohammed was also subjected to waterboarding, by his account on five occasions:

> I would be strapped to a special bed, which could be rotated into a vertical position. A cloth would be placed over my face. Cold water from a bottle that had been kept in a fridge was then poured onto the cloth by one of the guards so that I could not breathe.... The cloth was then removed and the bed was put into a vertical position. The whole process was then repeated during about one hour. Injuries to my ankles and wrists also occurred during the waterboarding as I struggled in the panic of not being able to breathe. Female interrogators were also present ... and a doctor was always present, standing out of sight behind the head of [the] bed, but I saw him when he came to fix a clip to my finger which was connected to a machine. I think it was to measure my pulse and oxygen content in my blood. So they could take me to [the] breaking point.

As with Zubaydah, the harshest sessions of interrogation involved the "alternative set of procedures" used in sequence and in combination, one technique intensifying the effects of the others:

> The beatings became worse and I had cold water directed at me from a hose-pipe by guards while I was still in my cell. The worst day was when I was beaten for about half an hour by one of the interrogators. My head was banged against the wall so hard that it started to bleed. Cold water was poured over my head. This was then repeated with other interrogators. Finally I was taken for a session of water boarding. The torture on that day was finally stopped by the intervention of the doctor. I was allowed to sleep for about one hour and then put back in my cell standing with my hands shackled above my head.

Reading the ICRC report, one becomes eventually somewhat inured to the "alternative set of procedures" as they are described: the cold and repeated violence grows numbing. Against this background, the descriptions of daily life of the detainees in the black sites, in which interrogation seems merely a periodic heightening of consistently imposed brutality, become more striking. Here again is Mohammed:

> After each session of torture I was put into a cell where I was allowed to lie on the floor and could sleep for a few minutes. However, due to shackles on my ankles and wrists I was never able to sleep very well. . . . The toilet consisted of a bucket in the cell, which I could use on request [he was shackled standing, his hands affixed to the ceiling], but I was not allowed to clean myself after toilet during the first month. . . . During the first month I was not provided with any food apart from on two occasions as a reward for perceived cooperation. I was given Ensure to drink every 4 hours. If I refused to drink then my mouth was forced open by the guard and it was poured down my throat by force. . . . At the time of my arrest I weighed 78kg. After one month in detention I weighed 60kg.
>
> I wasn't given any clothes for the first month. Artificial light was on 24 hours a day, but I never saw sunlight.

7.

> *Q:* Mr. President, . . . this is a moral question: Is torture ever justified?
>
> *President George W. Bush:* Look, I'm going to say it one more time. . . . Maybe I can be more clear. The instructions went out to our people to adhere to law. That ought to comfort you. We're a nation of law. We adhere to laws. We have laws on the books. You might look at these laws, and that might provide comfort for you.
>
> —Sea Island, Georgia, June 10, 2004

Abu Zubaydah, Walid Bin Attash, Khaled Shaik Mohammed—these men almost certainly have blood on their hands, a great deal of blood. There is strong reason to believe that they had critical parts in planning and organizing terrorist operations that caused the deaths of thousands of people. So in all likelihood did the other twelve "high-value detainees" whose treatment while secretly confined by agents of the U.S. government is described with such gruesome particularity in the report of the International Committee of the Red Cross. From everything we know, many or all of these men deserve to be tried and punished—to be "brought to justice," as President Bush, in his speech to the American people on September 6, 2006, vowed they would be.

It seems unlikely that they will be brought to justice anytime soon. In mid-January, Susan J. Crawford, who had been appointed by the Bush administration to decide which Guantánamo detainees should be tried before military commissions, declined to refer to trial Mohammed al-Qahtani, who was to have been among the September 11 hijackers but who had been turned back by immigration officials at Orlando International Airport. After he was captured in Afghanistan in late 2002, Qahtani was imprisoned in Guantánamo and interrogated by Department of Defense intelligence officers. Crawford, a retired judge and former general counsel of the army, told *The Washington Post* that she had concluded that Qahtani's "treatment met the legal definition of torture."

> The techniques they used were all authorized, but the manner in which they applied them was overly aggressive and too persistent. . . .

You think of torture, you think of some horrendous physical act done to an individual. This was not any one particular act; this was just a combination of things that had a medical impact on him, that hurt his health. It was abusive and uncalled for. And coercive. Clearly coercive. [14]

Qahtani's interrogation at Guantánamo, accounts of which have appeared in *Time* and *The Washington Post*, was intense and prolonged, stretching for fifty consecutive days beginning in the late fall of 2002, and led to his hospitalization on at least two occasions. Some of the techniques used, including longtime sitting in restraints, prolonged exposure to cold, loud music, and noise, and sleep deprivation, recall those described in the ICRC report. If the "coercive" and "abusive" interrogation of Qahtani makes trying him impossible, one may doubt that any of the fourteen "high-value detainees" whose accounts are given in this report will ever be tried and sentenced in an internationally recognized and sanctioned legal proceeding.

◅─ • ─▻

In the case of men who have committed great crimes, this seems to mark perhaps the most important and consequential sense in which "torture doesn't work." The use of torture deprives the society whose laws have been so egregiously violated of the possibility of rendering justice. Torture destroys justice. Torture in effect relinquishes this sacred right in exchange for speculative benefits whose value is, at the least, much disputed. John Kiriakou, the CIA officer who witnessed part of Zubaydah's interrogation, described to Brian Ross of ABC News what happened after Zubaydah was waterboarded:

He resisted. He was able to withstand the water boarding for quite some time. And by that I mean probably 30, 35 seconds. . . . And a short time afterwards, in the next day or so, he told his interrogator that Allah had visited him in his cell during the night and told him to cooperate because his cooperation would make it easier on the other brothers who had been captured. And from that day on he answered every question just like I'm sitting here speaking to you. . . .

The threat information that he provided disrupted a number of attacks, maybe dozens of attacks.

This claim, echoed by President Bush in his speech, is a matter of fierce
dispute. Bush's public version, indeed, was much more carefully circumscribed:
among other things, that Zubaydah's information confirmed the alias
("Muktar") of Khaled Shaik Mohammed, and thus helped lead to his capture; that it helped lead, indirectly, to the capture of Ramzi bin al-Shibh, a
Yemeni who was another key figure in planning the September 11 attacks;
and that it "helped us stop another planned attack within the United States."

At least some of this information, apparently, came during the early, non-
coercive interrogation led by FBI agents. Later, according to the reporter
Ron Suskind, Zubaydah

> named countless targets inside the U.S. to stop the pain, all of them
> immaterial. Indeed, think back to the sudden slew of alerts in the
> spring and summer of 2002 about attacks on apartment buildings,
> banks, shopping malls and, of course, nuclear plants.

Suskind is only the most prominent of a number of reporters with strong
sources in the intelligence community who argue that the importance of
the intelligence Zubaydah supplied, and indeed his importance within al
Qaeda, have been grossly and systematically exaggerated by government
officials, from President Bush on down.[15]

Though it seems highly unlikely that Zubaydah's information stopped
"maybe dozens of attacks," as Kiriakou said, the plain fact is that it is impossible, until a thorough investigation can be undertaken of the interrogations, to evaluate fully and fairly what intelligence the United States
actually received in return for all the severe costs, practical, political, legal,
and moral, the country incurred by instituting a policy of torture. There is
a sense in which the entire debate over what Zubaydah did or did not provide, and the attacks the information might or might not have prevented—
a debate driven largely by leaks by fiercely self-interested parties—itself
reflects an unvoiced acceptance, on both sides, of the centrality of the myth-
ical "ticking-bomb scenario" so beloved of those who argue that torture is
necessary, and so prized by the writers of television dramas like *24*. That is,

the argument centers on whether Zubaydah's interrogation directly "disrupted a number of attacks."

◄ • ►►

Perhaps unwittingly, Kiriakou is most revealing about the intelligence value of interrogation of "high-value detainees" when he discusses what the CIA actually got from Zubaydah:

> What he was able to provide was information on the al-Qaeda leadership. For example, if bin Laden were to do X, who would be the person to undertake such and such an operation? "Oh, logically that would be Mr. Y." And we were able to use that information to kind of get an idea of how al-Qaeda operated, how it came about conceptualizing its operations, and how it went about tasking different cells with carrying out operations. . . . His value was, it allowed us to have somebody who we could pass ideas onto for his comments or analysis.

This has the ring of truth, for this is how intelligence works—by the patient accruing of individual pieces of information, by building a picture that will help officers make sense of the other intelligence they receive. Could such "comments or analysis" from a high al Qaeda operative eventually help lead to the disruption of "a number of attacks, maybe dozens of attacks"? It seems possible—but if it did, the chain of cause and effect might not be direct, certainly not nearly so direct as the dramatic scenarios in newspapers and television dramas—and presidential speeches—suggest. The ticking bomb, about to explode and kill thousands or millions; the evil captured terrorist who alone has the information to find and disarm it; the desperate intelligence operative, forced to do whatever is necessary to gain that information—all these elements are well known and emotionally powerful, but where they appear most frequently is in popular entertainment, not in white rooms in Afghanistan.

There is a reverse side, of course, to the "ticking bomb" and torture: pain and ill-treatment, by creating an unbearable pressure on the detainee to say something, anything, to make the pain stop, increase the likelihood that he will fabricate stories, and waste time, or worse. At least some of the intelligence that came of the "alternative set of procedures," like Zubaydah's supposed "information" about attacks on shopping malls and banks, seems to have led the U.S. government to issue what turned out to be baseless warnings to Americans. Khaled Shaik Mohammed asserted this directly in his interviews with the ICRC. "During the harshest period of my interrogation," he said,

> I gave a lot of false information in order to satisfy what I believed the interrogators wished to hear in order to make the ill-treatment stop.... I'm sure that the false information I was forced to invent... wasted a lot of their time and led to several false red-alerts being placed in the U.S.

For all the talk of ticking bombs, very rarely, if ever, have officials been able to point to information gained by interrogating prisoners with "enhanced techniques" that enabled them to prevent an attack that had reached its "operational stage" (that is, had gone beyond reconnoitering and planning). Still, widespread perception that such techniques have prevented attacks, actively encouraged by the president and other officials, has been politically essential in letting the administration carry on with these policies after they had largely become public. Polls tend to show that a majority of Americans are willing to support torture only when they are assured that it will "thwart a terrorist attack." Because of the political persuasiveness of such scenarios it is vital that a future inquiry truly investigate claims that attacks have been prevented.

⤛ • ⤜

As I write, it is impossible to know what benefits—in intelligence, in national security, in disrupting al Qaeda—the president's approval of use of an "alternative set of procedures" might have brought to the United States. What we can say definitively is that the decision has harmed American interests in quite demonstrable ways. Some are practical and specific: for example, FBI agents, many of them professionals with great experience and skill in interrogation, were withdrawn, apparently after objections by the bureau's leaders, when it was decided to use the "alternative set of procedures" on Abu Zubaydah. Extensive leaks to the press, from both officials supportive of and critical of the "alternative set of procedures," undermined what was supposed to be a highly secret program; those leaks, in large part a product of the great controversy the program provoked within the national security bureaucracy, eventually helped make it unsustainable.

Finally, this bureaucratic weakness led officials of the CIA to destroy, apparently out of fear of eventual exposure and possible prosecution, a trove of as many as ninety-two video recordings that had been made of the interrogations, all but two of them of Abu Zubaydah. Whether or not the prosecutor investigating those actions determines that they were illegal, it is hard to believe that the recordings did not include valuable intelligence, which was sacrificed, in effect, for political reasons. These recordings doubtless could have played a critical part as well in the effort to determine what benefits, if any, the program brought to the security of the United States.

⤙ • ⤚

Far and away the greatest damage, though, was legal, moral, and political. In the wake of the ICRC report one can make several definitive statements:

1. Beginning in the spring of 2002 the United States government began to torture prisoners. This torture, approved by the President of the United States and monitored in its daily unfolding by senior officials, including the nation's highest law enforcement officer, clearly violated major treaty obligations of the United States, including the Geneva Conventions and the Convention Against Torture, as well as U.S. law.

2. The most senior officers of the U.S. government, President George W. Bush first among them, repeatedly and explicitly lied about this, both in reports to international institutions and directly to the public. The president lied about it in news conferences, interviews, and, most explicitly, in speeches expressly intended to set out the administration's policy on interrogation before the people who had elected him.

3. The U.S. Congress, already in possession of a great deal of information about the torture conducted by the administration—which had been covered widely in the press, and had been briefed, at least in part, from the outset to a select few of its members—passed the Military Commissions Act of

2006 and in so doing attempted to protect those responsible from criminal penalty under the War Crimes Act.

4. Democrats, who could have filibustered the bill, declined to do so—a decision that had much to do with the proximity of the midterm elections, in the run-up to which, they feared, the president and his Republican allies might gain advantage by accusing them of "coddling terrorists." One senator summarized the politics of the Military Commissions Act with admirable forthrightness:

> Soon, we will adjourn for the fall, and the campaigning will begin in earnest. And there will be 30-second attack ads and negative mail pieces, and we will be criticized as caring more about the rights of terrorists than the protection of Americans. And I know that the vote before us was specifically designed and timed to add more fuel to that fire. [16]

Senator Barack Obama was only saying aloud what every other legislator knew: that for all the horrified and gruesome exposés, for all the leaked photographs and documents and horrific testimony, when it came to torture in the September 11 era, the raw politics cut in the other direction. Most politicians remain convinced that still fearful Americans—given the choice between the image of *24*'s Jack Bauer, a latter-day Dirty Harry, fantasy symbol of untrammeled power doing "everything it takes" to protect them from that ticking bomb, and the image of weak liberals "reading Miranda rights to terrorists"—will choose Bauer every time. As Senator Obama said, after the bill he voted against had passed, "politics won today."

5. The political damage to the United States' reputation, and to the "soft power" of its constitutional and democratic ideals, has been, though difficult to quantify, vast and enduring. In a war that is essentially an insurgency fought on a worldwide scale—which is to say, a political war, in which the attitudes and allegiances of young Muslims are the critical target of opportunity—the United States' decision to use torture has resulted in an enormous self-administered defeat, undermining liberal sympathizers of the United States and convincing others that the country is exactly as its enemies paint it: a ruthless imperial power determined to suppress and

abuse Muslims. By choosing to torture, we freely chose to become the caricature they made of us.

8.

In the wake of the attacks of September 11, 2001, Cofer Black, the former head of the CIA's Counterterrorism Center and a famously colorful hardliner, appeared before the Senate Intelligence Committee and made the most telling pronouncement of the era: "All I want to say is that there was 'before' 9/11 and 'after' 9/11. After 9/11 the gloves come off." In the days after the attacks this phrase was everywhere. Columnists quoted it, television commentators flaunted it, interrogators at Abu Ghraib used it in their cables. ("The gloves are coming off gentlemen regarding these detainees, Col Boltz has made it clear that we want these individuals broken.")[17]

The gloves came off: four simple words. And yet they express a complicated thought. For if the gloves must come off, that means that before the attacks the gloves were on. There is something implicitly exculpatory in the image, something that made it particularly appealing to officials of an administration that endured, on its watch, the most lethal terrorist attack in the country's history. If the attack succeeded, it must have had to do not with the fact that intelligence was not passed on or that warnings were not heeded or that senior officials did not focus on terrorism as a leading threat. It must have been, at least in part, because the gloves were on—because the post-Watergate reforms of the 1970s, in which Congress sought to put limits on the CIA, on its freedom to mount covert actions with "deniability" and to conduct surveillance at home and abroad, had illegitimately circumscribed the president's power and thereby put the country dangerously at risk. It is no accident that two of the administration's most powerful officials, Dick Cheney and Donald Rumsfeld, served as young men in very senior positions in the Nixon and Ford administrations. They had witnessed firsthand the gloves going on and, in the weeks after the September 11 attacks, they argued powerfully that it was those limitations—and, it was implied, not a failure to heed warnings— that had helped lead, however indirectly, to the country's vulnerability to attack.

And so, after a devastating and unprecedented attack, the gloves came off. Guided by the president and his closest advisers, the United States transformed itself from a country that, officially at least, condemned torture to a country that practiced it. And this fateful decision, however much we may want it to, will not go away, any more than the fourteen "high-value detainees," tortured and thus unprosecutable, will go away. Like the grotesque stories in the ICRC report, the decision sits before us, a toxic fact, polluting our political and moral life.

≺≺∙ ≻≻

Since the inauguration of President Obama, the previous administration's "alternative procedures" have acquired a prominence in the press, particularly on cable television, that they rarely achieved when they were actually being practiced on detainees. This is especially the case with waterboarding, which according to the former director of the CIA has not been used since 2003. On his first day in office, President Obama issued executive orders that stopped the use of these techniques and provided for task forces to study U.S. government policies on rendition, detention, and interrogation, among others.

Meantime, Democratic leaders in Congress, who have been in control since 2006, have at last embarked on serious investigations. Senators Dianne Feinstein and Christopher Bond, the chair and ranking member of the Intelligence Committee, have announced a "review of the CIA's detention and interrogation program," which would study, among other questions, "how the CIA created, operated, and maintained its detention and interrogation program," make "an evaluation of intelligence information gained through the use of enhanced and standard interrogation techniques," and investigate "whether the CIA accurately described the detention and interrogation program to other parts of the US government"—including, notably, "the Senate Intelligence Committee." The hearings, according to reports, are unlikely to be public.

In February, Senator Patrick Leahy, chairman of the Judiciary Committee, called for the establishment of what he calls a "nonpartisan commission of inquiry," better known as a "Truth and Reconciliation Committee," to investigate "how our detention policies and practices, from Guantánamo to Abu Ghraib, have seriously eroded fundamental American principles of the rule of law." Since Senator Leahy's commission is intended above all to investigate and make public what was done—"in order to restore our moral leadership," as he said, "we must acknowledge what was done in our name"—he would offer grants of immunity to public officials in exchange for their truthful testimony. He seeks not prosecution and justice but knowledge and exposure: "We cannot turn the page until we have read the page."

Many officials of human rights organizations, who have fought long and valiantly to bring attention and law to bear on these issues, strongly reject any proposal that includes widespread grants of immunity. They urge investigations and prosecutions of Bush administration officials. The choices are complicated and painful. From what we know, officials acted with the legal sanction of the U.S. government and under orders from the highest political authority, the elected President of the United States. Political decisions, made by elected officials, led to these crimes. But political opinion, within the government and increasingly, as time passed, without, to some extent allowed those crimes to persist. If there is a need for prosecution there is also a vital need for education. Only a credible investigation into what was done and what information was gained can begin to alter the political calculus around torture by replacing the public's attachment to the ticking bomb with an understanding of what torture is and what is gained, and lost, when the United States reverts to it.

President Obama, while declaring that "nobody's above the law, and if there are clear instances of wrongdoing . . . people should be prosecuted," has also expressed his strong preference for "looking forward" rather than "looking backwards." One can understand the sentiment but even some of the decisions his administration has already made—concerning state secrecy, for example—show the extent to which he and his Department of Justice will be haunted by what his predecessor did. Consider the uncompromising words of Eric Holder, the attorney general, who in reply to a direct question at his confirmation hearings had declared, "Waterboarding is torture." There is nothing ambiguous about this statement—nor about the equally blunt statements of several high Bush administration officials, including the former vice-president and the director of the CIA, confirming unequivocally that the administration had ordered and directed that prisoners under its control be waterboarded. We are all living, then, with a terrible contradiction, an enduring one, and it is not subtle, any more than the accounts in the ICRC report are subtle. "It was," as Mr. Cheney said of waterboarding, "a no-brainer for me." Now Abu Zubaydah and his fellow detainees have stepped forward out of the darkness to link hands with the former vice-president and testify to his truthfulness.

—March 12, 2009

NOTES

1. See "Restoring Trust in the Justice System: The Senate Judiciary Committee's Agenda in the 111th Congress," 2009 Marver Bernstein Lecture, Georgetown University, February 9, 2009.

2. See "President Discusses Creation of Military Commissions to Try Suspected Terrorists," September 6, 2006, East Room, White House, available at cfr.org.

3. See, for the authoritative account, Dana Priest, "CIA Holds Terror Suspects in Secret Prisons," *The Washington Post*, November 2, 2005.

4. See Jonathan Alter, "Time to Think About Torture: It's a New World, and Survival May Well Require Old Techniques That Seemed Out of the Question," *Newsweek*, November 5, 2001. See also Raymond Bonner, Don Van Natta Jr., and Amy Waldman, "Interrogations: Questioning Terror Suspects in a Dark and Surreal World," *The New York Times*, March 9, 2003.

5. "President Bush's News Conference," *The New York Times*, September 15, 2006.

6. From "CIA–Abu Zubaydah. Interview with John Kiriakou." This is the rough and undated transcript of a video interview conducted by Brian Ross of ABC News, apparently in December 2007, available at abcnews.go.com. Quotations from this document have been edited very slightly for clarity. See also Richard Esposito and Brian Ross, "Coming in from the Cold: CIA Spy Calls Waterboarding Necessary But Torture," ABC News, December 10, 2007.

7. See "Working Group Report on Detainee Interrogations in the Global War on Terrorism: Assessment of Legal, Historical, Policy, and Operational Considerations," April 4, 2003, in Mark Danner, *Torture and Truth: America, Abu Ghraib, and the War on Terror* (New York Review Books, 2004), 190–192. A great many of these documents, collected in this book and elsewhere, were leaked in the wake of the publication of the Abu Ghraib photographs, and have been public since late spring or early summer of 2004.

8. See David Johnston, "At a Secret Interrogation, Dispute Flared Over Tactics," *The New York Times*, September 10, 2006.

9. See Mark Hosenball, "How Good Is Abu Zubaydah's Information?" *Newsweek* Web Exclusive, April 27, 2002.

10. See Johnston, "At a Secret Interrogation, Dispute Flared Over Tactics."

11. See KUBARK, *Counterintelligence Interrogation—July 1963* and *Human Resource Exploitation Training Manual—1983,* both archived at "Prisoner Abuse: Patterns from the Past," National Security Archive Electronic Briefing Book No. 122. For the historical roots of the "alternative set of procedures," see Alfred W. McCoy, *A Question of Torture: CIA Interrogation, from the Cold War to the War on Terror* (Metropolitan, 2006); and Jane Mayer, *The Dark Side: The Inside Story of How the War on Terror Turned into a War on American Ideals* (Doubleday, 2008), especially 167–174. See also my "The Logic of Torture," *The New York Review*, June 24, 2004, and *Torture and Truth*.

12. See Jan Crawford Greenburg, Howard L. Rosenberg, and Ariane de Vogue, "Sources: Top Bush Advisors Approved 'Enhanced Interrogation,'" ABC News, April 9, 2008.

13. The bracketed comment appears in the ICRC report.

14. See Bob Woodward, "Detainee Tortured, Says U.S. Official: Trial Overseer Cites 'Abusive' Methods Against 9/11 Suspect," *The Washington Post*, January 14, 2009.

15. See Ron Suskind, "The Unofficial Story of the al-Qaeda 14," *Time,* September 10, 2006. See also Suskind's *The One Percent Doctrine: Deep Inside America's Pursuit of Its Enemies Since 9/11* (Simon & Schuster, 2006), 99–101, and Mayer, *The Dark Side,* 175–177.

16. See "Statement on Military Commission Legislation: Remarks by Senator Barack Obama," September 28, 2006.

17. See my *Torture and Truth*, 33.

PERMISSIONS

CONTRIBUTORS

Steve Brodner is a freelance illustrator specializing in political satire. His work has appeared in numerous publications, including *The New Yorker*, *The Atlantic Monthly*, *Harper's*, *Mother Jones*, *Esquire*, *Business Week*, and *The New York Times Book Review*. His political work is collected in the book *Freedom Fries*.

Michelle Cottle is a senior editor at *The New Republic* and a contributing editor to *Washington Monthly*. She is also a regular panelist for the PBS political affairs show, *Tucker Carlson Unfiltered*.

Mark Danner is a frequent contributor to *The New York Review of Books* and the author of numerous books, including *Torture and Truth: America, Abu Ghraib and the War on Terror* and *The Secret Way to War: The Downing Street Memo and the Iraq War's Buried History*. He is a professor of journalism at the University of California at Berkeley and Henry R. Luce Professor of Human Rights and Journalism at Bard College.

Brian Doherty is a senior editor at *Reason* and author of the books *This Is Burning Man*, *Radicals for Capitalism*, and *Gun Control on Trial*.

Robert Draper is a correspondent for *GQ* and the author of *Dead Certain: The Presidency of George W. Bush*.

Dexter Filkins, a foreign correspondent for *The New York Times*, covered the Afghanistan invasion from 2001 to 2002 and the Iraq war from 2003 to 2006. The author of the book *The Forever War*, he is currently a fellow at the Carr Center for Human Rights Policy at Harvard University.

James K. Galbraith holds the Lloyd M. Bentsen Jr. Chair in Government/Business Relations at the LBJ School of Public Affairs at the University of Texas at Austin. He is also a senior scholar with the Jerome Levy Economics Institute and chair of Economists for Peace and Security, a global professional association. He has authored numerous books including, most recently, *The Predator State: How Conservatives Abandoned the Free Market and Why Liberals Should Too.*

Ilan Goldenberg was recently appointed to be the Pentagon's special adviser to the deputy assistant secretary of defense for the Middle East. Prior to that, he was policy director of the National Security Network, a national security think tank. A regular contributor to the foreign policy blog *Defense Arsenal*, he is a frequent commentator in print and new media.

Joshua Green is a senior editor at the *Atlantic Monthly* and a contributing editor to *Washington Monthly*. His work has also appeared in *Esquire, The New Yorker, The American Prospect,* and *Rolling Stone* magazine. He is the coauthor, with Representative Henry Waxman, of *The Waxman Report: How Congress Really Works.*

Michael Hastings is a contributing editor to *GQ* magazine. A former war correspondent in Iraq for *Newsweek*, he is the author of the book *I Lost My Love in Baghdad.* His writing has also appeared in *Slate, Salon, Foreign Policy,* and *The Los Angeles Times.*

Christopher Hitchens writes for *Slate* and *The Daily Mirror* and is a contributing editor to *Vanity Fair* and *The Atlantic Monthly*. He is the author of numerous books including, most recently, *God Is Not Great: How Religion Poisons Everything.*

Paul Krugman is a professor of economics and international affairs at Princeton University and an op-ed columnist for the *New York Times*. The author of numerous books, including *The Conscience of a Liberal* and *The Return of Depression Economics and the Crisis of 2008,* he was awarded the Nobel Prize for Economics in 2008.

Ryan Lizza is *The New Yorker's* Washington correspondent. Formerly the White House correspondent for *The New Republic*, he has also been a correspondent for *GQ* and a contributing editor to *New York* and has written for the *New York Times, Washington Monthly,* and the *Atlantic Monthly.*

Larissa MacFarquhar is a staff writer for *The New Yorker.*

Jane Mayer is a staff writer for *The New Yorker.* She is the author of several books including, most recently, *The Dark Side: The Inside Story of How the War on Terror Turned into a War on American Ideals.*

George Packer is a staff writer for *The New Yorker.* His work has also appeared in *Mother Jones, The Nation, Harper's,* and the *New York Times Magazine.* He is the author of several books including, most recently, *The Assassin's Gate: America in Iraq*, and a play, *Betrayed*, based on his work as journalist in Iraq.

John H. Richardson is a writer-at-large for *Esquire*.

Terence Samuel is deputy editor of *TheRoot.com*, an online magazine aimed at African American readers, and a political columnist for the online edition of *The American Prospect*. He is a former senior editor and chief congressional correspondent for *U.S. News and World Report*.

Jennifer Senior is a contributing editor to *New York* magazine.

Adam Sternbergh is an editor-at-large at *New York* magazine and the coauthor of *Hey! It's That Guy: The Fametracker.com Guide to Character Actors*.

Joseph E. Stiglitz is a professor of economics at Columbia University, where he also holds appointments in the schools of business and international and public affairs. A former senior vice president and chief economist at the World Bank, he was awarded the Nobel Prize for Economics in 2001. He is the author of numerous books, including *Globalization and Its Discontents*.

Lisa Taddeo is a frequent contributor to *Esquire* and other magazines.

Matt Taibbi is a contributing editor to *Rolling Stone*. He is the author of several books including, most recently, *The Great Derangement: A Terrifying True Story of War, Politics, and Religion*.

Michael Wolff is a contributing editor to *Vanity Fair*. He is the author of *Autumn of the Moguls* and *Burn Rate: How I Survived the Gold Rush Years on the Internet*.

ABOUT THE EDITOR

Royce Flippin is the series editor of *The Best American Political Writing*. A former senior editor at *American Health* magazine, he has written for various publications, including the *New York Times*, *Men's Journal*, *Self*, and *Parents* magazine. This is his eighth year as the editor of the series.